INSANELY AWESOME MAD®

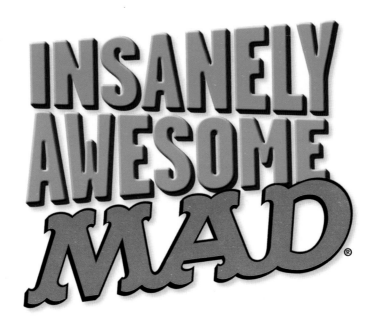

Also available from MAD Books

MAD About Comic Strips

MAD About Super Heroes Vol. 2

MAD About The Fifties

MAD About The Sixties

MAD About The Mob

MAD About The Oscars

MAD Neumanisms

MAD Bathroom Companion Number Two

MAD Monster Book of Horrifying Clichés

MAD Archives Vol. 1

INSANELY AWESOME MAD

By
"The Usual Gang of Idiots"

MAD
NEW YORK
BOOKS™

MAD BOOKS

William Gaines Founder
John Ficarra Editor
Charlie Kadau, Joe Raiola Senior Editors
Dave Croatto Associate Editor
Sam Viviano Art Director
Ryan Flanders Assistant Art Director
Doug Thomson Production Artist

ADMINISTRATION

CONTRIBUTING WRITERS AND ARTISTS:
"The Usual Gang of Idiots"

Compilation and new material © 2011 by E.C. Publications, Inc. All Rights Reserved.

MAD, Boy's Head Design, and all related indicia are trademarks of E.C. Publications, Inc.

Published by MAD Books. An imprint of E.C. Publications, Inc., 1700 Broadway, New York, NY 10019.
A Warner Bros. Entertainment Company.

CARTOON NETWORK and the logo TM & © Cartoon Network.

Printed by RR Donnelley, Salem, VA, USA. 7/22/11. First Printing.
ISBN: 978-1-4012-3348-8

SUSTAINABLE FORESTRY INITIATIVE
Certified Chain of Custody
Promoting Sustainable
Forest Management
www.sfiprogram.org
Fiber used in this product line meets the
sourcing requirements of the SFI program.
www.sfiprogram.org SGS-SFI/COC-US10/81072

Visit MAD online at: www.madmag.com

Though Alfred E. Neuman wasn't the first to say "A fool and his money are soon parted," here's your chan[ce] ...
subscribe to MAD! Simply call 1-800-4-MADMAG and mention code AWFMDIA. Operators are standing by ...

3 0646 00182 3636

CONTENTS

SERGIO ARAGONES PRESENTS A MAD LOOK AT

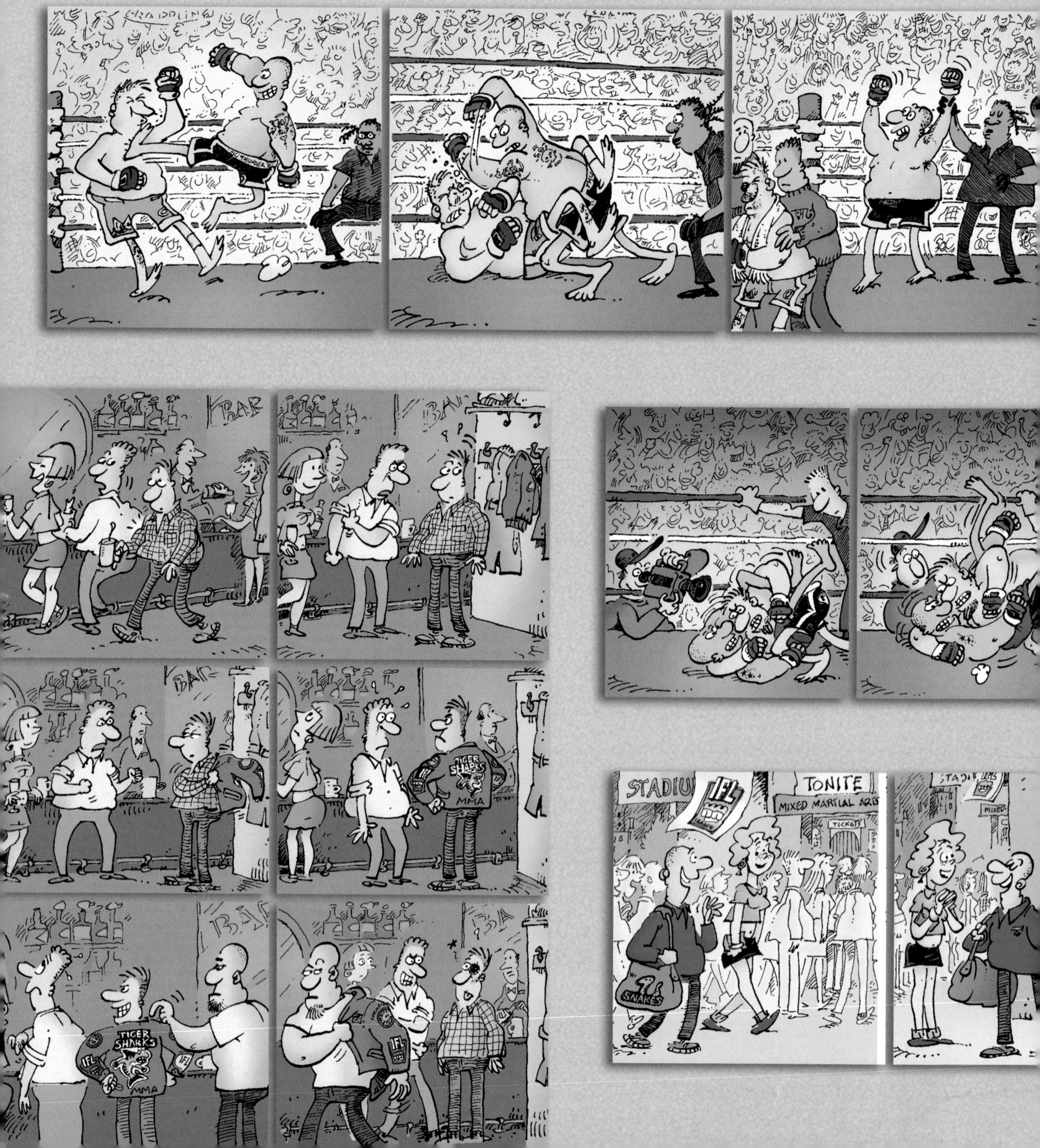
BAR
TIGER SHARKS
MMA
TONITE
MIXED MARTIAL ARTS
TICKETS
SNAKES

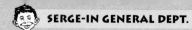

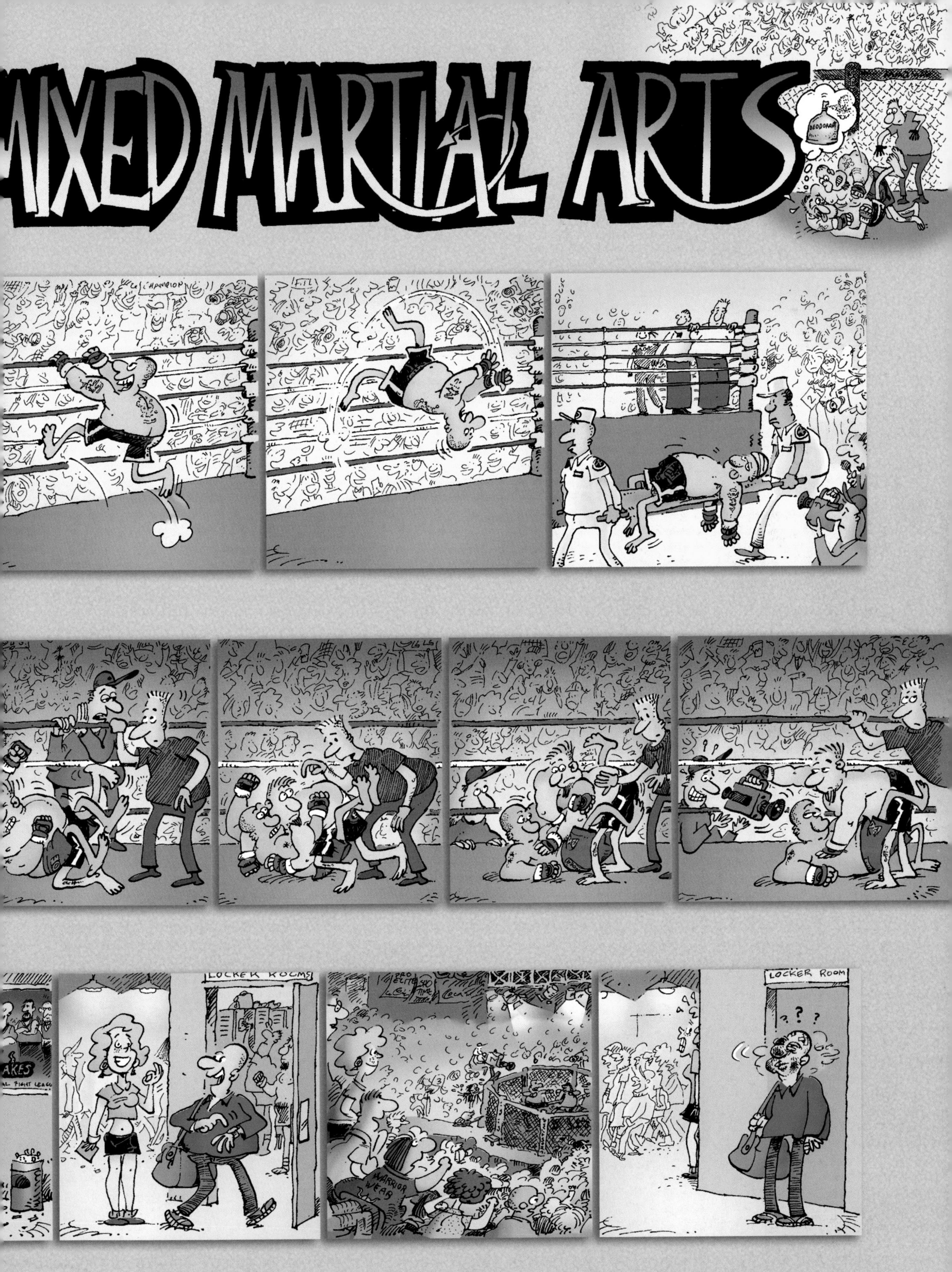
MIXED MARTIAL ARTS
DEODORANT
CHAMPION
LOCKER ROOMS
WARRIOR WEAR
LOCKER ROOM
? ? ?

WRITER AND ARTIST: SERGIO ARAGONES

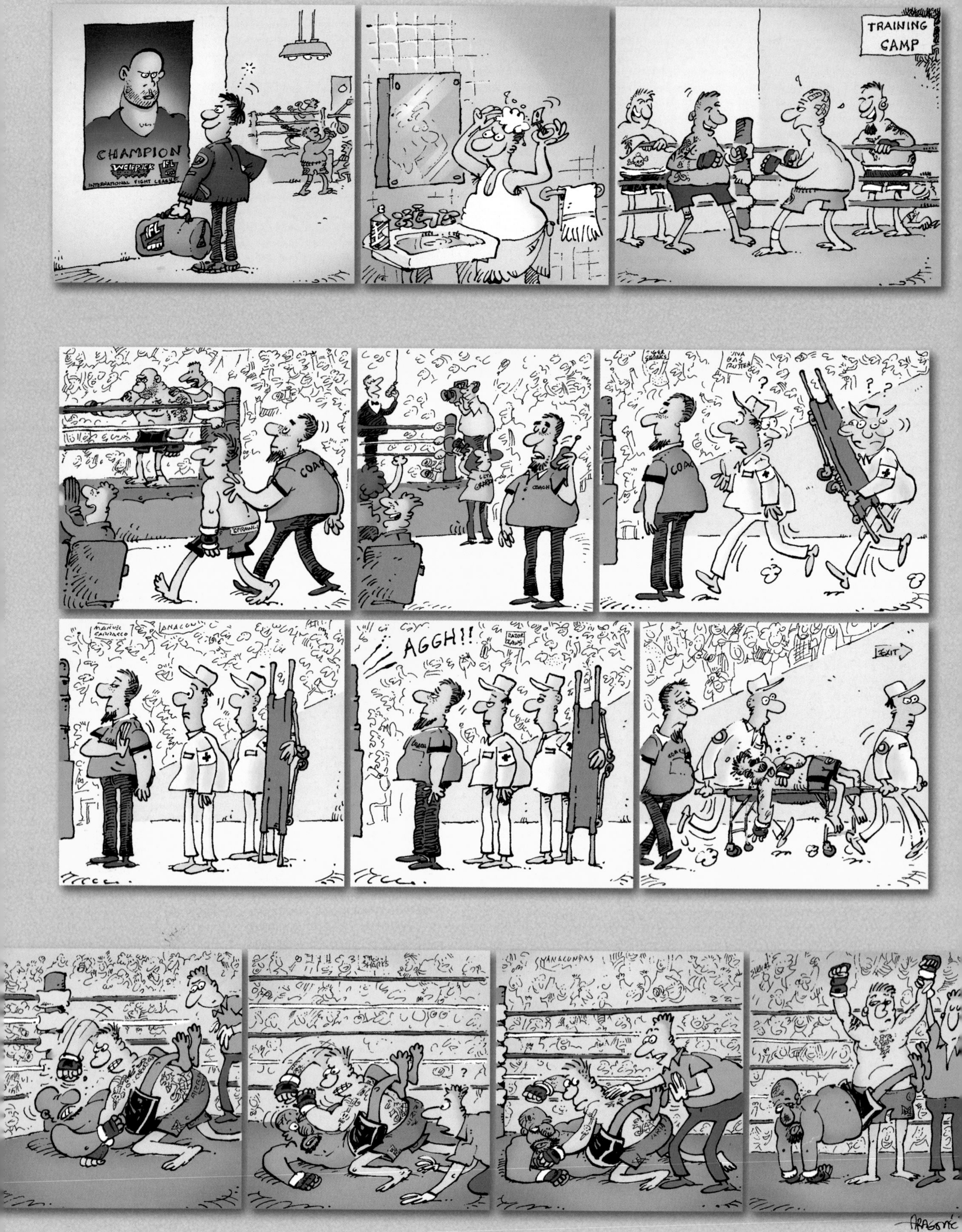
CHAMPION
IFL
INTERNATIONAL FIGHT LEAGUE
TRAINING CAMP
COACH
AGGH!!
EXIT
ARAGONÉS

JOKE AND DAGGER DEPT.

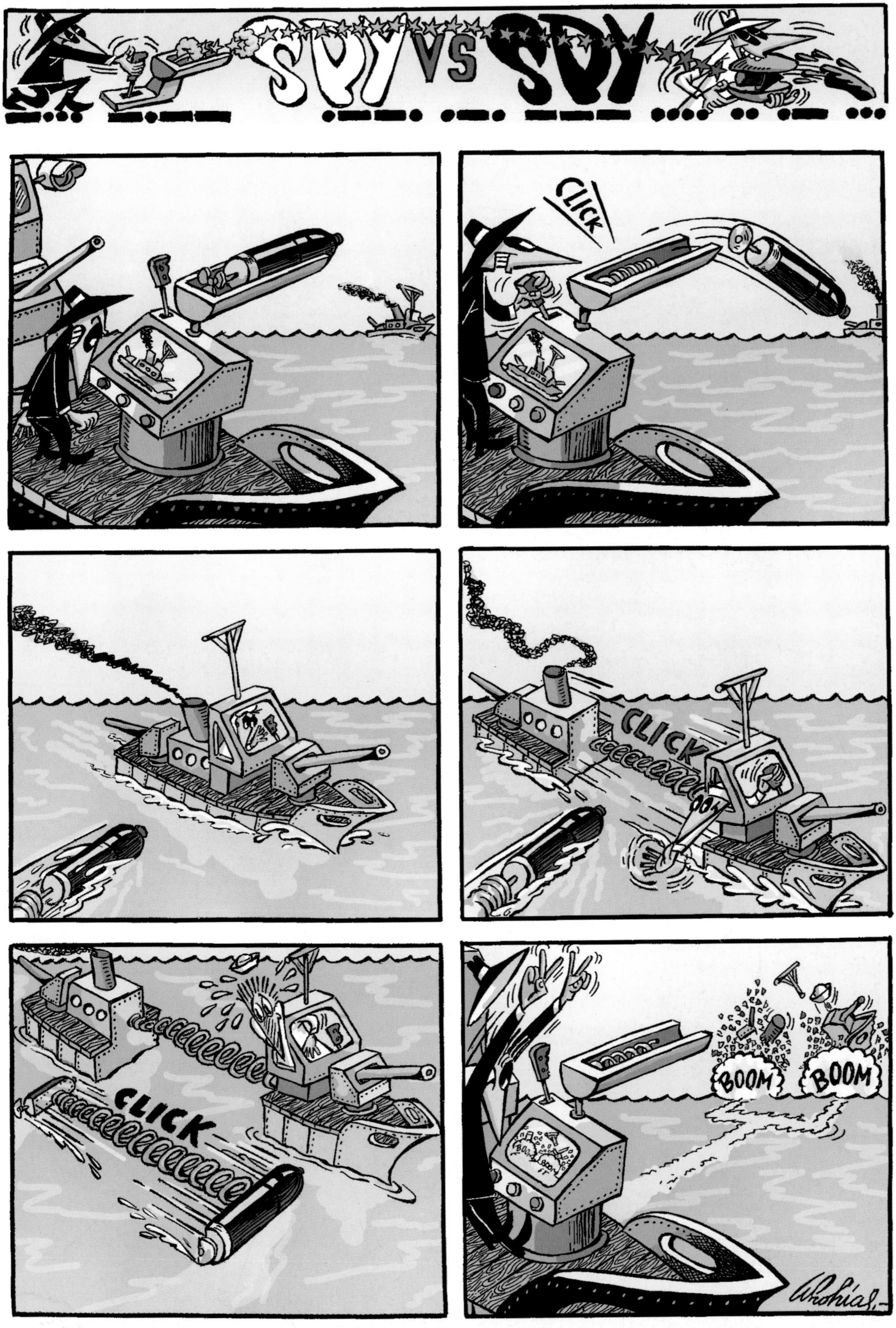
SPY VS SPY
CLICK
CLICK
CLICK
BOOM
BOOM
Prohias

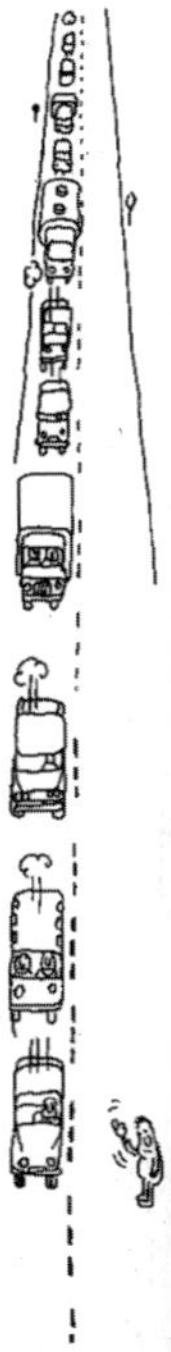

WRITER AND ARTIST: ANTONIO PROHIAS

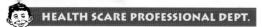

School nurses are special people — kind, caring...oh, who are we kidding? Most school nurses are about as qualified as Barry Bonds is lovable! So how does YOURS stack up? Before it's too late, find out with...

SIGNS YOU HAVE A LOUSY SCHOOL NURSE

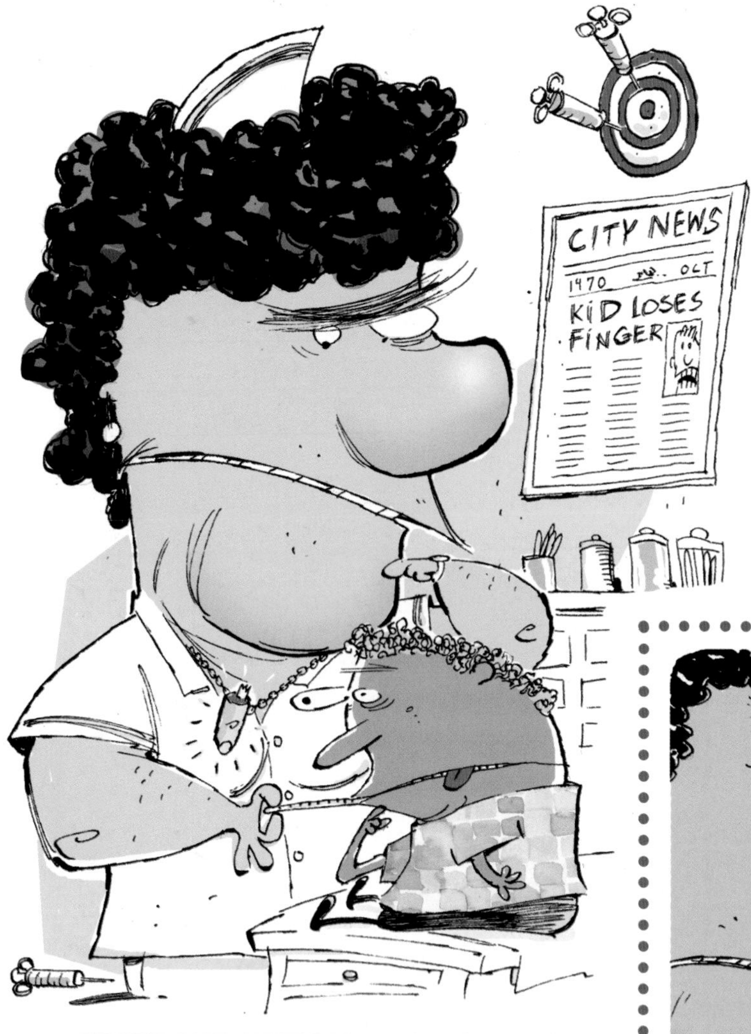
CITY NEWS
1970 OCT
KiD LOSES FiNGER

She proudly wears the severed finger from an 8th grade shop student around her neck.

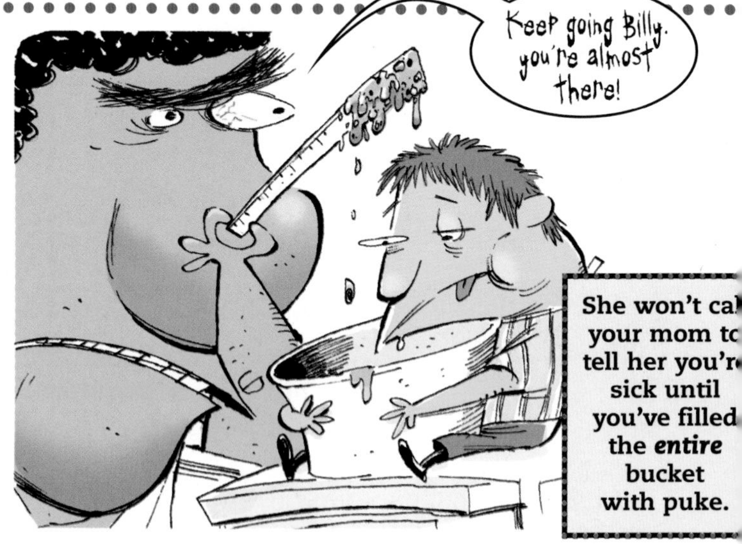
Keep going Billy. you're almost there!

She won't call your mom to tell her you're sick until you've filled the *entire* bucket with puke.

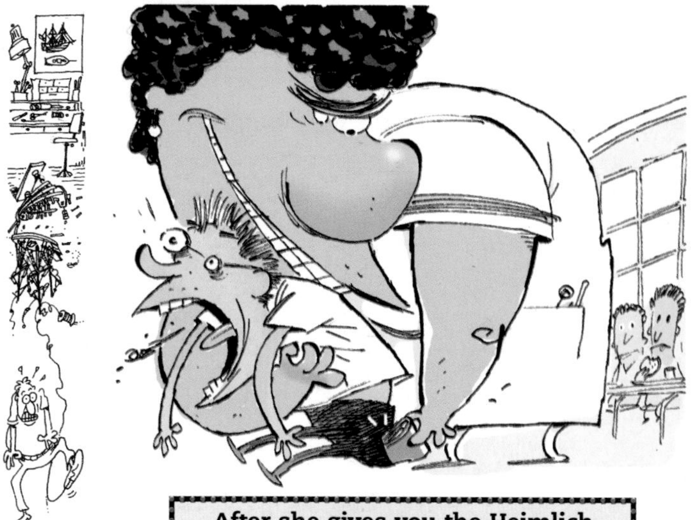

After she gives you the Heimlich maneuver in the school cafeteria, you realize your wallet is missing.

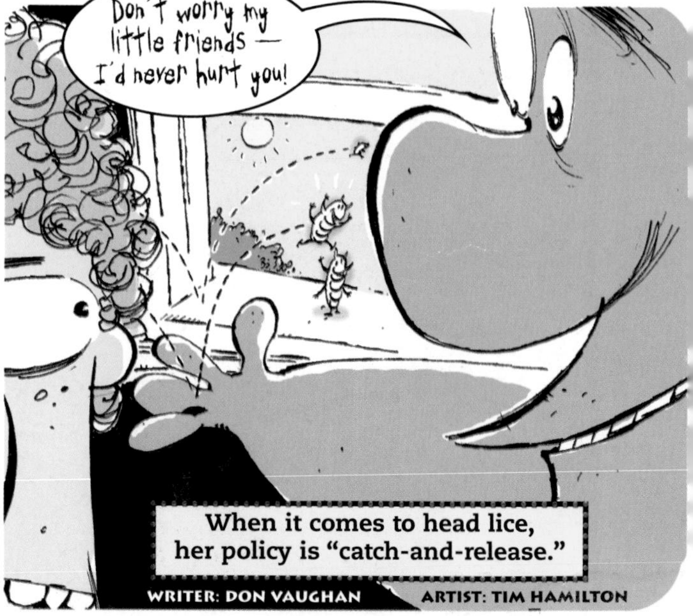
Don't worry my little friends — I'd never hurt you!

When it comes to head lice, her policy is "catch-and-release."

WRITER: DON VAUGHAN ARTIST: TIM HAMILTON

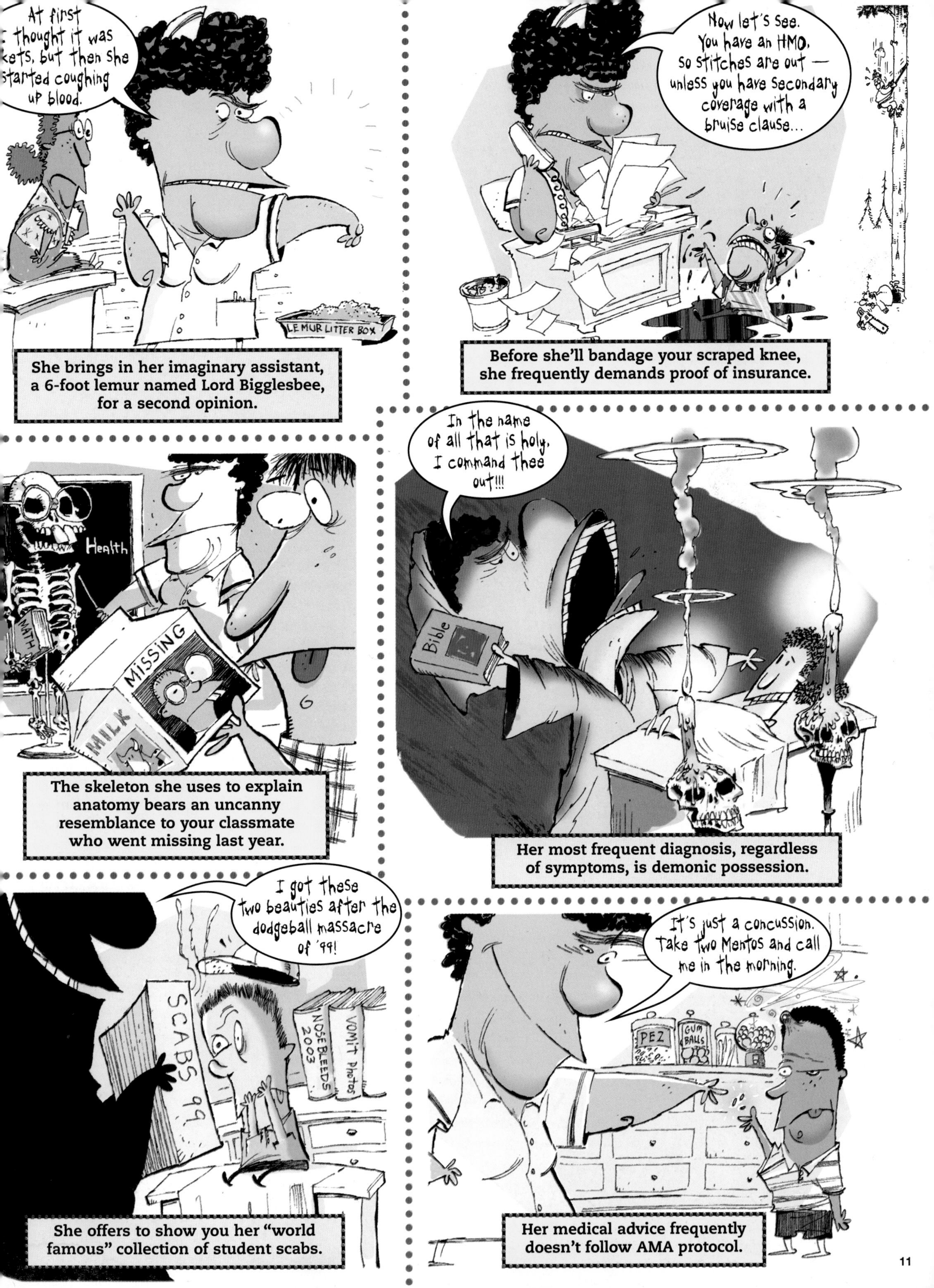
At first
thought it was
kets, but then she
started coughing
up blood.
LEMUR LITTER BOX
She brings in her imaginary assistant, a 6-foot lemur named Lord Bigglesbee, for a second opinion.
Now let's see. You have an HMO, so stitches are out — unless you have secondary coverage with a bruise clause...
Before she'll bandage your scraped knee, she frequently demands proof of insurance.
Health
MATH
MISSING
MILK
The skeleton she uses to explain anatomy bears an uncanny resemblance to your classmate who went missing last year.
In the name of all that is holy, I command thee out!!!
Bible
Her most frequent diagnosis, regardless of symptoms, is demonic possession.
I got these two beauties after the dodgeball massacre of '99!
SCABS 99
NOSE BLEEDS 2003
VOMIT Photos
She offers to show you her "world famous" collection of student scabs.
It's just a concussion. Take two Mentos and call me in the morning.
PEZ
GUM BALLS
Her medical advice frequently doesn't follow AMA protocol.

Let's face it, for every one Batman, there are fifteen other less notable muscle-heads in gaudy outfits out there fighting evil. And while these crime-fighters may enjoy certain super-hero powers, at the end of the day they're really just like the rest of us in having to put up with the petty annoyances of life. The only difference is, what drives us up the wall is less unusual than what gets their spandex in a twist. Here's...

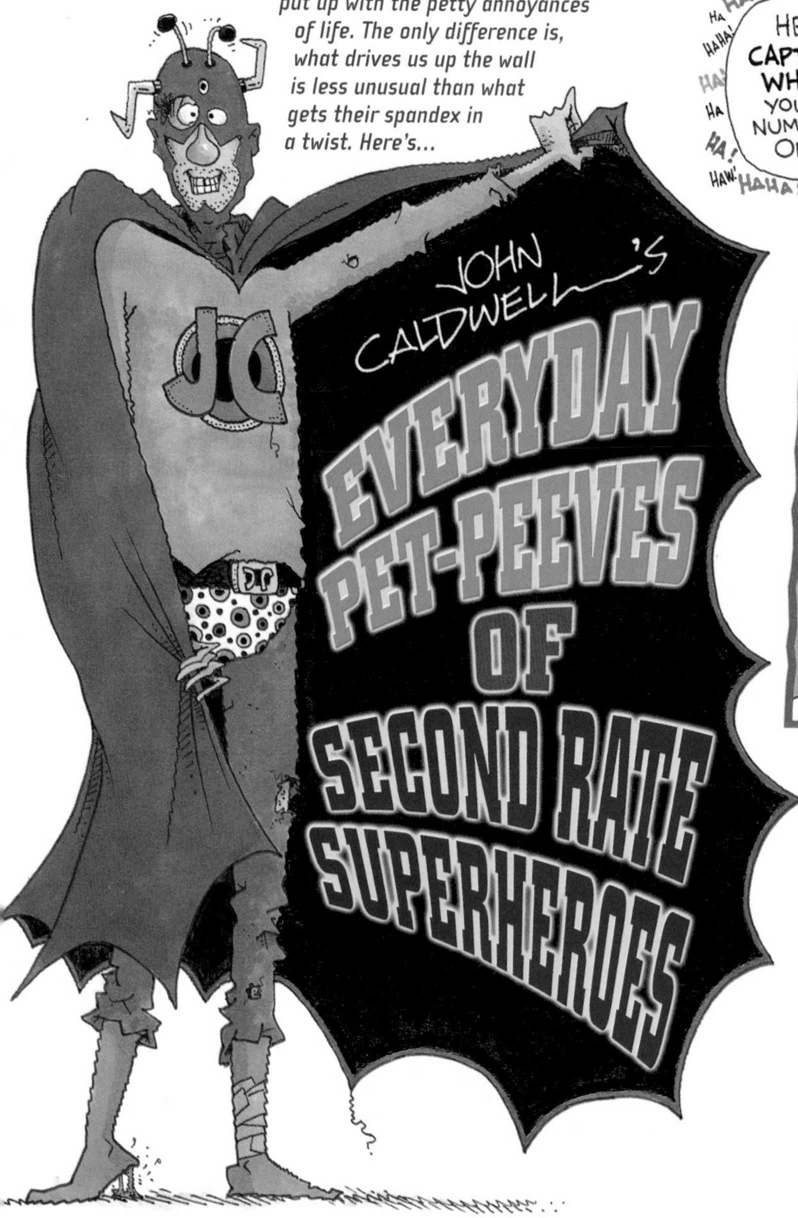
JOHN CALDWELL'S
EVERYDAY PET-PEEVES OF SECOND RATE SUPERHEROES

ARTIST AND WRITER: JOHN CALDWELL

People w
make fu
his nan

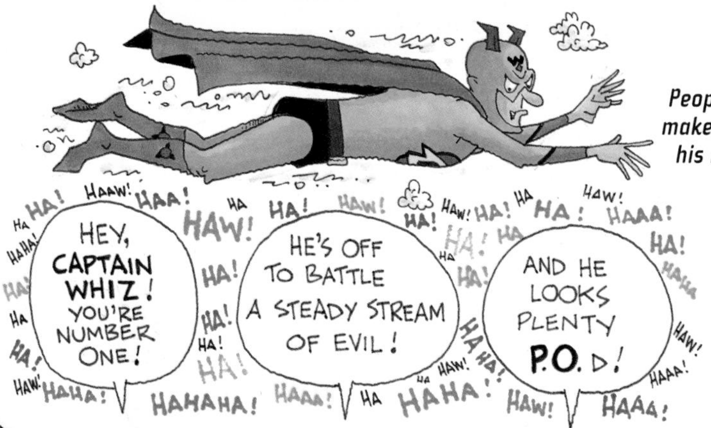
HEY, CAPTAIN WHIZ! YOU'RE NUMBER ONE!
HE'S OFF TO BATTLE A STEADY STREAM OF EVIL!
AND HE LOOKS PLENTY P.O.'D!

Mistaking sidewalk snot for the mystery element that renders him powerless

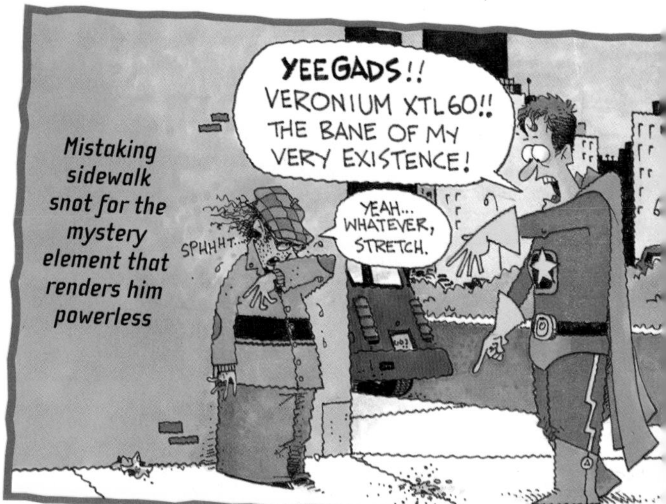
YEEGADS!! VERONIUM XTL60!! THE BANE OF MY VERY EXISTENCE!
YEAH... WHATEVER, STRETCH.
SPHHHT...

When the low budget film of his daring exploits goes straight to video because they cast Jon Lovitz in the feature role

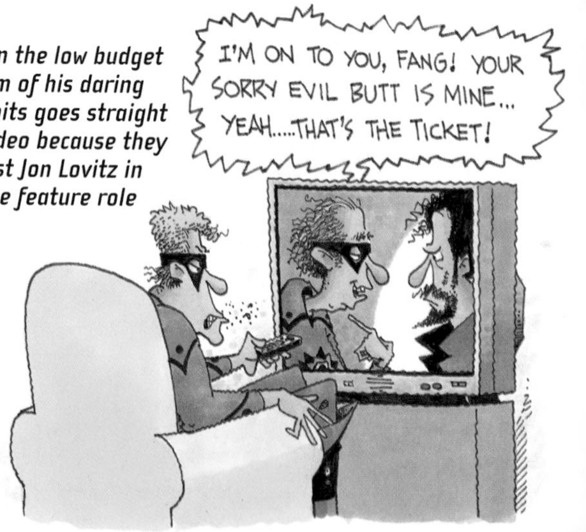
I'M ON TO YOU, FANG! YOUR SORRY EVIL BUTT IS MINE... YEAH.....THAT'S THE TICKET!

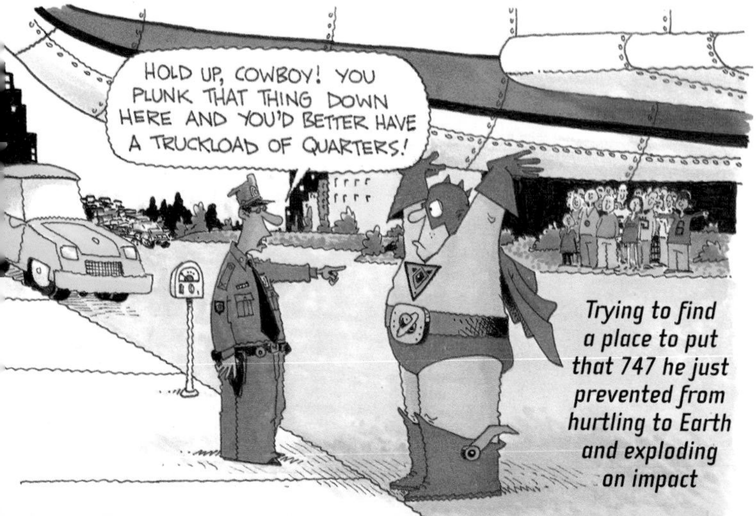
HOLD UP, COWBOY! YOU PLUNK THAT THING DOWN HERE AND YOU'D BETTER HAVE A TRUCKLOAD OF QUARTERS!

Trying to find a place to put that 747 he just prevented from hurtling to Earth and exploding on impact

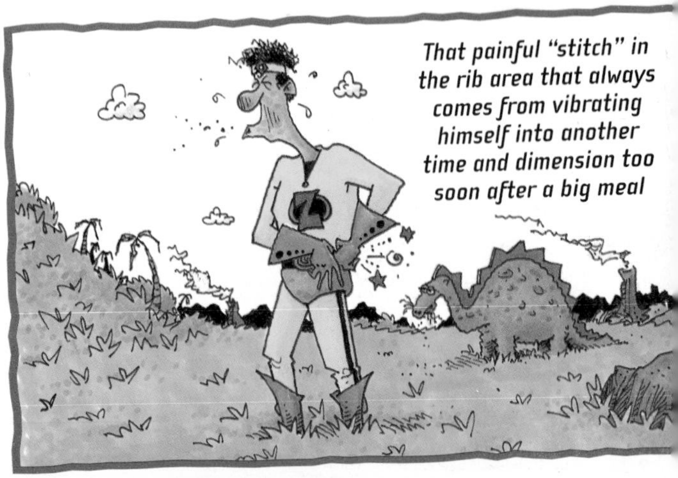

That painful "stitch" in the rib area that always comes from vibrating himself into another time and dimension too soon after a big meal

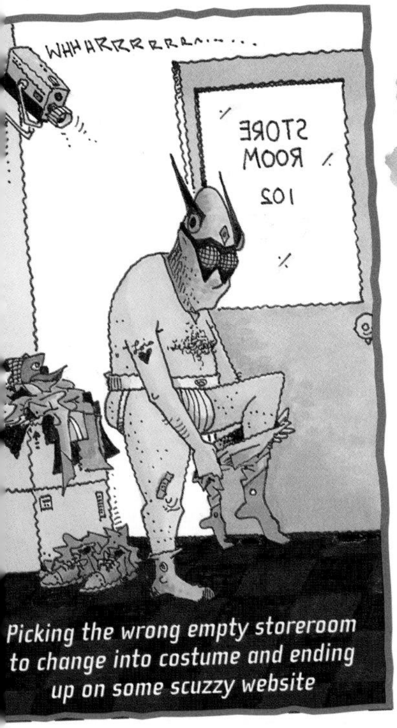
WHHARRRRRRR.....
STORE ROOM 102
Picking the wrong empty storeroom to change into costume and ending up on some scuzzy website

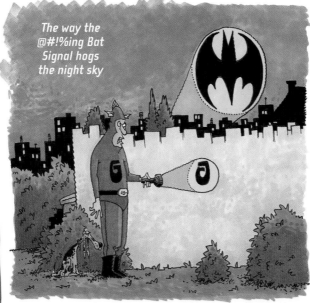

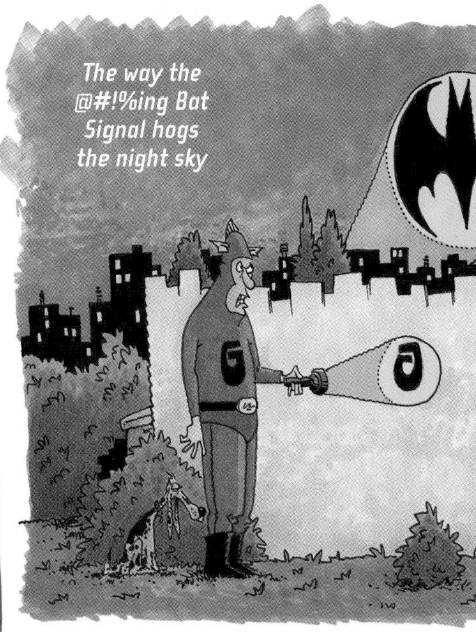
The way the @#!%ing Bat Signal hogs the night sky

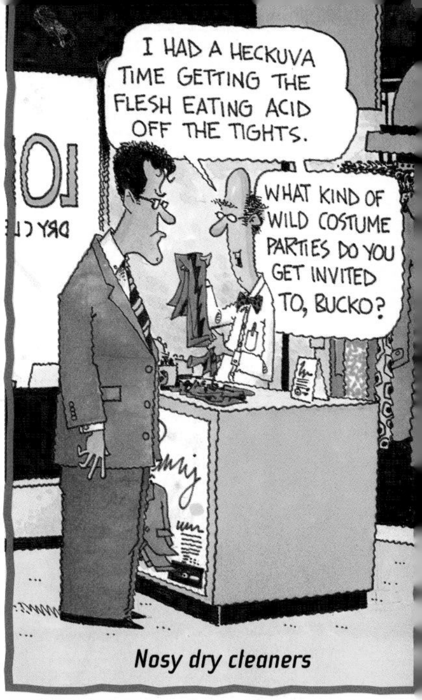
I HAD A HECKUVA TIME GETTING THE FLESH EATING ACID OFF THE TIGHTS.
WHAT KIND OF WILD COSTUME PARTIES DO YOU GET INVITED TO, BUCKO?
Nosy dry cleaners

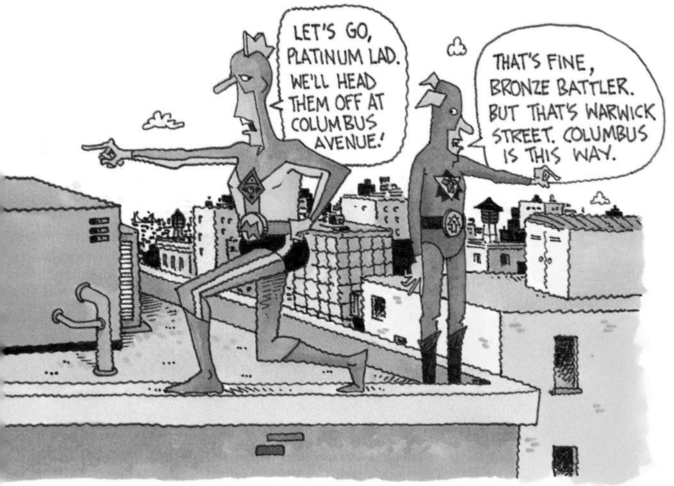
LET'S GO, PLATINUM LAD. WE'LL HEAD THEM OFF AT COLUMBUS AVENUE!
THAT'S FINE, BRONZE BATTLER. BUT THAT'S WARWICK STREET. COLUMBUS IS THIS WAY.
The fact that the city refuses to do squat with regard to his petition to put street signs on rooftops

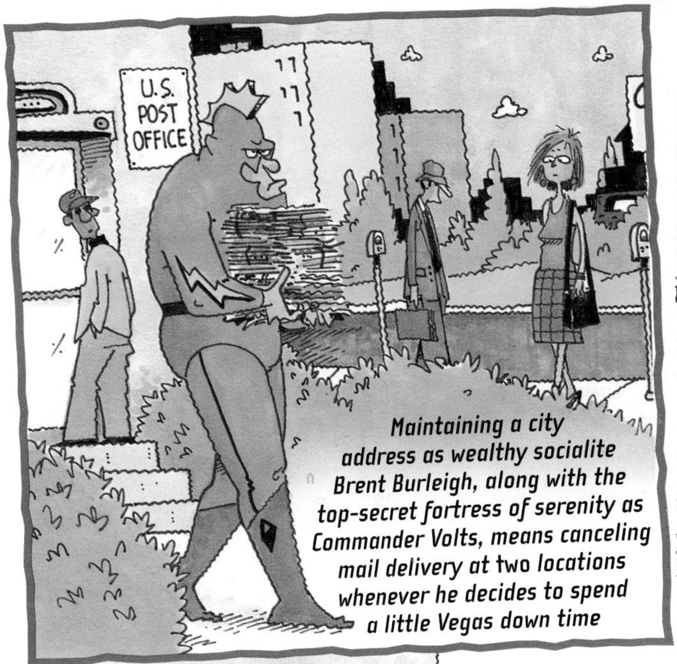
U.S. POST OFFICE
Maintaining a city address as wealthy socialite Brent Burleigh, along with the top-secret fortress of serenity as Commander Volts, means canceling mail delivery at two locations whenever he decides to spend a little Vegas down time

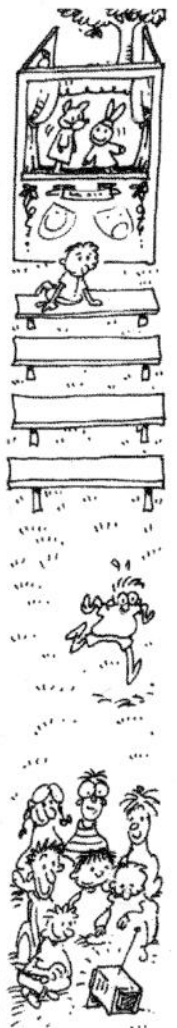

Fast food morons who act like it's the first time anyone ever asked if he wanted something Super Sized

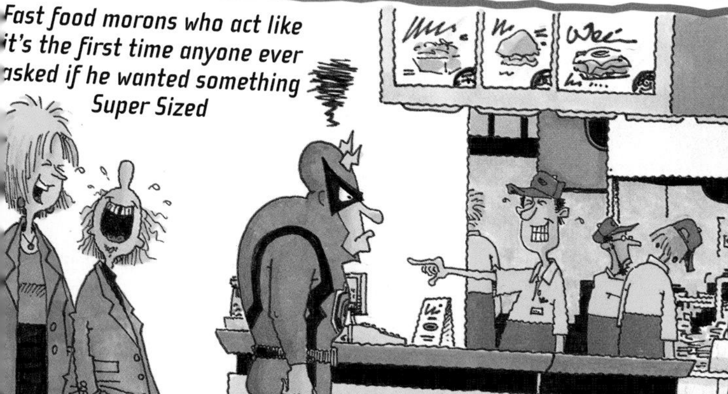

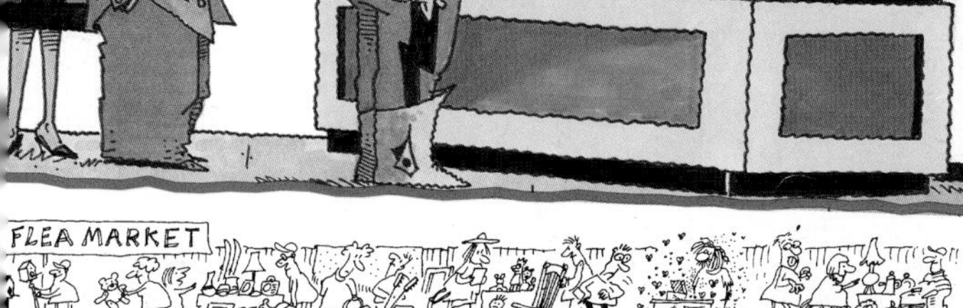
FLEA MARKET

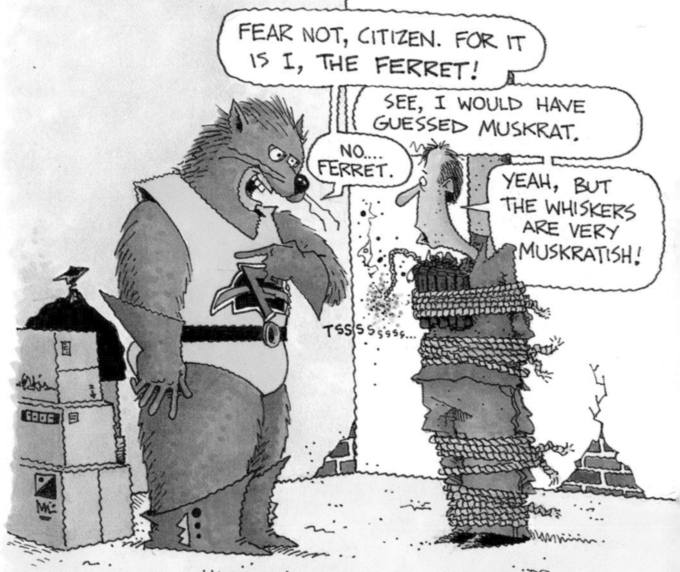
FEAR NOT, CITIZEN. FOR IT IS I, THE FERRET!
SEE, I WOULD HAVE GUESSED MUSKRAT.
NO.... FERRET.
YEAH, BUT THE WHISKERS ARE VERY MUSKRATISH!
TSSSSSSSS...
Poorly designed costumes

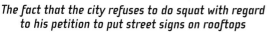

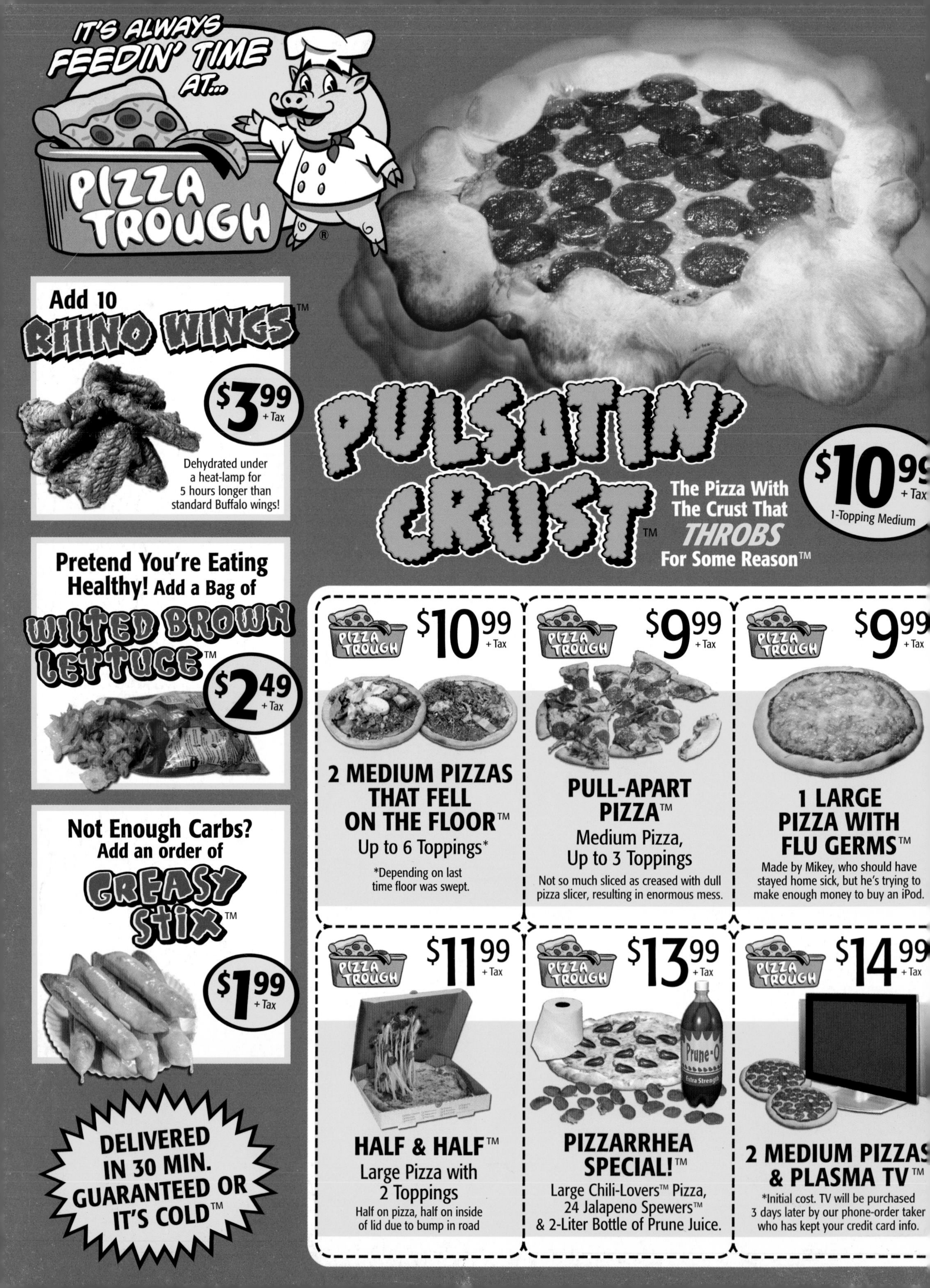

IT'S ALWAYS FEEDIN' TIME AT...
PIZZA TROUGH®
Add 10 RHINO WINGS™
$3.99 + Tax
Dehydrated under a heat-lamp for 5 hours longer than standard Buffalo wings!
Pretend You're Eating Healthy! Add a Bag of WILTED BROWN LETTUCE™
$2.49 + Tax
Not Enough Carbs? Add an order of GREASY STIX™
$1.99 + Tax
DELIVERED IN 30 MIN. GUARANTEED OR IT'S COLD™
PULSATIN' CRUST™
The Pizza With The Crust That THROBS For Some Reason™
$10.99 + Tax
1-Topping Medium
PIZZA TROUGH $10.99 + Tax
2 MEDIUM PIZZAS THAT FELL ON THE FLOOR™
Up to 6 Toppings*
*Depending on last time floor was swept.
PIZZA TROUGH $9.99 + Tax
PULL-APART PIZZA™
Medium Pizza, Up to 3 Toppings
Not so much sliced as creased with dull pizza slicer, resulting in enormous mess.
PIZZA TROUGH $9.99 + Tax
1 LARGE PIZZA WITH FLU GERMS™
Made by Mikey, who should have stayed home sick, but he's trying to make enough money to buy an iPod.
PIZZA TROUGH $11.99 + Tax
HALF & HALF™
Large Pizza with 2 Toppings
Half on pizza, half on inside of lid due to bump in road
PIZZA TROUGH $13.99 + Tax
Prune-O
Extra Strength
PIZZARRHEA SPECIAL!™
Large Chili-Lovers™ Pizza, 24 Jalapeno Spewers™ & 2-Liter Bottle of Prune Juice.
PIZZA TROUGH $14.99 + Tax
2 MEDIUM PIZZAS & PLASMA TV™
*Initial cost. TV will be purchased 3 days later by our phone-order taker who has kept your credit card info.

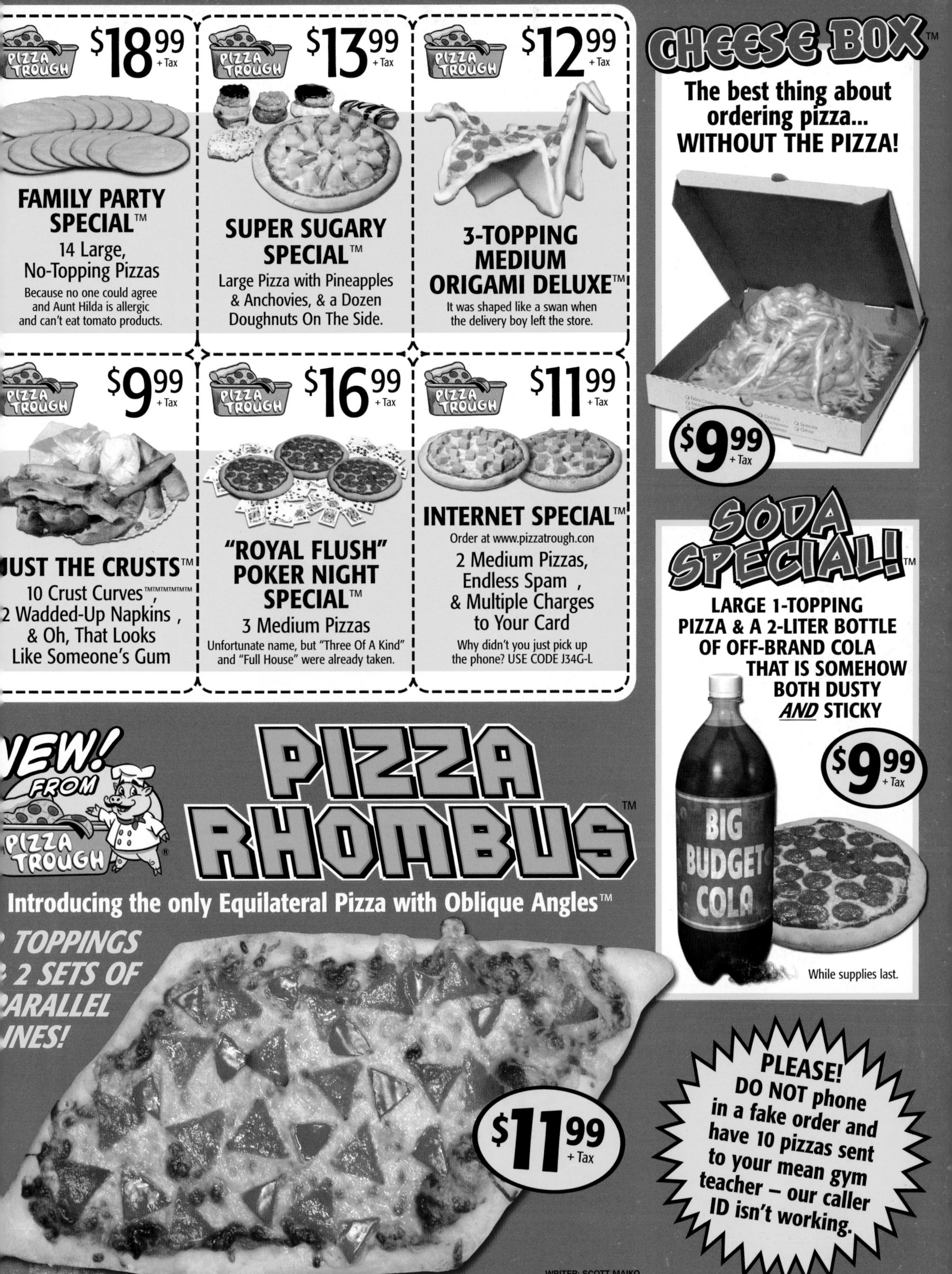
PIZZA TROUGH
$18.99 + Tax
FAMILY PARTY SPECIAL™
14 Large, No-Topping Pizzas
Because no one could agree and Aunt Hilda is allergic and can't eat tomato products.
PIZZA TROUGH
$13.99 + Tax
SUPER SUGARY SPECIAL™
Large Pizza with Pineapples & Anchovies, & a Dozen Doughnuts On The Side.
PIZZA TROUGH
$12.99 + Tax
3-TOPPING MEDIUM ORIGAMI DELUXE™
It was shaped like a swan when the delivery boy left the store.
PIZZA TROUGH
$9.99 + Tax
JUST THE CRUSTS™
10 Crust Curves™™™™™™, 2 Wadded-Up Napkins , & Oh, That Looks Like Someone's Gum
PIZZA TROUGH
$16.99 + Tax
"ROYAL FLUSH" POKER NIGHT SPECIAL™
3 Medium Pizzas
Unfortunate name, but "Three Of A Kind" and "Full House" were already taken.
PIZZA TROUGH
$11.99 + Tax
INTERNET SPECIAL™
Order at www.pizzatrough.con
2 Medium Pizzas, Endless Spam , & Multiple Charges to Your Card
Why didn't you just pick up the phone? USE CODE J34G-L
CHEESE BOX™
The best thing about ordering pizza... WITHOUT THE PIZZA!
$9.99 + Tax
SODA SPECIAL!™
LARGE 1-TOPPING PIZZA & A 2-LITER BOTTLE OF OFF-BRAND COLA THAT IS SOMEHOW BOTH DUSTY AND STICKY
$9.99 + Tax
BIG BUDGET COLA
While supplies last.
EW! FROM PIZZA TROUGH®
PIZZA RHOMBUS™
Introducing the only Equilateral Pizza with Oblique Angles™
TOPPINGS
2 SETS OF
ARALLEL
INES!
$11.99 + Tax
PLEASE! DO NOT phone in a fake order and have 10 pizzas sent to your mean gym teacher – our caller ID isn't working.

WRITER: SCOTT MAIKO
ARTIST: SCOTT BRICHER

Hey, gameboy, it's time for you to put down your memory cards, cheat codes and oversized Xbox controllers! Yep, as painful as it is, it's time to make at least a half-hearted attempt to have an *actual* experience in the *actual* world, you know, the one outside your television screen! What's that, you say? You've been gaming so long you don't remember how to function out there? Well, fear not, you indolent dweeb! It's for your benefit that we provide...

THE
TO FUNCTIONING IN

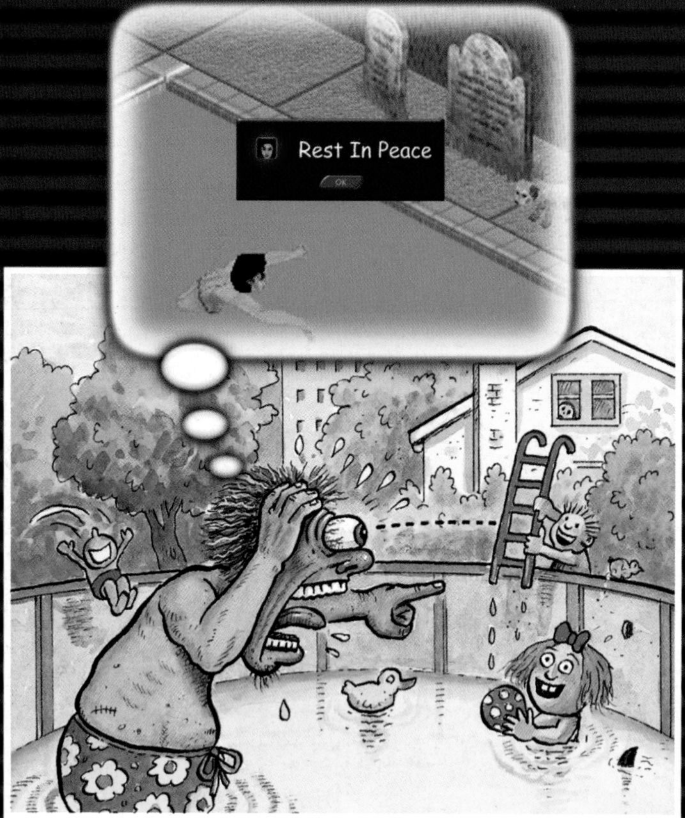
Rest In Peace
OK

Should you find yourself in a swimming pool when the ladder is removed, relax. It doesn't point to a plot by someone to kill you.

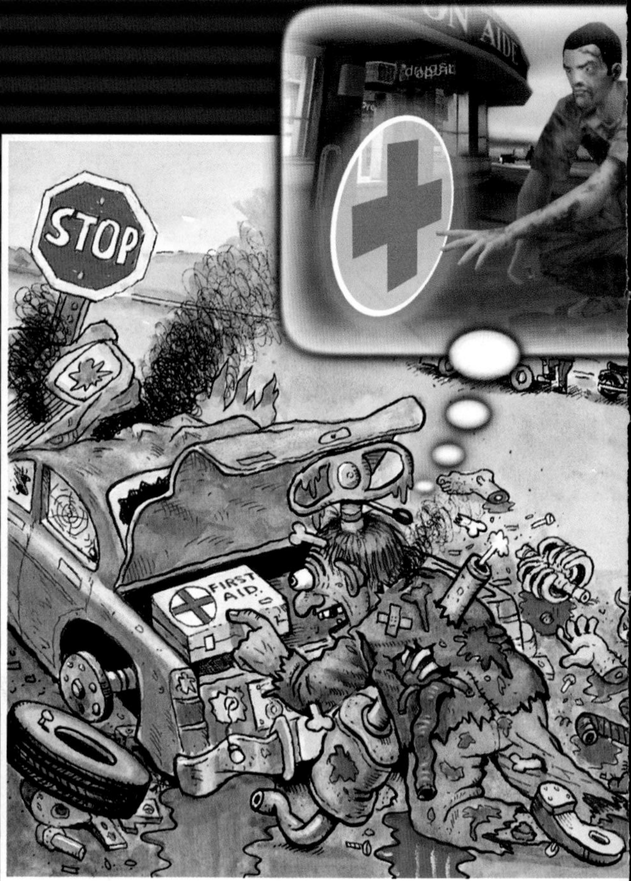
STOP
FIRST AID

If you are seriously injured, seek medical attention from a health care professional. Merely touching a first aid kit with a big red cross on it will not be sufficient.

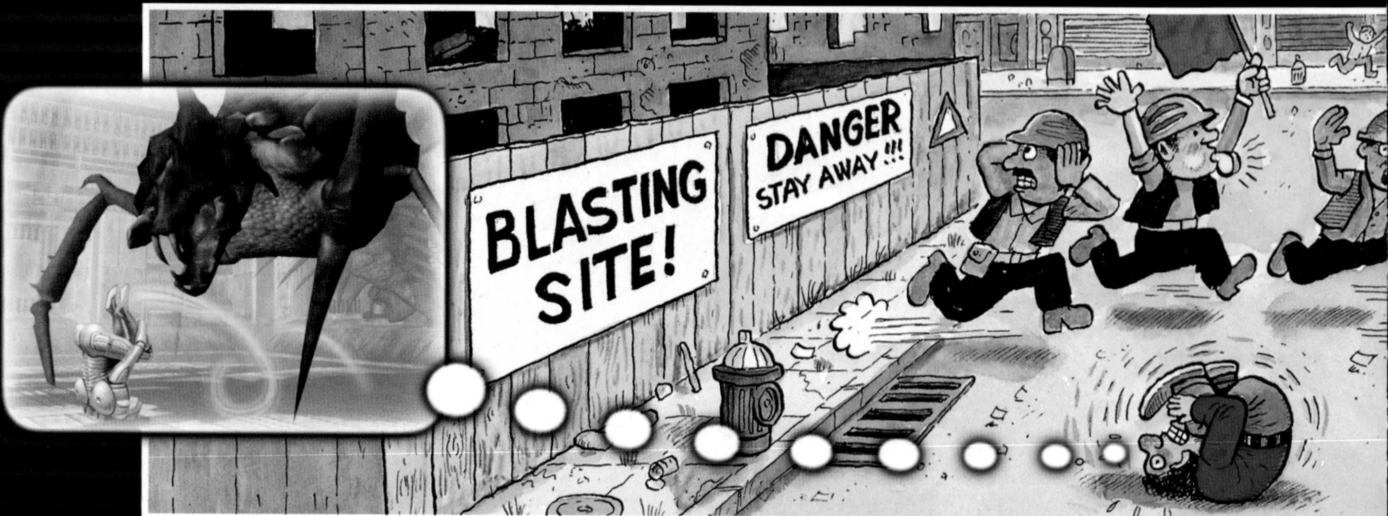
BLASTING SITE!
DANGER STAY AWAY!!!

Curling into a ball and rolling away to escape danger is considered cowardly, as well as highly ineffective.

GAMER'S GUIDE THE REAL WORLD

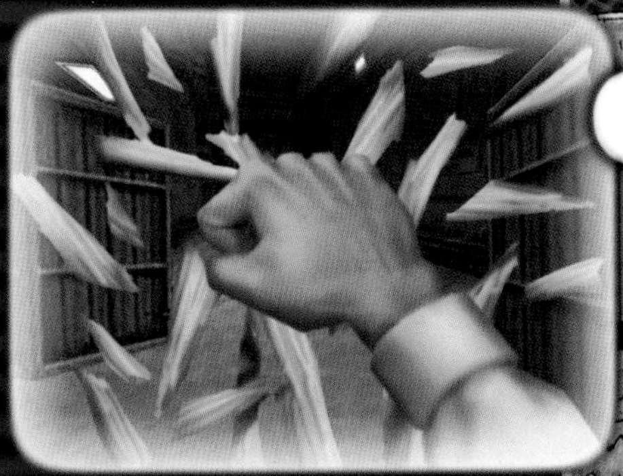

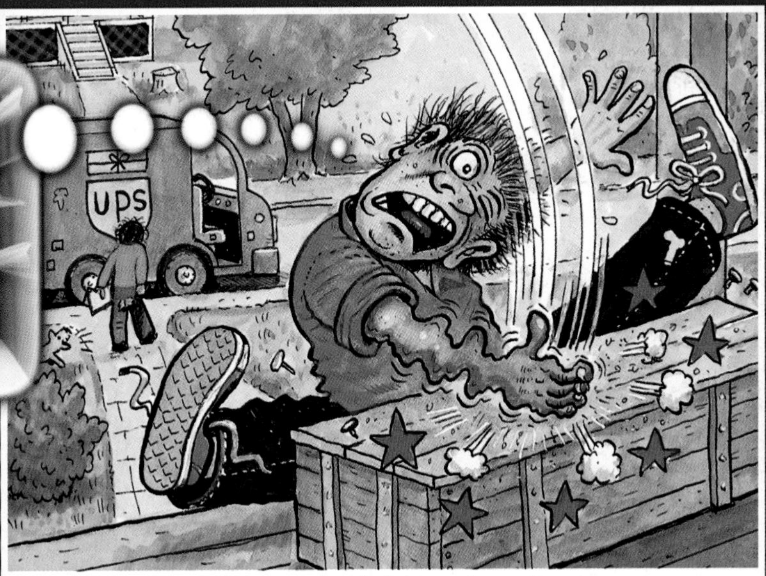
UPS

Smashing open sealed crates is much more difficult than you think. It often requires more than a single blow to completely shatter the wood.

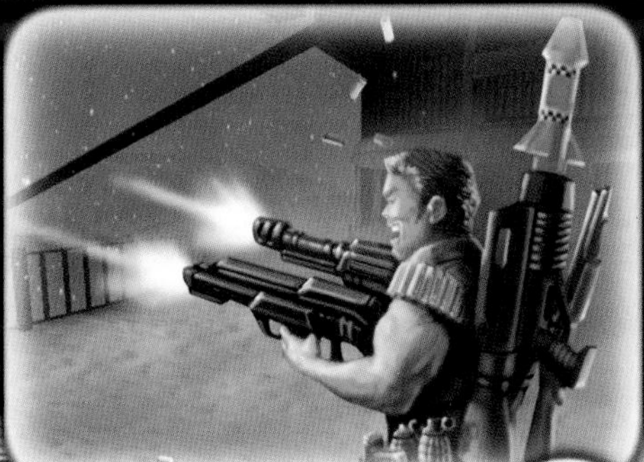

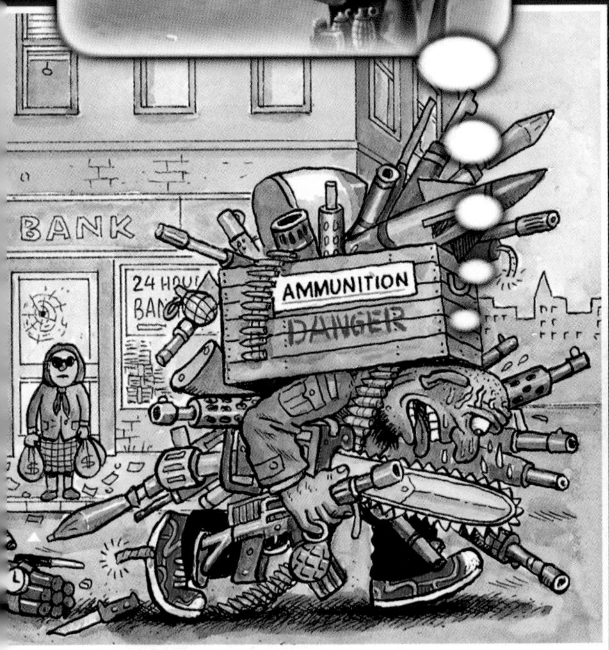
BANK
AMMUNITION
DANGER

Carrying a revolver, shotgun, Luger pistol, sniper rifle and anti-aircraft rocket launcher at the same time is virtually impossible. And even if you could, it would result in an unbearably painful hernia.

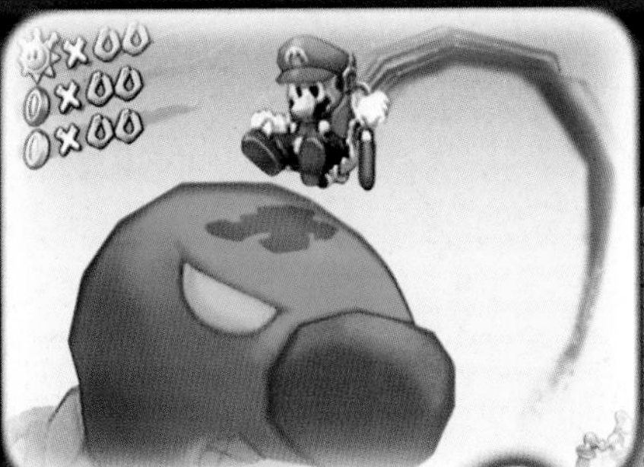

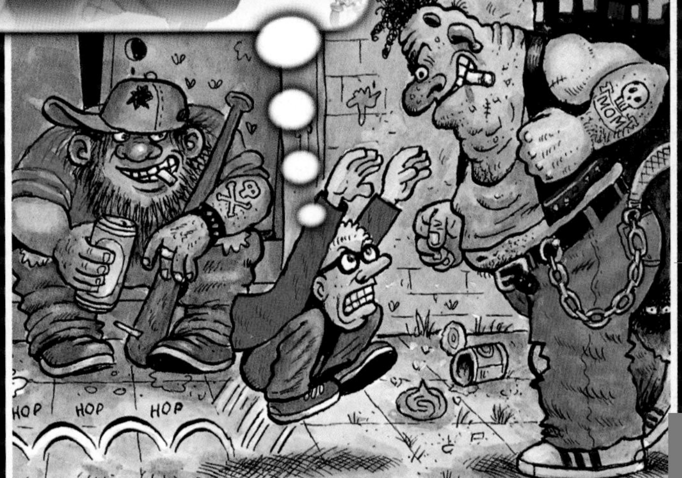
MOM
HOP HOP HOP

Do not attempt to rid yourself of hostile enemies by leaping onto their heads. There is a good chance you cannot jump this high.

TISTS: TOM BUNK AND SCOTT BRICHER WRITER: KENNY BYERLY

THE GAMER'S GUIDE TO FUNCTIONING IN THE REAL WORLD

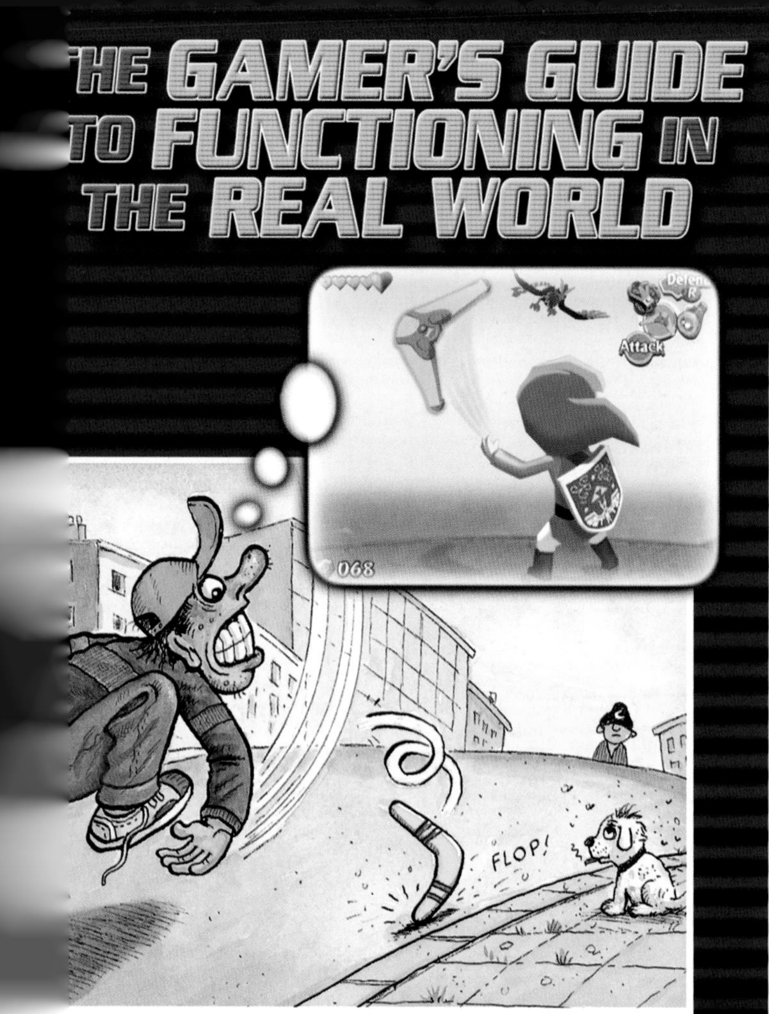
Attack
068
FLOP!

Real boomerangs are almost impossible to throw. They must be thrown a certain way, and even then, they rarely work right. Real boomerangs suck.

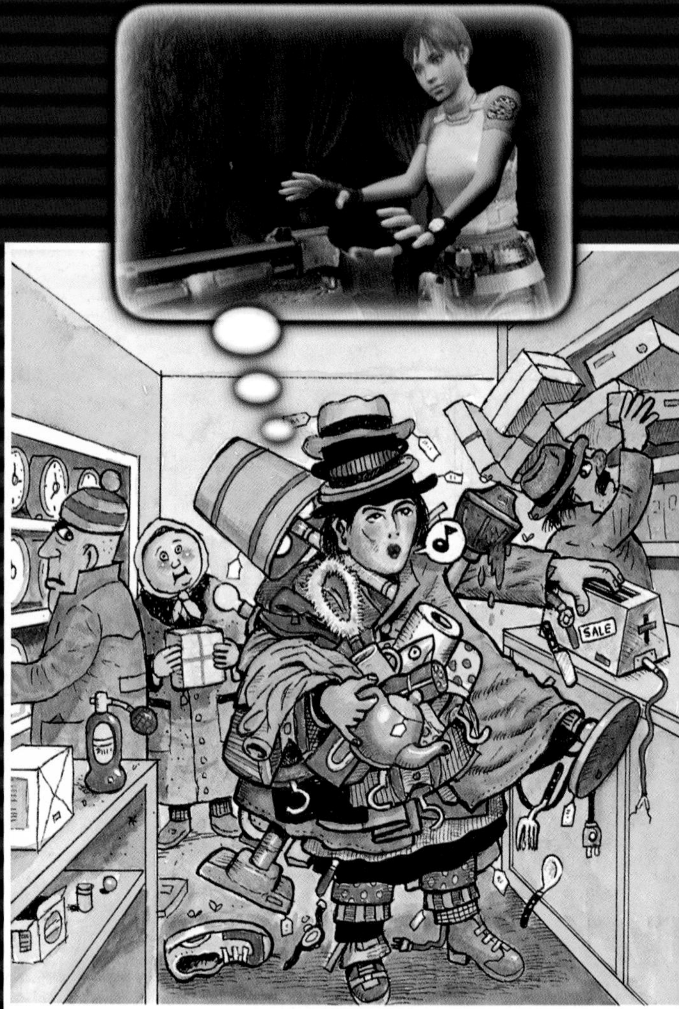
SALE

Picking up items wherever you find them is often a useful strategy in role-playing adventure games, but in reality this behavior is known as kleptomania.

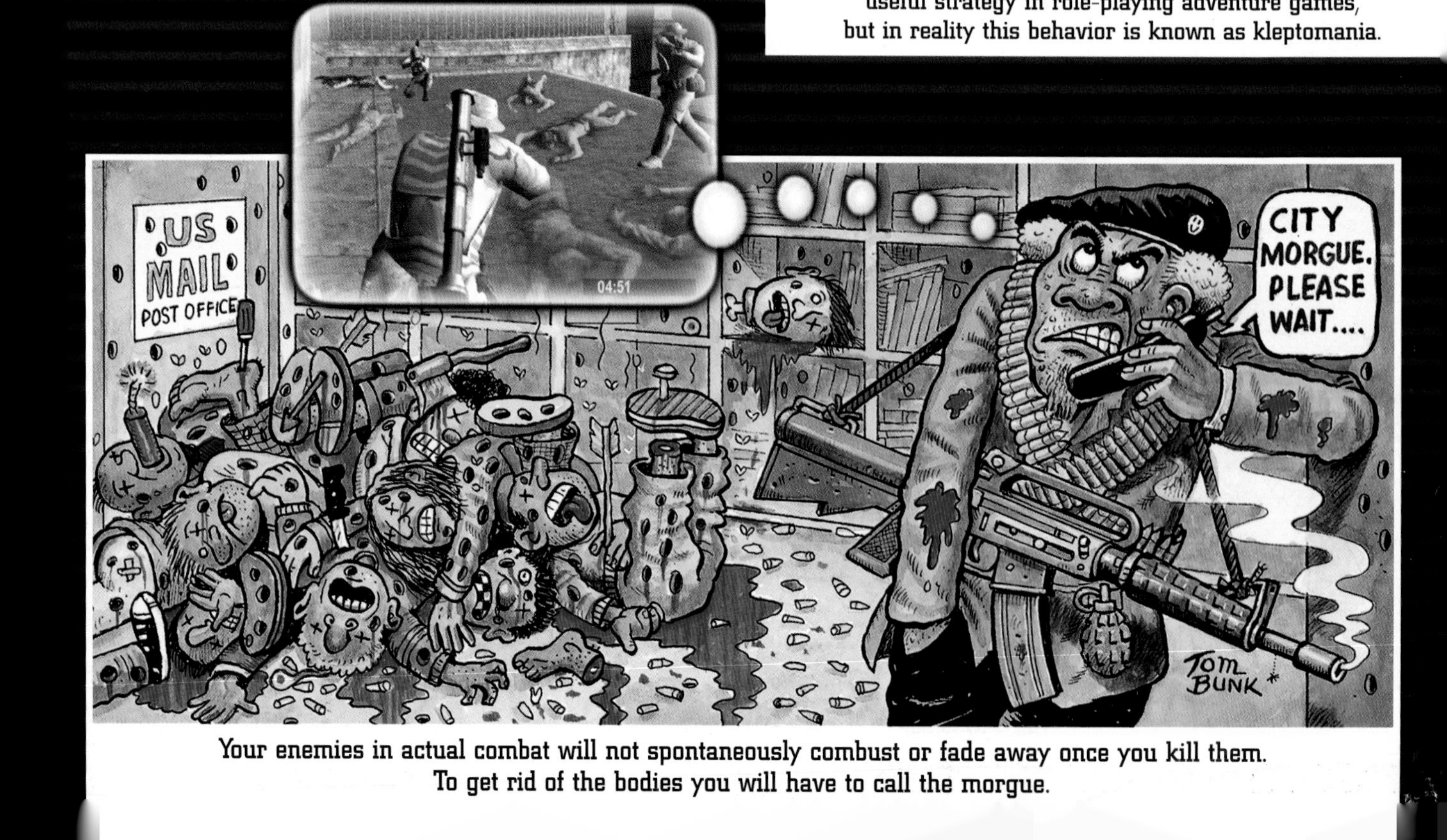
04:51
US MAIL
POST OFFICE
CITY MORGUE. PLEASE WAIT....
TOM BUNK

Your enemies in actual combat will not spontaneously combust or fade away once you kill them. To get rid of the bodies you will have to call the morgue.

ONE EVENING IN A BATHTUB

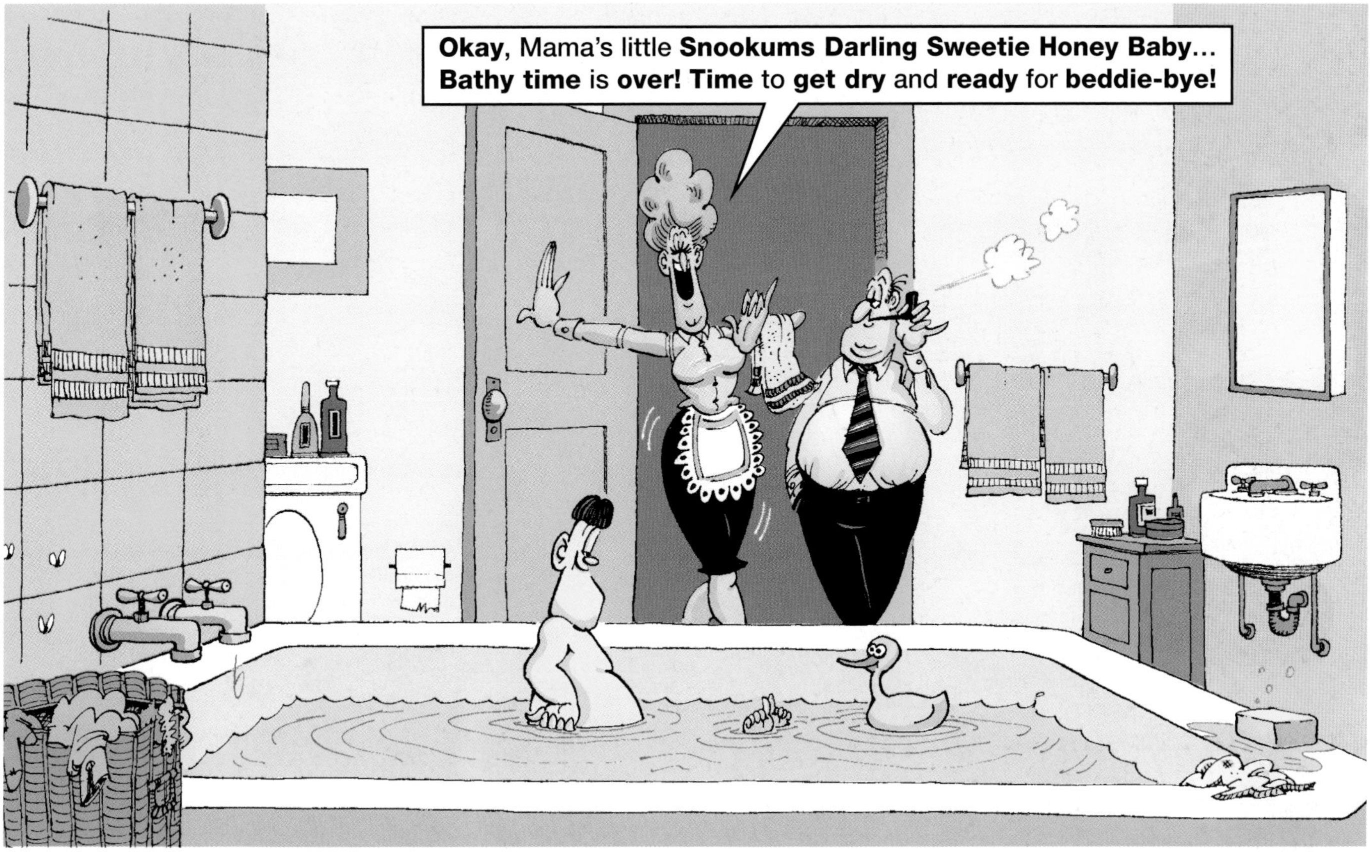
Okay, Mama's little **Snookums Darling Sweetie Honey Baby**... **Bathy time** is **over! Time** to **get dry** and **ready** for **beddie-bye!**

WRITER AND ARTIST: DON MARTIN

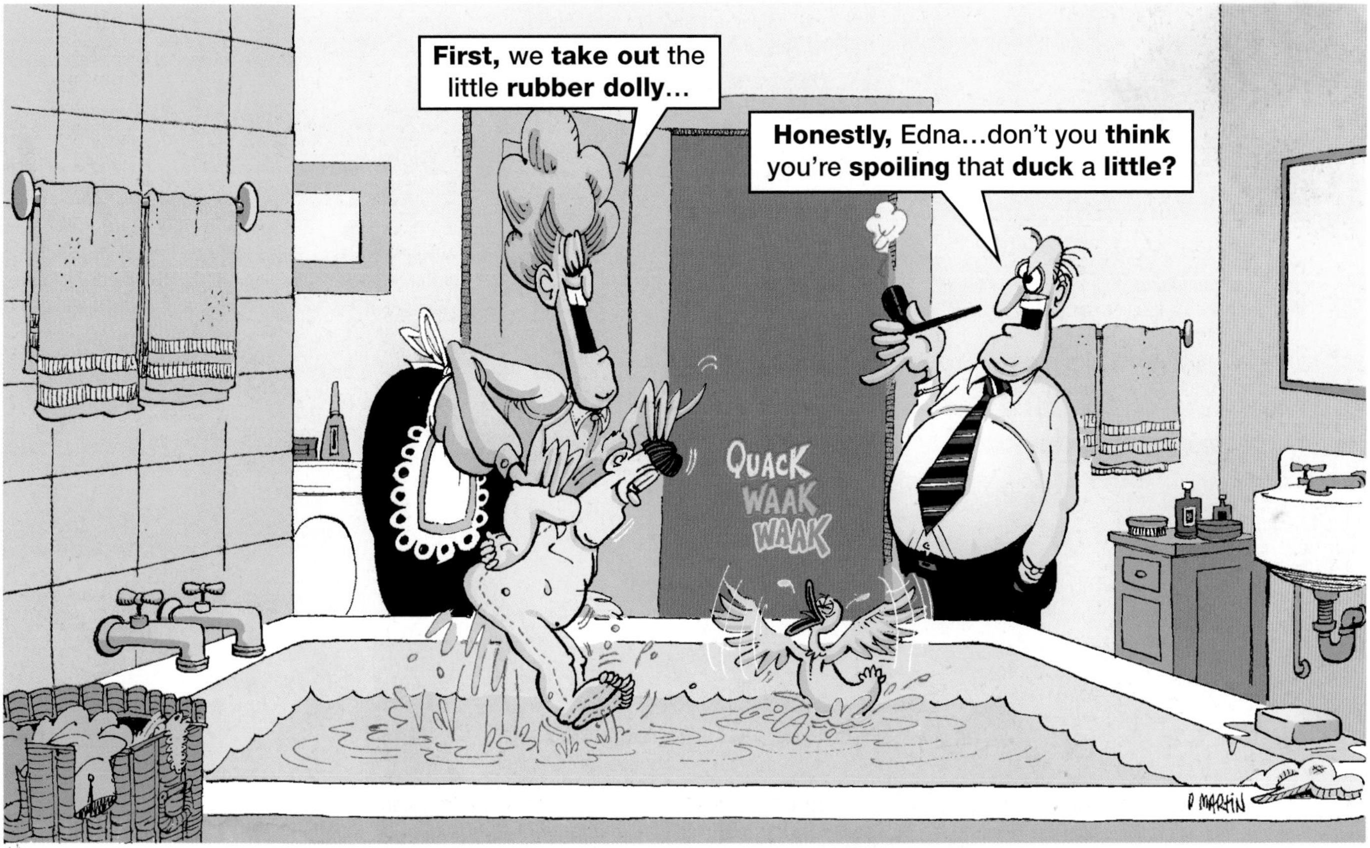
First, we **take out** the little **rubber dolly**...
Honestly, Edna...don't you **think** you're **spoiling** that **duck a little?**
QUACK
WAAK
WAAK

FIELD OF SCHEMES DEPT.

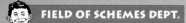

When the Baltimore Orioles unveiled Camden Yards in 1992, the stadium received the kind of nauseatingly over-the-top praise usually reserved for Cal Ripken, Jr. Camden was hailed as a one-of-a-kind marvel and quickly inspired even *more* obscenely expensive imitations. Now it seems a gimmick-laden new park opens every year, featuring such monstrosities as swimming pools, rock-climbing walls and, in the case of the Padres' Petco Park, David Wells! Here's...

WHAT TO
SPANKING

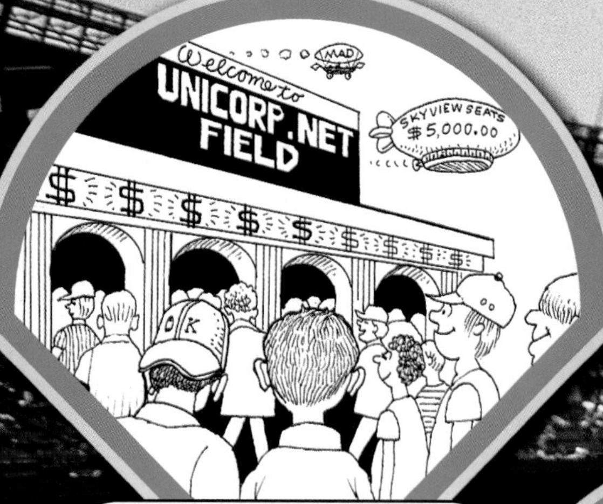
Welcome to
MAD
UNICORP.NET FIELD
SKYVIEW SEATS $5,000.00
OK

The inevitable corporate title — because nothing says "old-fashioned baseball fun" like "Unicorp.net Field."

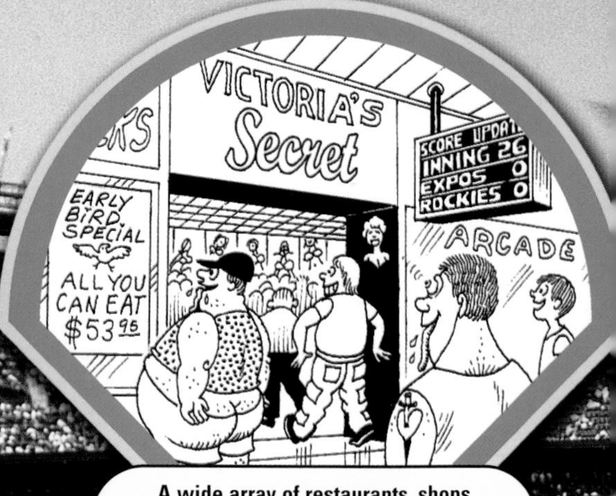
VICTORIA'S Secret
SCORE UPDAT
INNING 26
EXPOS 0
ROCKIES 0
EARLY BIRD SPECIAL
ALL YOU CAN EAT $53.95
ARCADE

A wide array of restaurants, shops and activities — anything to help you forget that you're wasting an evening watching the lowly Rockies play the pathetic Expos.

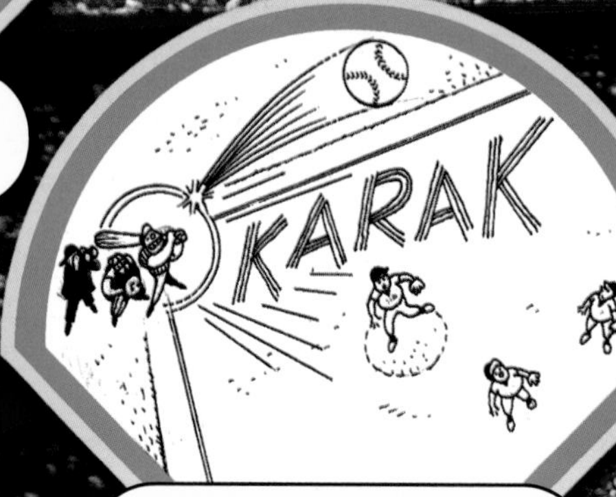
KARAK

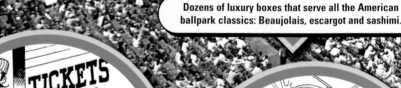

Natural grass fields — because artificial turf has no place in a game filled with doped-up sluggers crushing juiced balls over shortened fences.

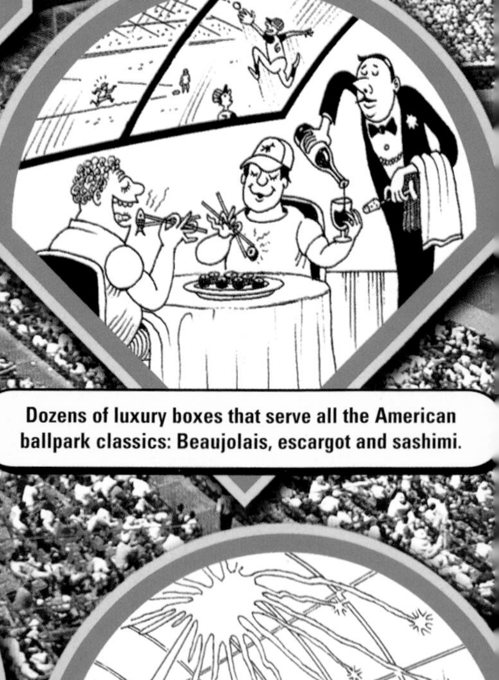

Dozens of luxury boxes that serve all the American ballpark classics: Beaujolais, escargot and sashimi.

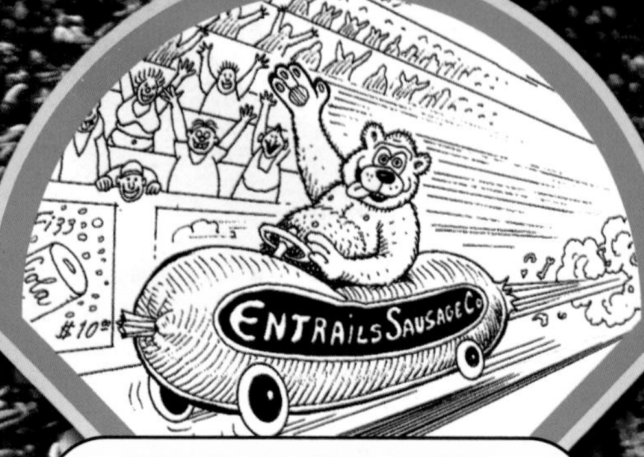
ENTRAILS SAUSAGE Co
$10

Unique features, like a neon liberty bell or racing sausages, that emphasize a team's special relationship with its city — even though the club would've bolted said city in a second if they didn't get a new park.

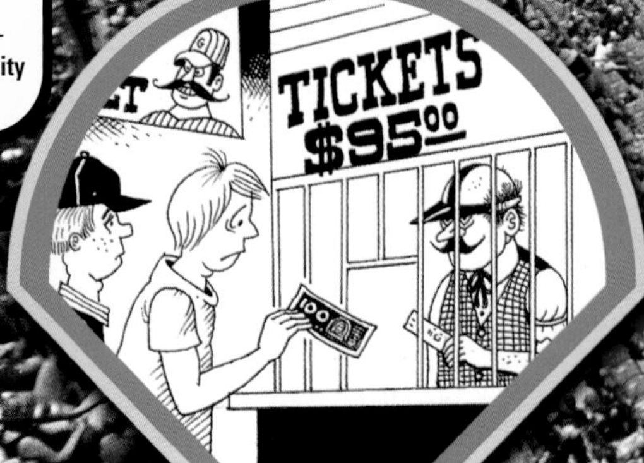
TICKETS $95.00
100

A quaint ballpark atmosphere that transports you back to the 1930s, and ticket prices that rocket you into the 2030s.

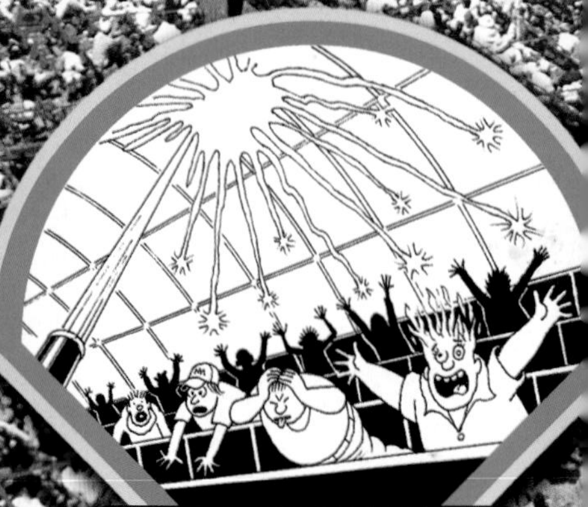

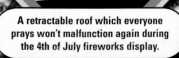

A retractable roof which everyone prays won't malfunction again during the 4th of July fireworks display.

EXPECT AT YOUR TEAM'S NEW $450 MILLION BALLPARK

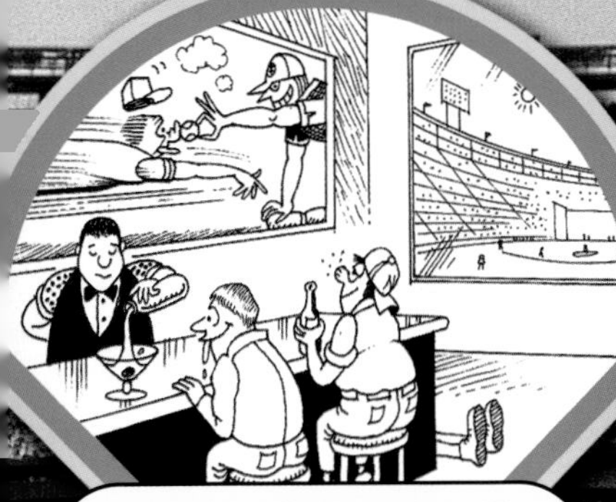

A state-of-the-art sports bar with a giant, wide-screen TV, so you can relax and follow all of the action as if you weren't even at the stadium.

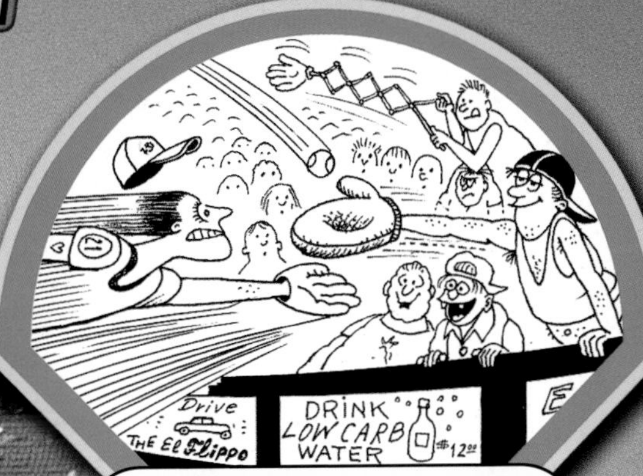

Drive THE El Flippo
DRINK LOW CARB WATER

Seats that are closer to the field than ever before, significantly increasing the odds that some misguided pinhead will ruin your team's pennant chances by interfering with a play in a crucial late-season game.

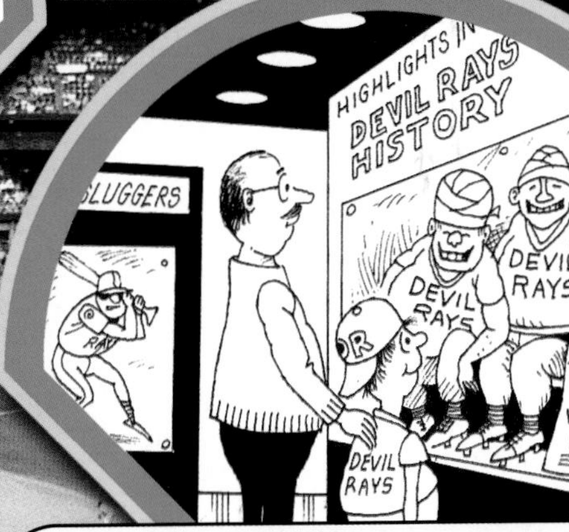

HIGHLIGHTS IN DEVIL RAYS HISTORY
SLUGGERS
DEVIL RAYS
DEVIL RAYS
DEVIL RAYS
DEVIL RAYS WIN ON BALK
DEVIL RAYS

Informative exhibits that highlight the proudest moments in the home team's history, like the Indians' 1954 pennant run, the Pirates' World Series win in 1960, and that time the Devil Rays broke a 14-game losing streak when the opposing pitcher hit three consecutive batters and then balked-in the game's only run.

ARTIST: AL JAFFEE
WRITER: JACOB LAMBERT
PHOTO: GETTY IMAGES

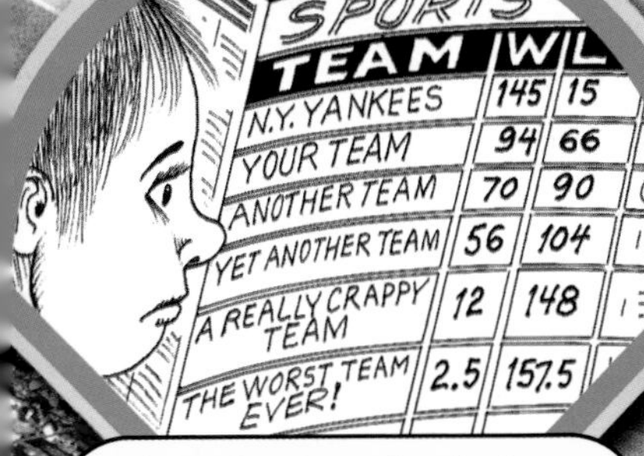

SPORTS
TEAM W L
N.Y. YANKEES 145 15
YOUR TEAM 94 66
ANOTHER TEAM 70 90
YET ANOTHER TEAM 56 104
A REALLY CRAPPY TEAM 12 148
THE WORST TEAM EVER! 2.5 157.5

A solid home team that, thanks to the new ballpark revenue, can finally be competitive enough to take one out of every seven from the Yankees.

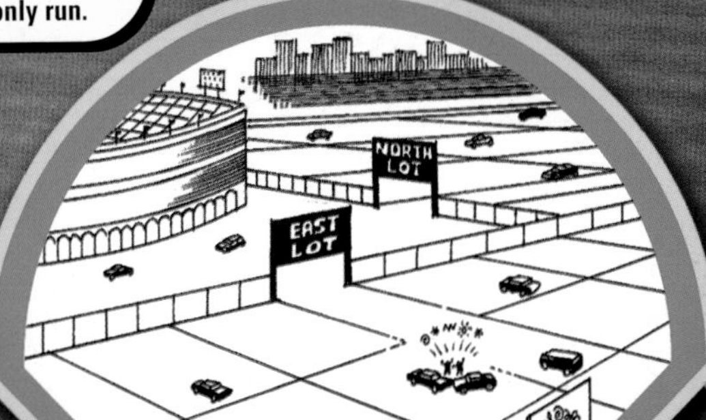

NORTH LOT
EAST LOT

Ample parking to handle crowds of 40,000 or, more accurately, the 14,000 who will actually show up once the stadium's novelty inevitably wears off.

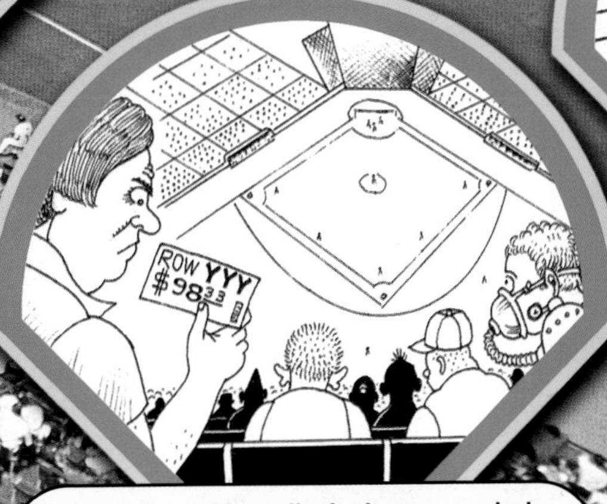

ROW YYY
$98.33

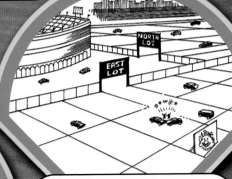

For the team's blue-collar fan base, upper-deck "cheap seats" that are more expensive than those in the old park's behind-the-plate VIP section.

GET RICH OR DIE BUYING DEPT.

The MAD WORLD of...

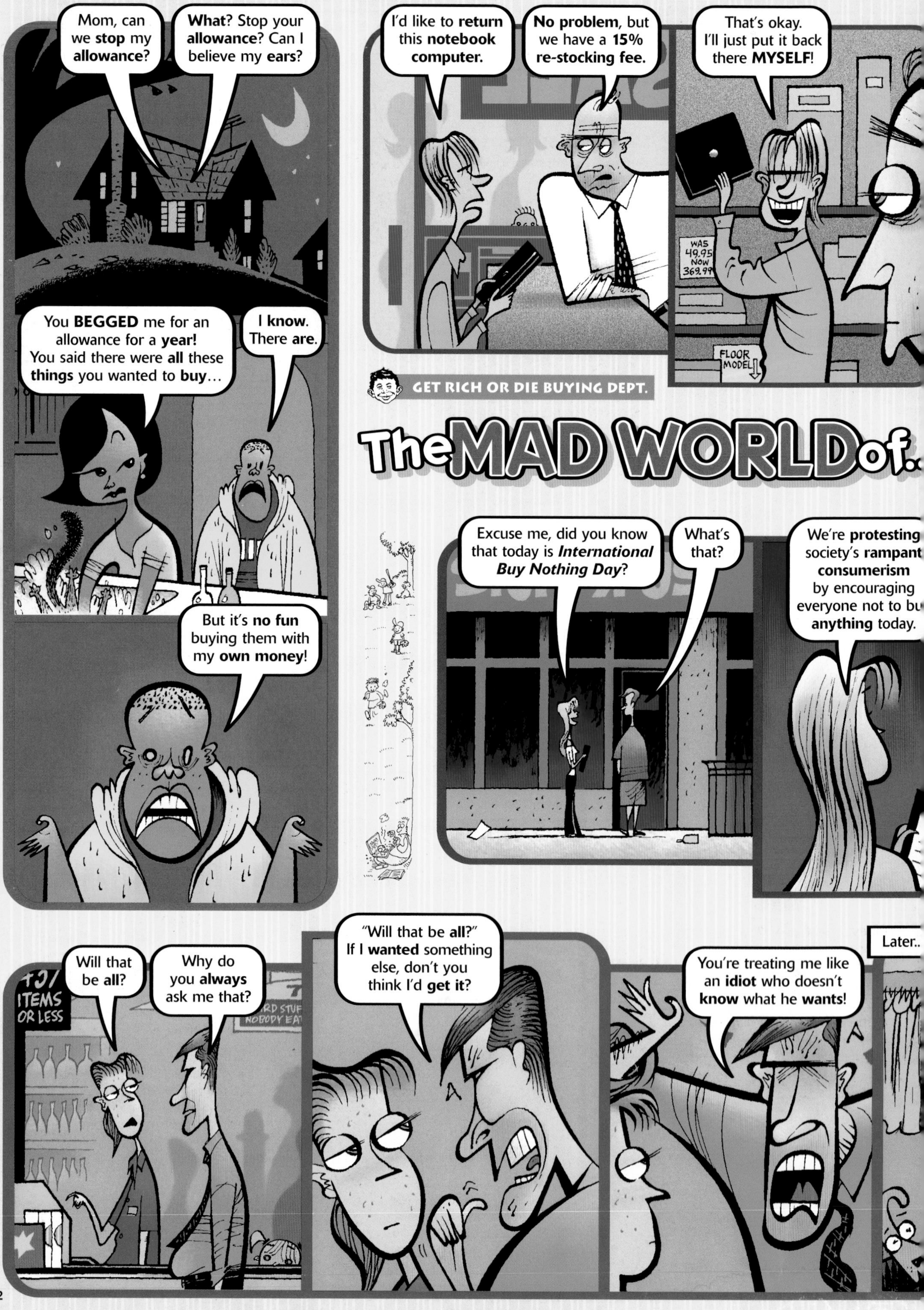

Mom, can we **stop** my **allowance**?
What? Stop your **allowance**? Can I believe my **ears**?
You **BEGGED** me for an allowance for a **year!** You said there were **all** these **things** you wanted to **buy**…
I **know**. There **are**.
But it's **no fun** buying them with my **own money**!
I'd like to **return** this **notebook computer.**
No problem, but we have a **15% re-stocking fee.**
That's okay. I'll just put it back there **MYSELF**!
WAS 49.95 NOW 369.99
FLOOR MODEL
Excuse me, did you know that today is ***International Buy Nothing Day***?
What's that?
We're **protesting** society's **rampant consumerism** by encouraging everyone not to bu
anything today.
ITEMS OR LESS
Will that be **all**?
Why do you **always** ask me that?
"Will that be **all**?" If I **wanted** something else, don't you think I'd **get it**?
Later..
You're treating me like an **idiot** who doesn't **know** what he **wants**!

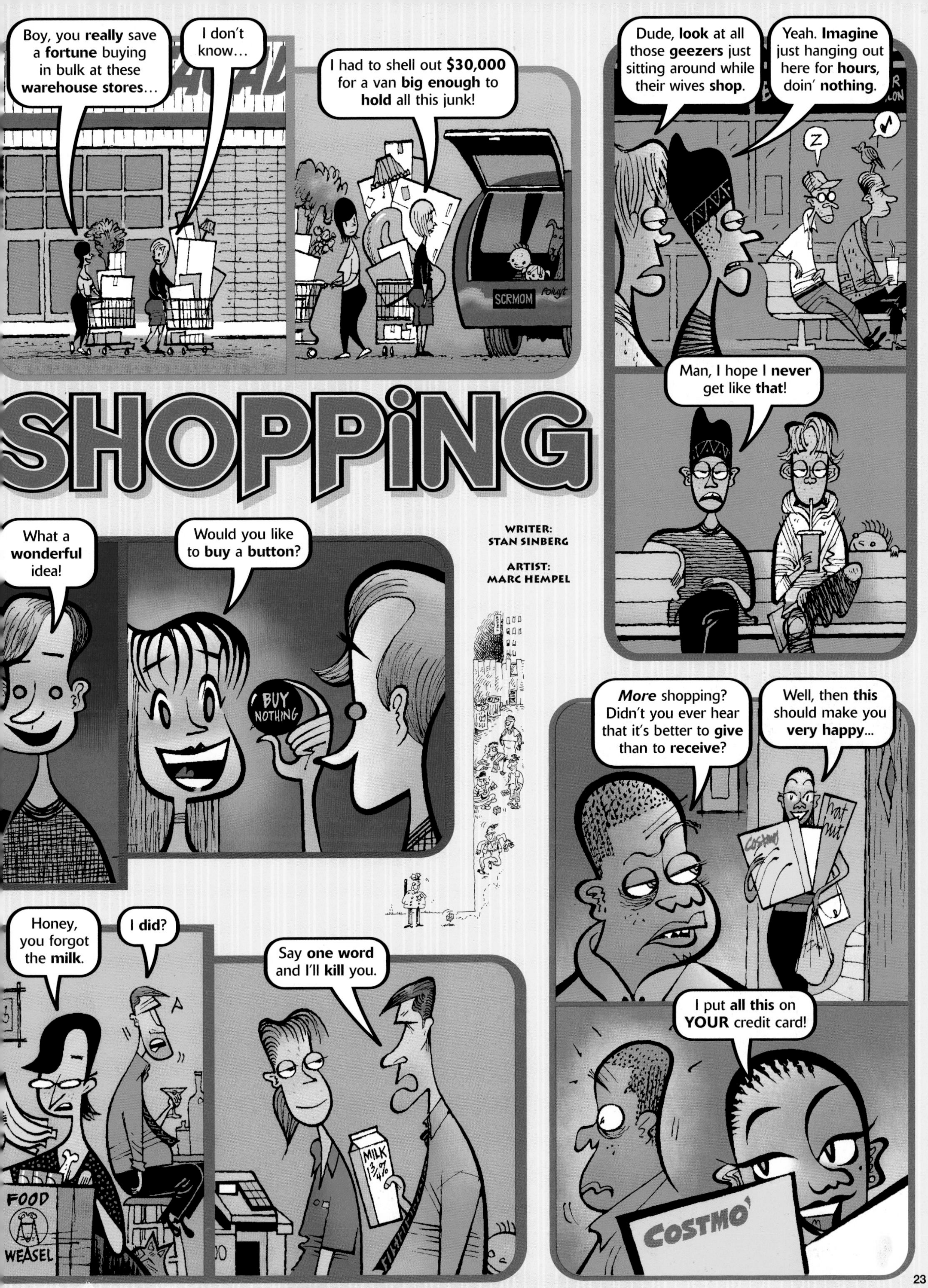

Boy, you really save a fortune buying in bulk at these warehouse stores…
I don't know…
I had to shell out $30,000 for a van big enough to hold all this junk!
SCRMOM
Dude, look at all those geezers just sitting around while their wives shop.
Yeah. Imagine just hanging out here for hours, doin' nothing.
Z
Man, I hope I never get like that!
SHOPPiNG
WRITER: STAN SINBERG
ARTIST: MARC HEMPEL
What a wonderful idea!
Would you like to buy a button?
BUY NOTHING
More shopping? Didn't you ever hear that it's better to give than to receive?
Well, then this should make you very happy...
COSTMO
I put all this on YOUR credit card!
COSTMO'
Honey, you forgot the milk.
I did?
Say one word and I'll kill you.
MILK 1 3/4 %
FOOD WEASEL

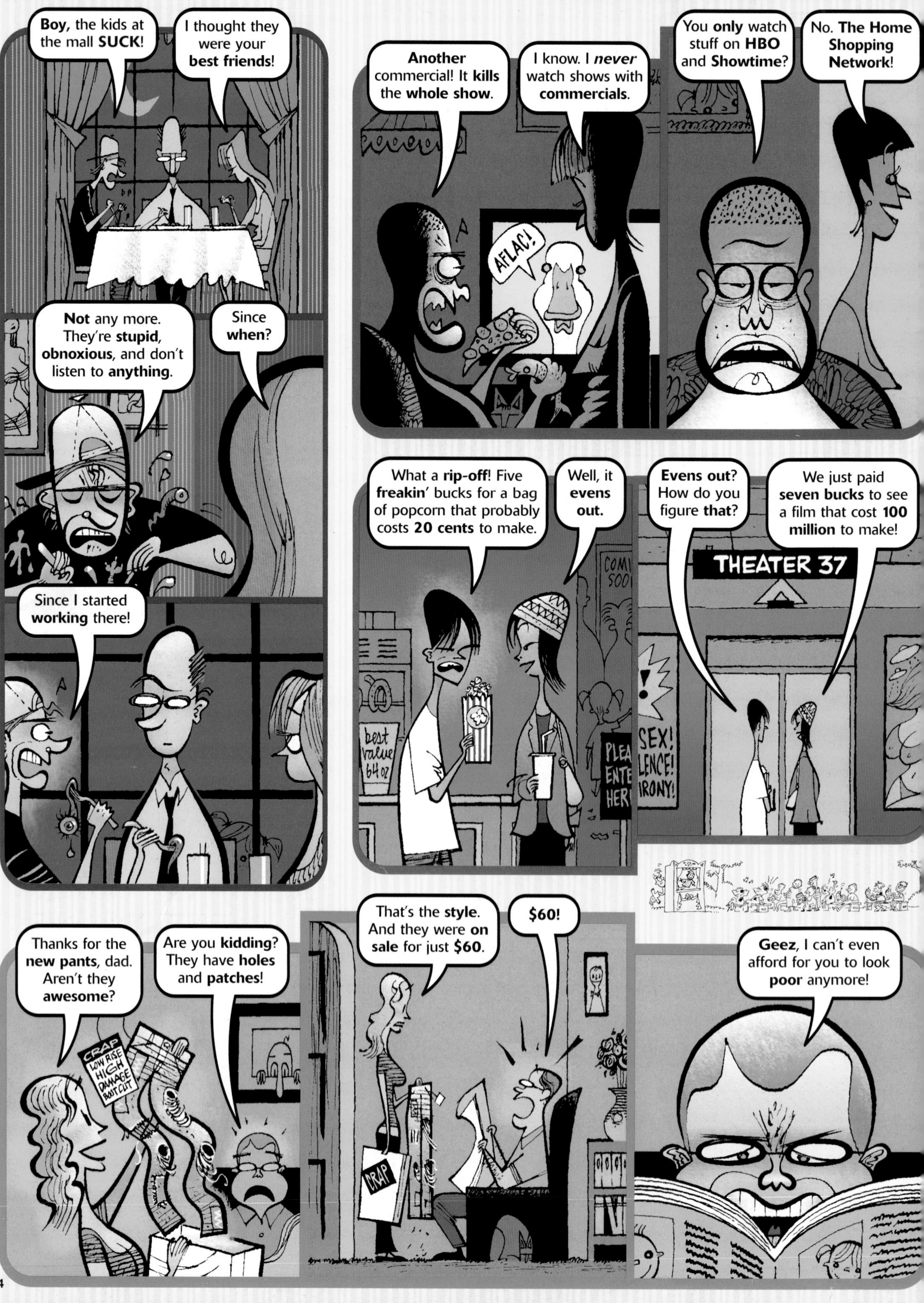

Boy, the kids at the mall SUCK!
I thought they were your best friends!
Not any more. They're stupid, obnoxious, and don't listen to anything.
Since when?
Since I started working there!
Another commercial! It kills the whole show.
I know. I never watch shows with commercials.
AFLAC!
You only watch stuff on HBO and Showtime?
No. The Home Shopping Network!
What a rip-off! Five freakin' bucks for a bag of popcorn that probably costs 20 cents to make.
Well, it evens out.
best value 64 oz
Evens out? How do you figure that?
We just paid seven bucks to see a film that cost 100 million to make!
THEATER 37
IRONY!
Thanks for the new pants, dad. Aren't they awesome?
CRAP LOW RISE HIGH DAMAGE BOOT CUT
Are you kidding? They have holes and patches!
That's the style. And they were on sale for just $60.
$60!
CRAP
Geez, I can't even afford for you to look poor anymore!

THE ZIT

ARTIST: TOM BUNK WRITER: MICHAEL GALLAGHER

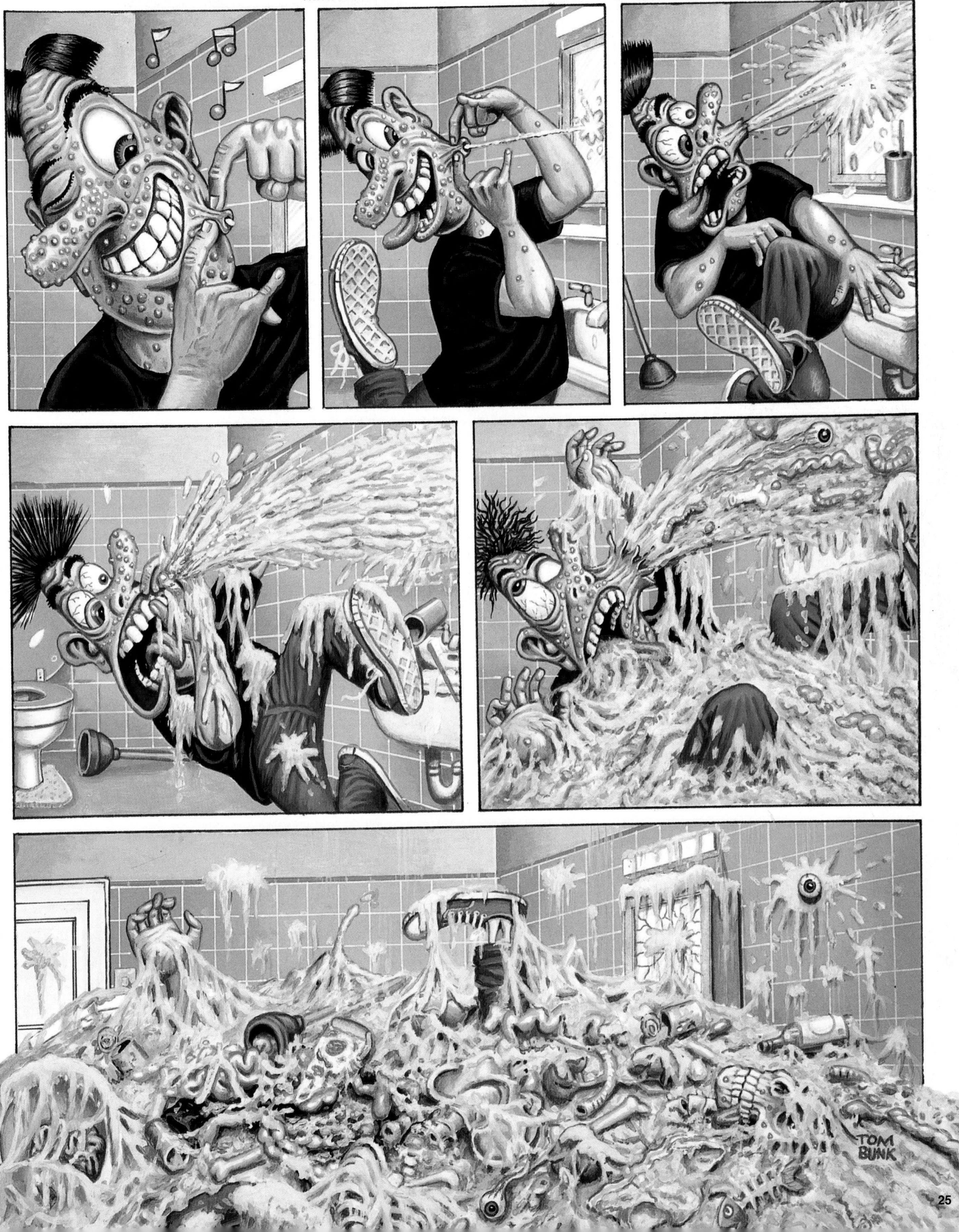
TOM BUNK

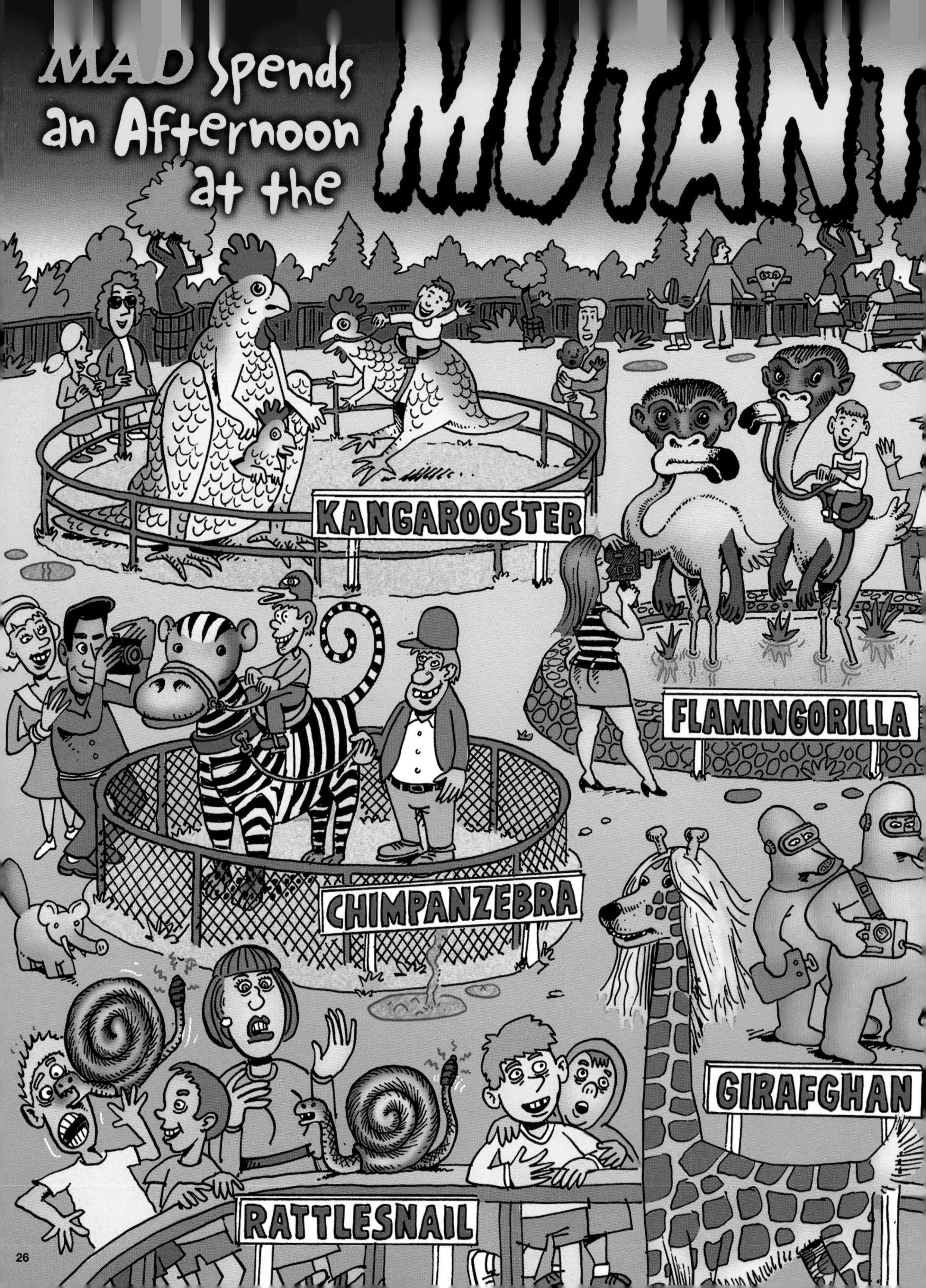
MAD Spends an Afternoon at the
MUTAN
KANGAROOSTER
FLAMINGORILLA
CHIMPANZEBRA
GIRAFGHAN
RATTLESNAIL

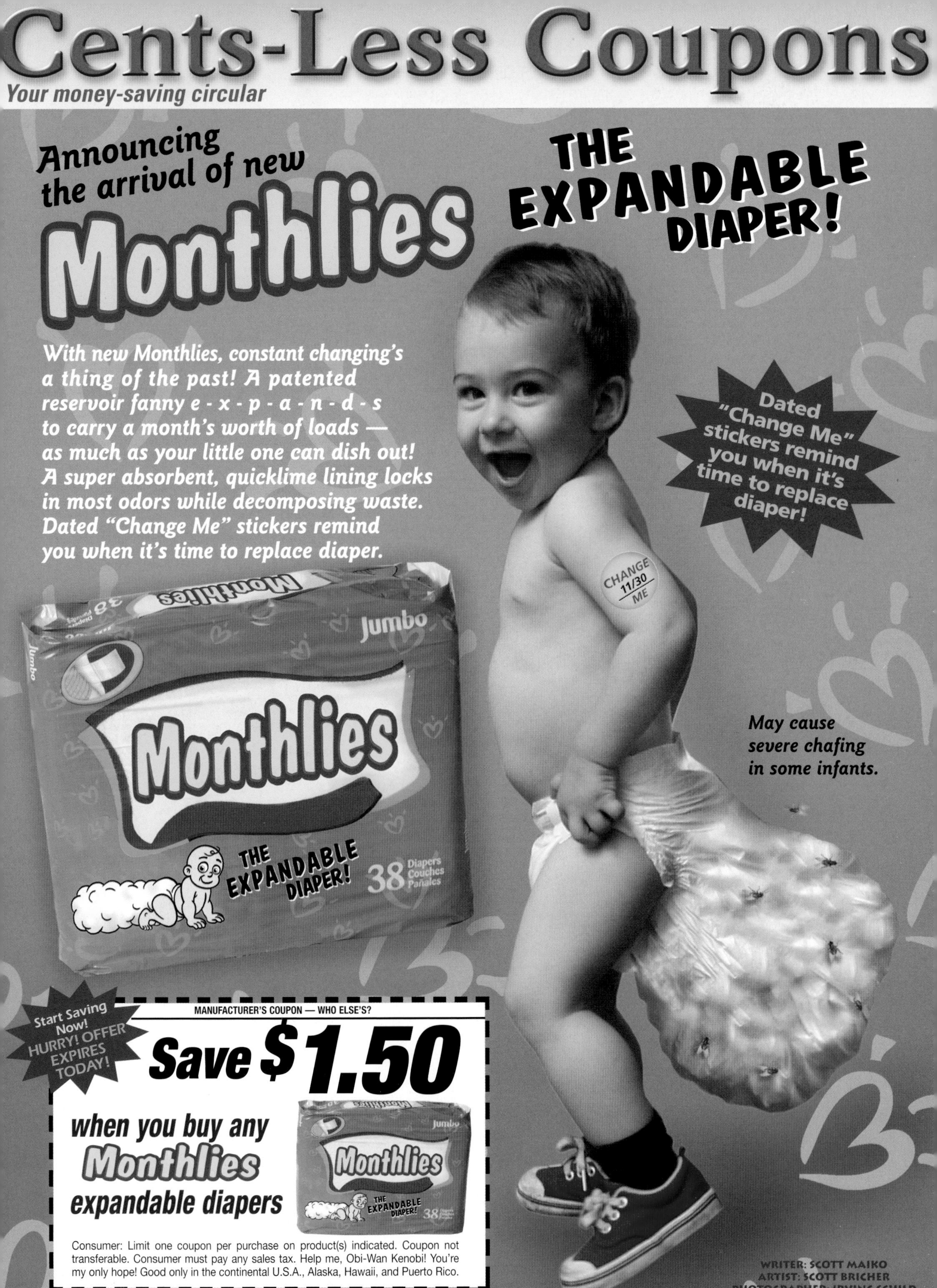

Cents-Less Coupons
Your money-saving circular
Announcing the arrival of new
Monthlies
THE EXPANDABLE DIAPER!
With new Monthlies, constant changing's a thing of the past! A patented reservoir fanny e-x-p-a-n-d-s to carry a month's worth of loads — as much as your little one can dish out! A super absorbent, quicklime lining locks in most odors while decomposing waste. Dated "Change Me" stickers remind you when it's time to replace diaper.
Dated "Change Me" stickers remind you when it's time to replace diaper!
CHANGE 11/30 ME
Monthlies
Jumbo
Monthlies
THE EXPANDABLE DIAPER!
38 Diapers Couches Pañales
May cause severe chafing in some infants.
Start Saving Now! HURRY! OFFER EXPIRES TODAY!
MANUFACTURER'S COUPON — WHO ELSE'S?
Save $1.50
when you buy any Monthlies expandable diapers
Consumer: Limit one coupon per purchase on product(s) indicated. Coupon not transferable. Consumer must pay any sales tax. Help me, Obi-Wan Kenobi! You're my only hope! Good only in the continental U.S.A., Alaska, Hawaii, and Puerto Rico.

WRITER: SCOTT MAIKO
ARTIST: SCOTT BRICHER
PHOTOGRAPHER: IRVING SCHILD

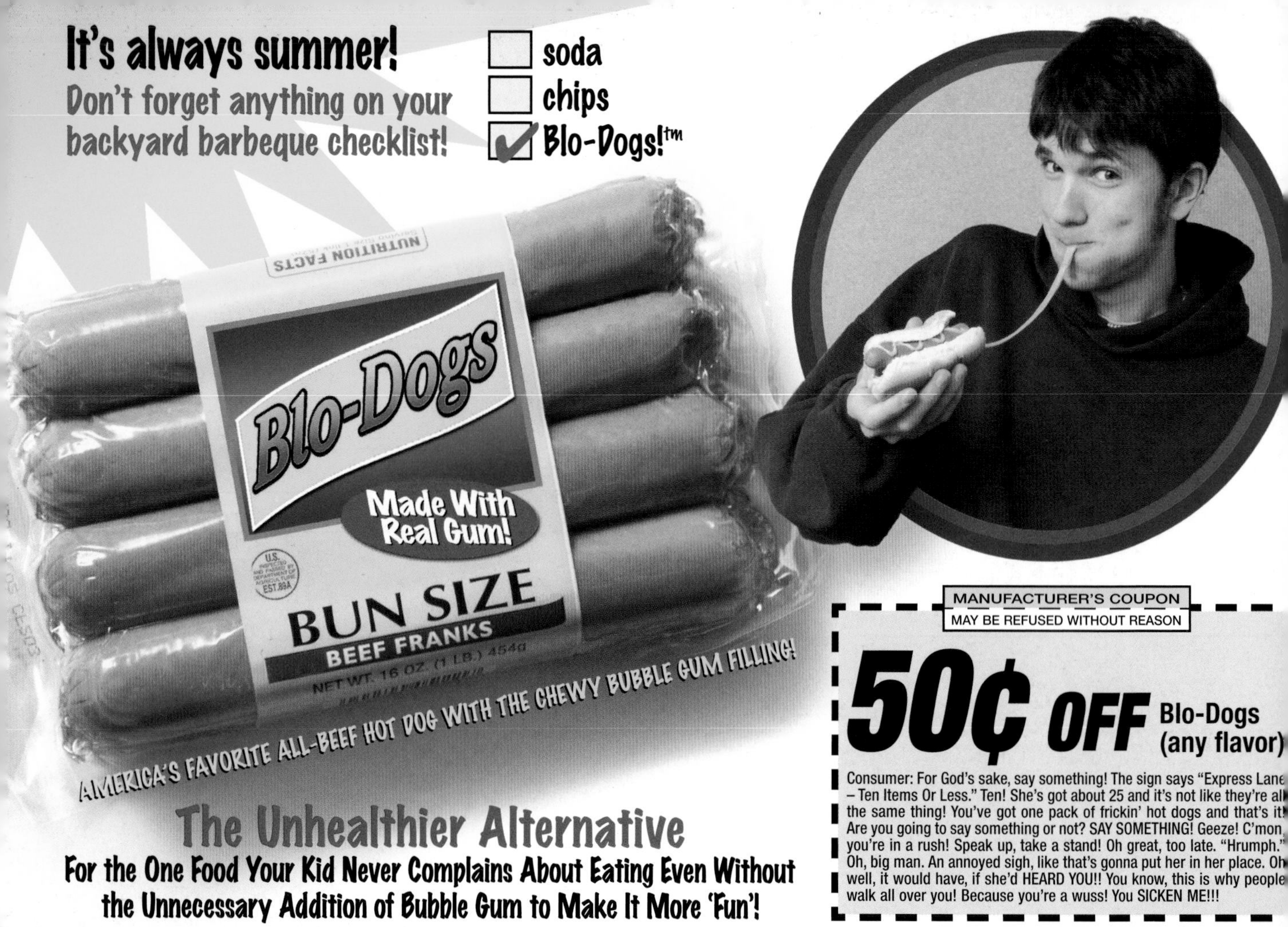
It's always summer!
Don't forget anything on your backyard barbeque checklist!
soda
chips
Blo-Dogs!™
NUTRITION FACTS
Blo-Dogs
Made With Real Gum!
BUN SIZE
BEEF FRANKS
NET WT. 16 OZ. (1 LB.) 454g
AMERICA'S FAVORITE ALL-BEEF HOT DOG WITH THE CHEWY BUBBLE GUM FILLING!
The Unhealthier Alternative
For the One Food Your Kid Never Complains About Eating Even Without the Unnecessary Addition of Bubble Gum to Make It More 'Fun'!
MANUFACTURER'S COUPON
MAY BE REFUSED WITHOUT REASON
50¢ OFF Blo-Dogs (any flavor)
Consumer: For God's sake, say something! The sign says "Express Lane – Ten Items Or Less." Ten! She's got about 25 and it's not like they're all the same thing! You've got one pack of frickin' hot dogs and that's it! Are you going to say something or not? SAY SOMETHING! Geeze! C'mon, you're in a rush! Speak up, take a stand! Oh great, too late. "Hrumph." Oh, big man. An annoyed sigh, like that's gonna put her in her place. Oh well, it would have, if she'd HEARD YOU!! You know, this is why people walk all over you! Because you're a wuss! You SICKEN ME!!!

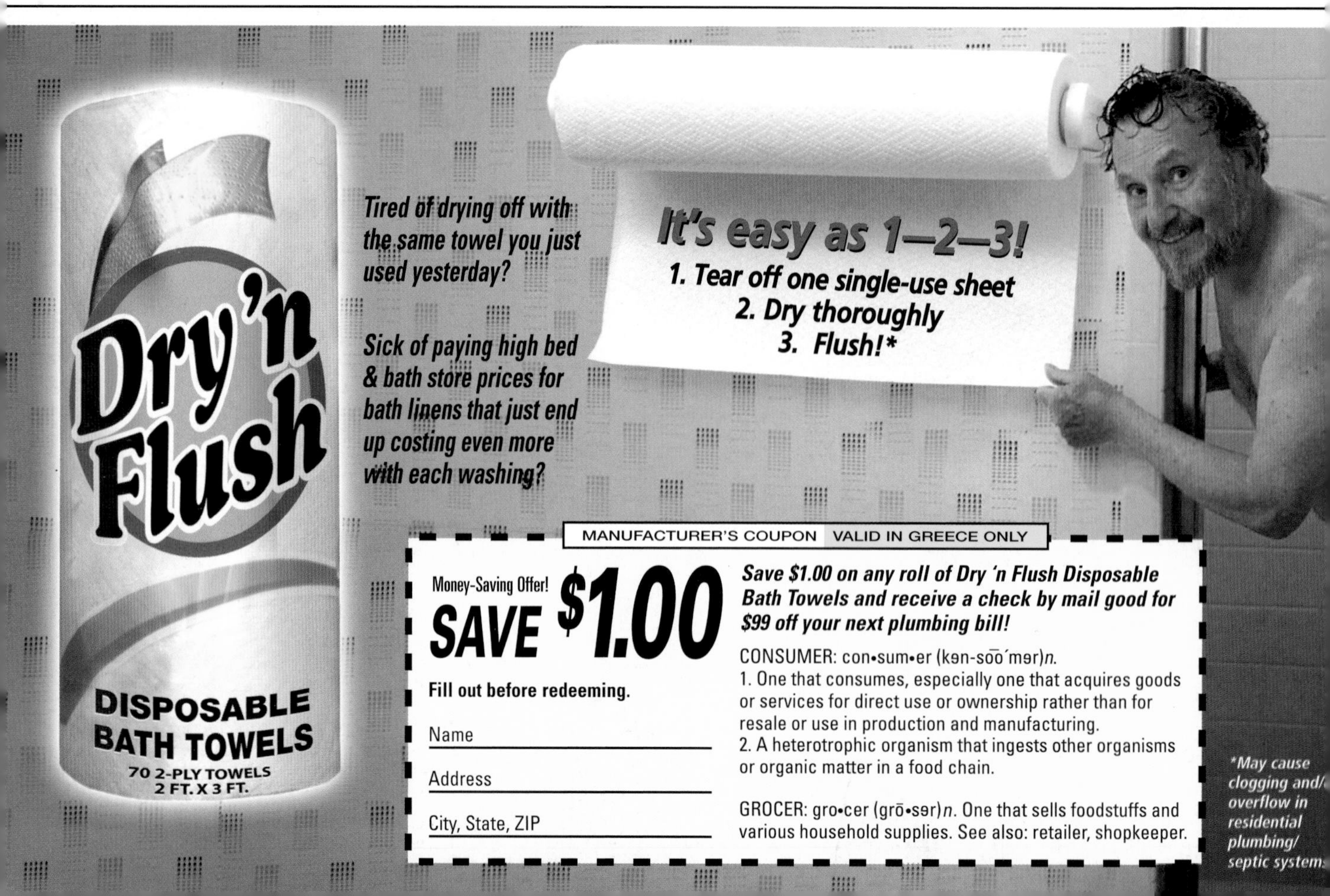
Dry 'n Flush
DISPOSABLE BATH TOWELS
70 2-PLY TOWELS
2 FT. X 3 FT.
Tired of drying off with the same towel you just used yesterday?
Sick of paying high bed & bath store prices for bath linens that just end up costing even more with each washing?
It's easy as 1—2—3!
1. Tear off one single-use sheet
2. Dry thoroughly
3. Flush!*
MANUFACTURER'S COUPON
VALID IN GREECE ONLY
Money-Saving Offer!
SAVE $1.00
Fill out before redeeming.
Name
Address
City, State, ZIP
Save $1.00 on any roll of Dry 'n Flush Disposable Bath Towels and receive a check by mail good for $99 off your next plumbing bill!
CONSUMER: con•sum•er (kən-sōō´mər)n.
1. One that consumes, especially one that acquires goods or services for direct use or ownership rather than for resale or use in production and manufacturing.
2. A heterotrophic organism that ingests other organisms or organic matter in a food chain.
GROCER: gro•cer (grō•sər)n. One that sells foodstuffs and various household supplies. See also: retailer, shopkeeper.
*May cause clogging and/or overflow in residential plumbing/septic systems

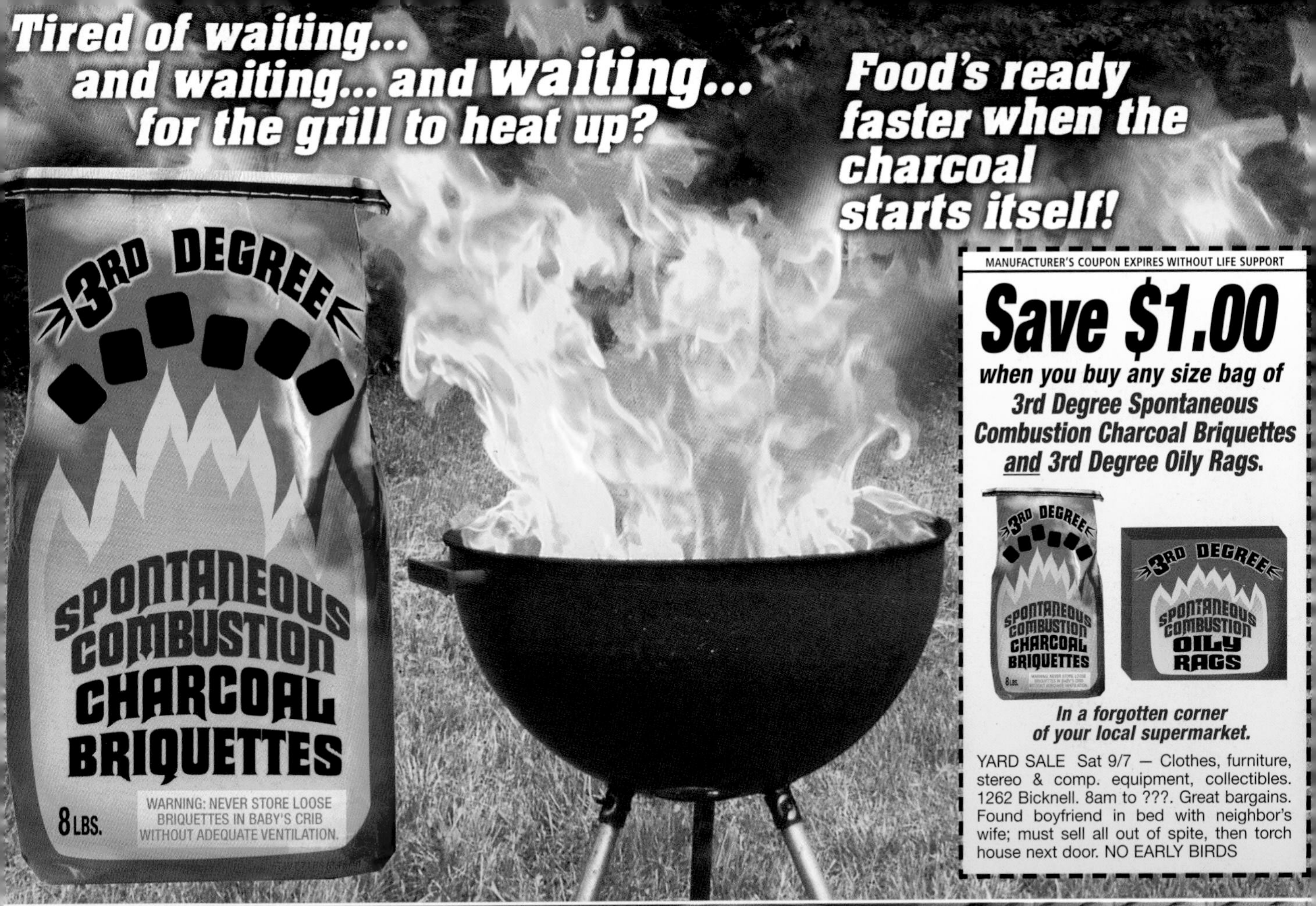
Tired of waiting...
and waiting... and waiting...
for the grill to heat up?
Food's ready faster when the charcoal starts itself!
3RD DEGREE
SPONTANEOUS COMBUSTION CHARCOAL BRIQUETTES
8 LBS.
WARNING: NEVER STORE LOOSE BRIQUETTES IN BABY'S CRIB WITHOUT ADEQUATE VENTILATION.
MANUFACTURER'S COUPON EXPIRES WITHOUT LIFE SUPPORT
Save $1.00
when you buy any size bag of 3rd Degree Spontaneous Combustion Charcoal Briquettes and 3rd Degree Oily Rags.
3RD DEGREE SPONTANEOUS COMBUSTION CHARCOAL BRIQUETTES
8 LBS.
3RD DEGREE SPONTANEOUS COMBUSTION OILY RAGS
In a forgotten corner of your local supermarket.
YARD SALE Sat 9/7 — Clothes, furniture, stereo & comp. equipment, collectibles. 1262 Bicknell. 8am to ???. Great bargains. Found boyfriend in bed with neighbor's wife; must sell all out of spite, then torch house next door. NO EARLY BIRDS

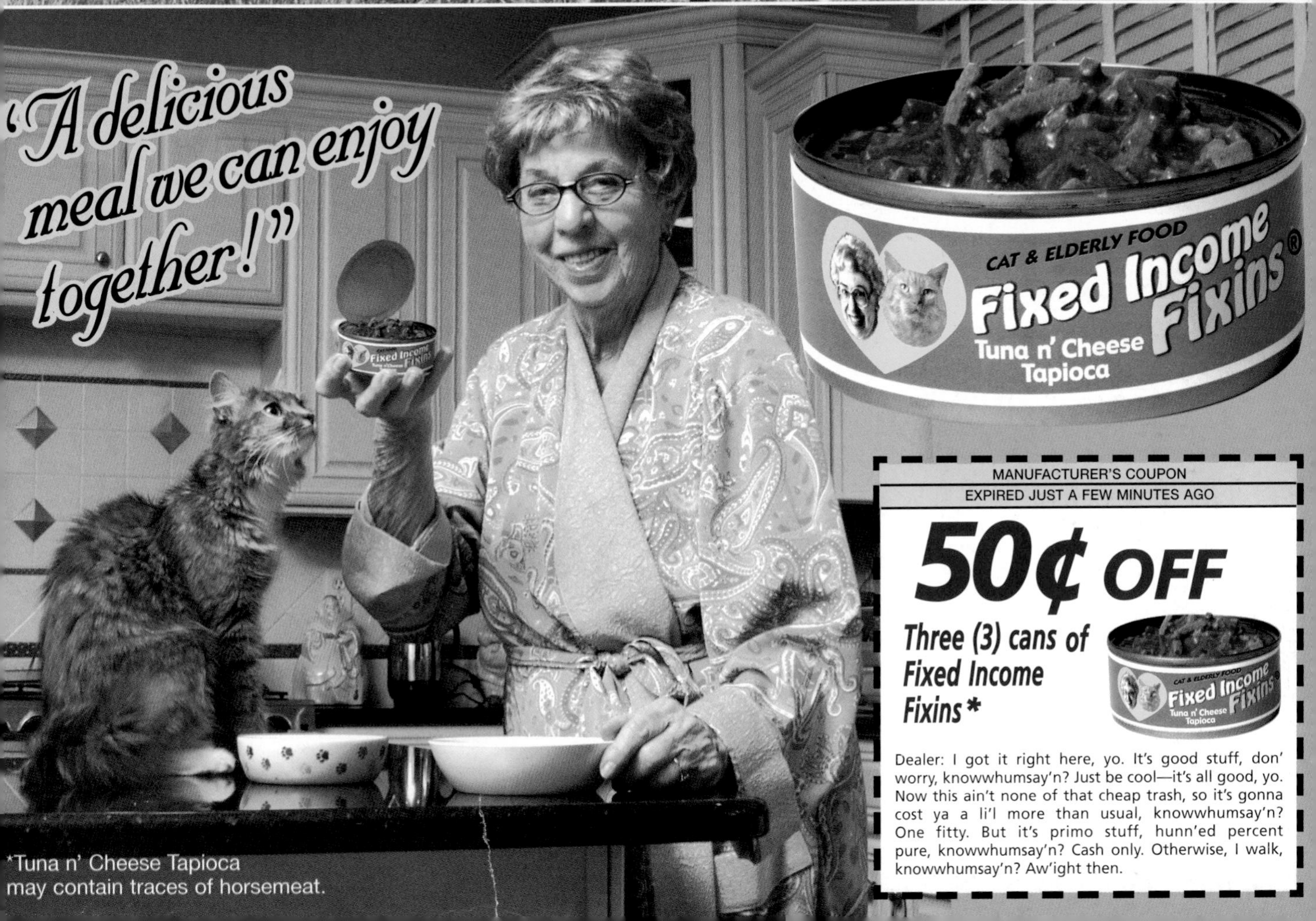
"A delicious meal we can enjoy together!"
CAT & ELDERLY FOOD
Fixed Income Fixins®
Tuna n' Cheese Tapioca
MANUFACTURER'S COUPON
EXPIRED JUST A FEW MINUTES AGO
50¢ OFF
Three (3) cans of Fixed Income Fixins*
Dealer: I got it right here, yo. It's good stuff, don' worry, knowwhumsay'n? Just be cool—it's all good, yo. Now this ain't none of that cheap trash, so it's gonna cost ya a li'l more than usual, knowwhumsay'n? One fitty. But it's primo stuff, hunn'ed percent pure, knowwhumsay'n? Cash only. Otherwise, I walk, knowwhumsay'n? Aw'ight then.
*Tuna n' Cheese Tapioca may contain traces of horsemeat.

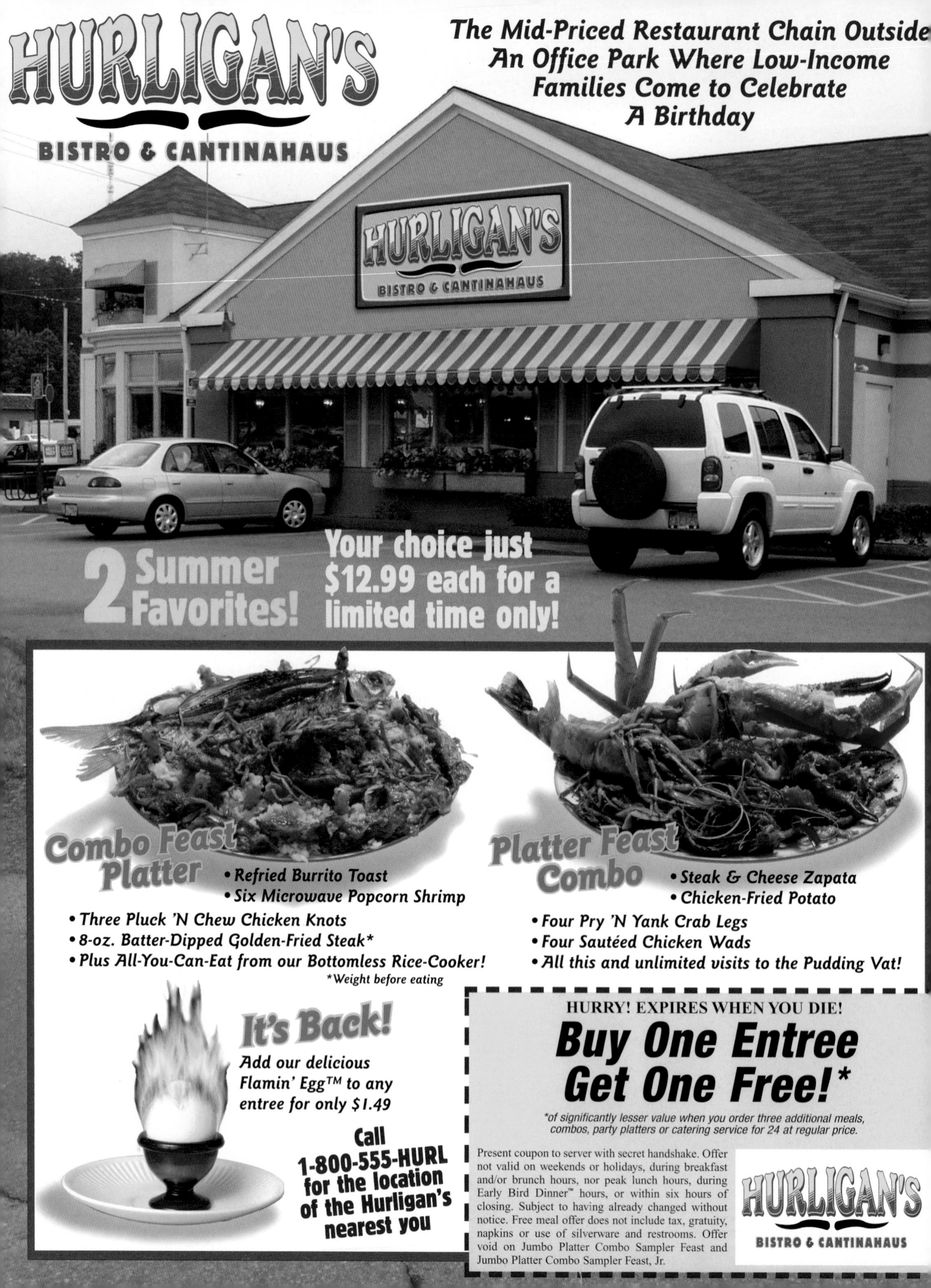
HURLIGAN'S
BISTRO & CANTINAHAUS
The Mid-Priced Restaurant Chain Outside An Office Park Where Low-Income Families Come to Celebrate A Birthday
HURLIGAN'S
BISTRO & CANTINAHAUS
2 Summer Favorites!
Your choice just $12.99 each for a limited time only!
Combo Feast Platter
• Refried Burrito Toast
• Six Microwave Popcorn Shrimp
• Three Pluck 'N Chew Chicken Knots
• 8-oz. Batter-Dipped Golden-Fried Steak*
• Plus All-You-Can-Eat from our Bottomless Rice-Cooker!
*Weight before eating
Platter Feast Combo
• Steak & Cheese Zapata
• Chicken-Fried Potato
• Four Pry 'N Yank Crab Legs
• Four Sautéed Chicken Wads
• All this and unlimited visits to the Pudding Vat!
It's Back!
Add our delicious Flamin' Egg™ to any entree for only $1.49
Call 1-800-555-HURL for the location of the Hurligan's nearest you
HURRY! EXPIRES WHEN YOU DIE!
Buy One Entree Get One Free!*
*of significantly lesser value when you order three additional meals, combos, party platters or catering service for 24 at regular price.
Present coupon to server with secret handshake. Offer not valid on weekends or holidays, during breakfast and/or brunch hours, nor peak lunch hours, during Early Bird Dinner™ hours, or within six hours of closing. Subject to having already changed without notice. Free meal offer does not include tax, gratuity, napkins or use of silverware and restrooms. Offer void on Jumbo Platter Combo Sampler Feast and Jumbo Platter Combo Sampler Feast, Jr.
HURLIGAN'S
BISTRO & CANTINAHAUS

ON THE BEACH AT LOW TIDE

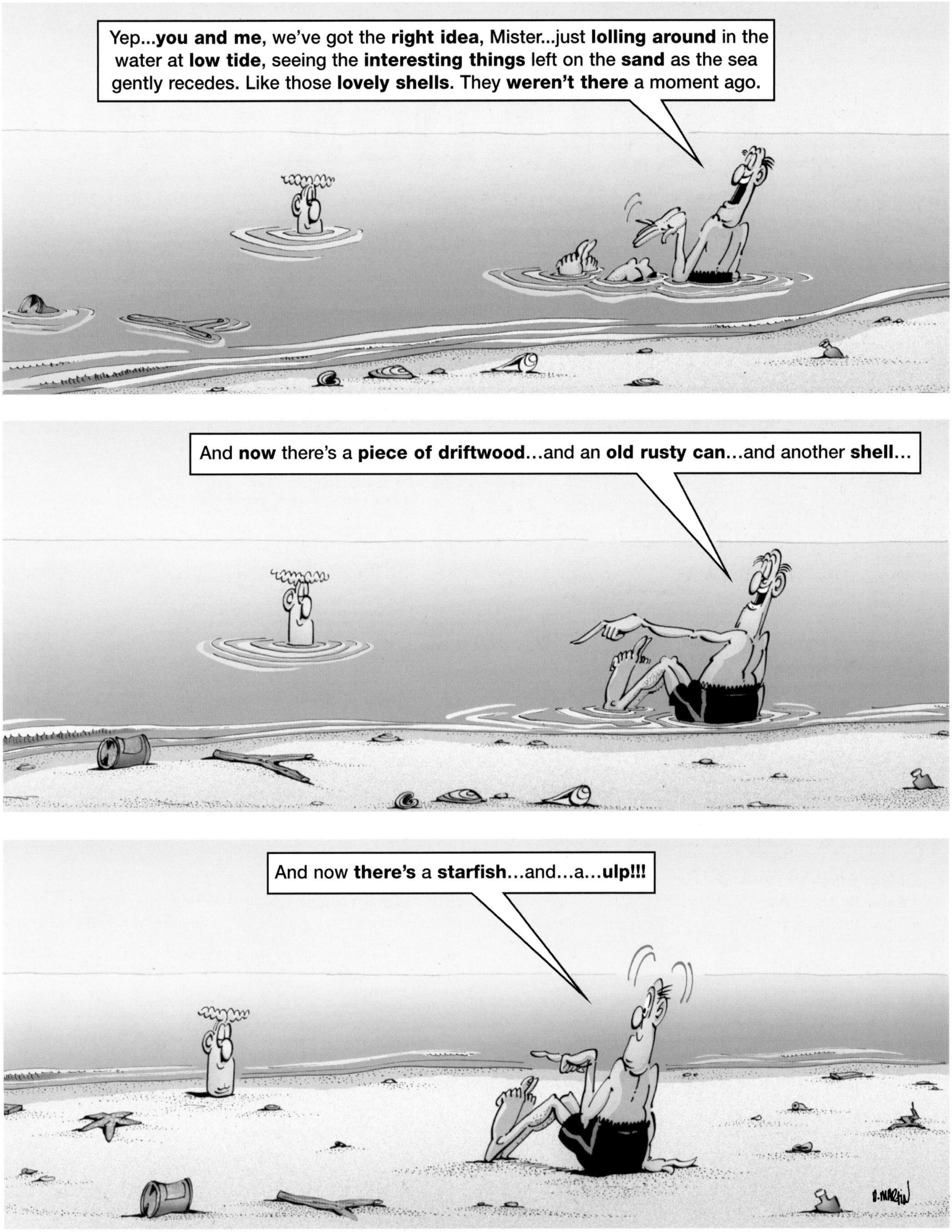
Yep...you and me, we've got the right idea, Mister...just lolling around in the water at low tide, seeing the interesting things left on the sand as the sea gently recedes. Like those lovely shells. They weren't there a moment ago.
And now there's a piece of driftwood...and an old rusty can...and another shell...
And now there's a starfish...and...a...ulp!!!

SEZ EDUCATION DEPT.

Your teachers talk, talk, talk. All day long, they drone on about denominators and zygotes and hidden meanings in *A Separate Peace*. It's enough to make you feel good that you never listen to a word they say! But, in the unlikely event that you actually pay attention for a second or two, well, then you should be able to understand them! That's why you absolutely need…

MAD's TEACHER TRANSLATION GUIDE

When a teacher says…
"You should all use *her* as an example."

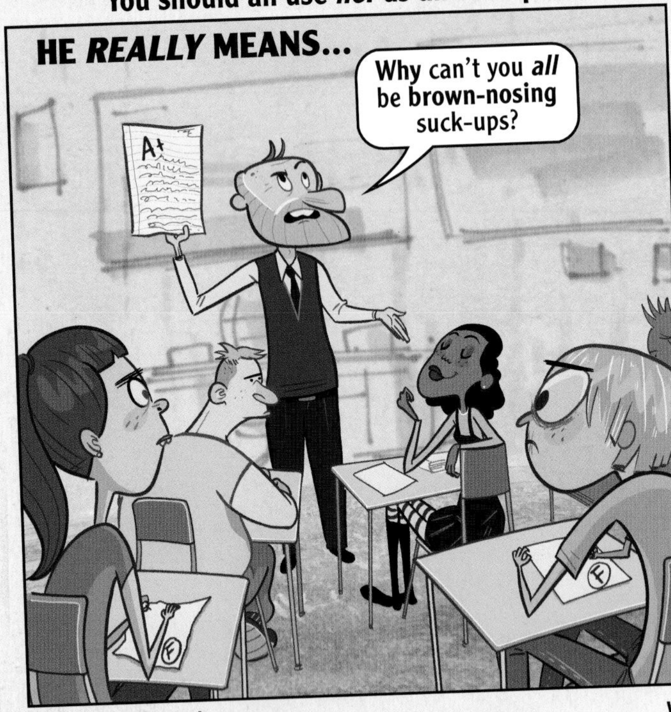
HE *REALLY* MEANS…
Why can't you *all* be brown-nosing suck-ups?
A+

When a teacher says…
"Students today just don't concentrate."

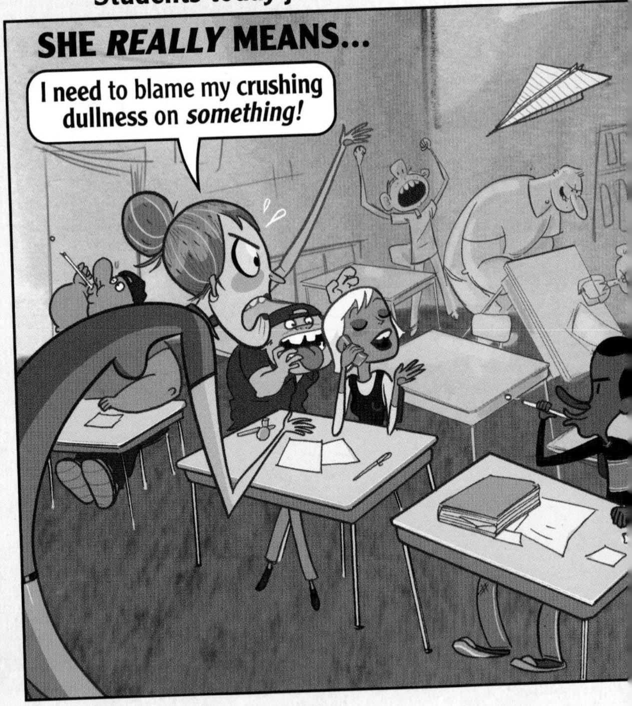
SHE *REALLY* MEANS…
I need to blame my crushing dullness on *something!*

When a teacher says…
"Hmm… I disagree with you, but we don't really have the time to get into it."

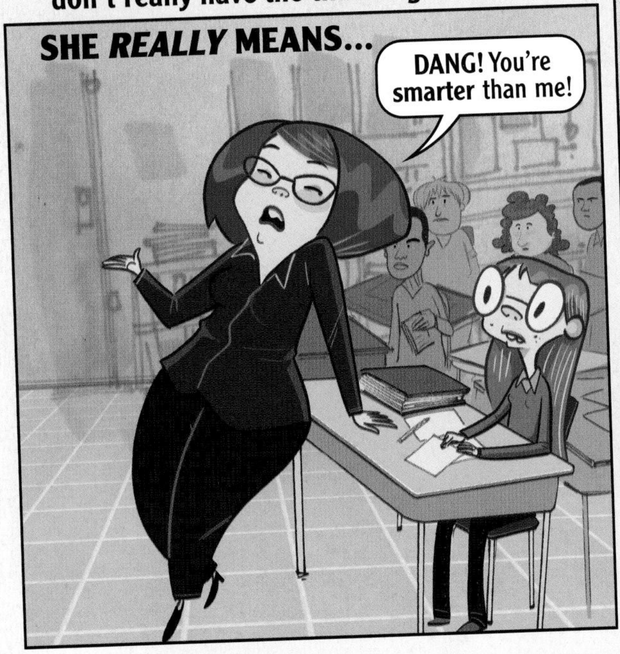
SHE *REALLY* MEANS…
DANG! You're smarter than me!

When a teacher says…
"We'll be watching a movie in class today."

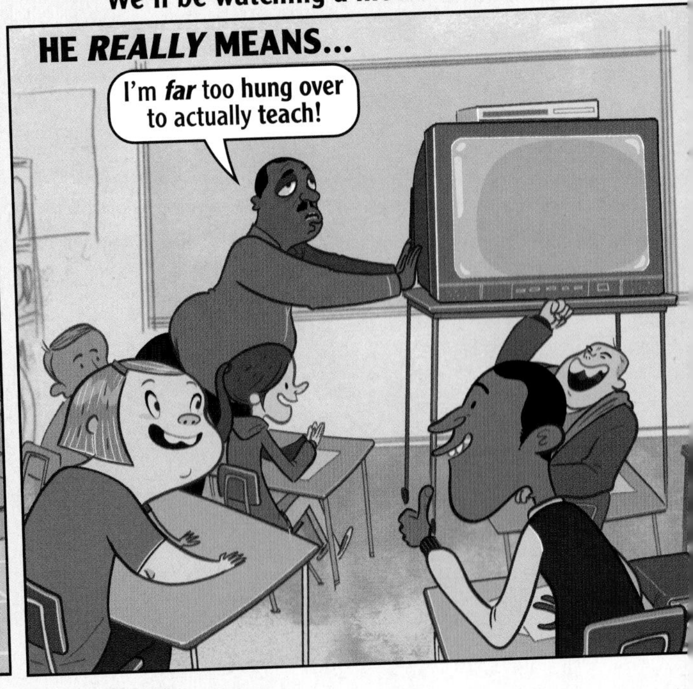
HE *REALLY* MEANS…
I'm *far* too hung over to actually teach!

WRITER: JACOB LAMBERT   ARTIST: JOSE GARIBALDI

When a teacher says…
"Would anyone like to elaborate on what she just said?"

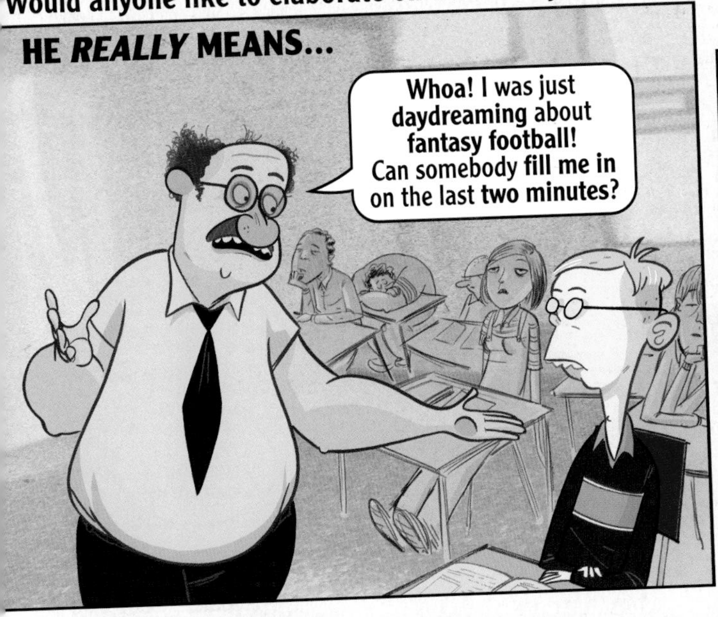
HE *REALLY* MEANS…
Whoa! I was just daydreaming about fantasy football! Can somebody fill me in on the last two minutes?

When a teacher says…
"I'm getting *sick and tired* of these constant failing test grades!"

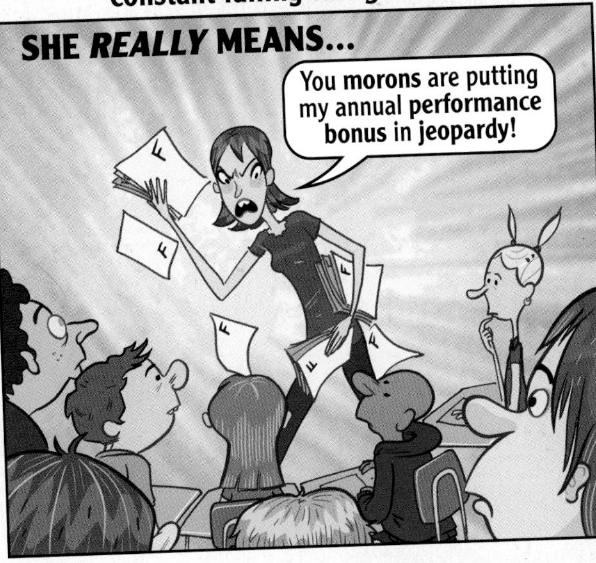
SHE *REALLY* MEANS…
You morons are putting my annual performance bonus in jeopardy!

When a teacher says…
"I know I promised to return your tests today, but I've decided to give them back tomorrow."

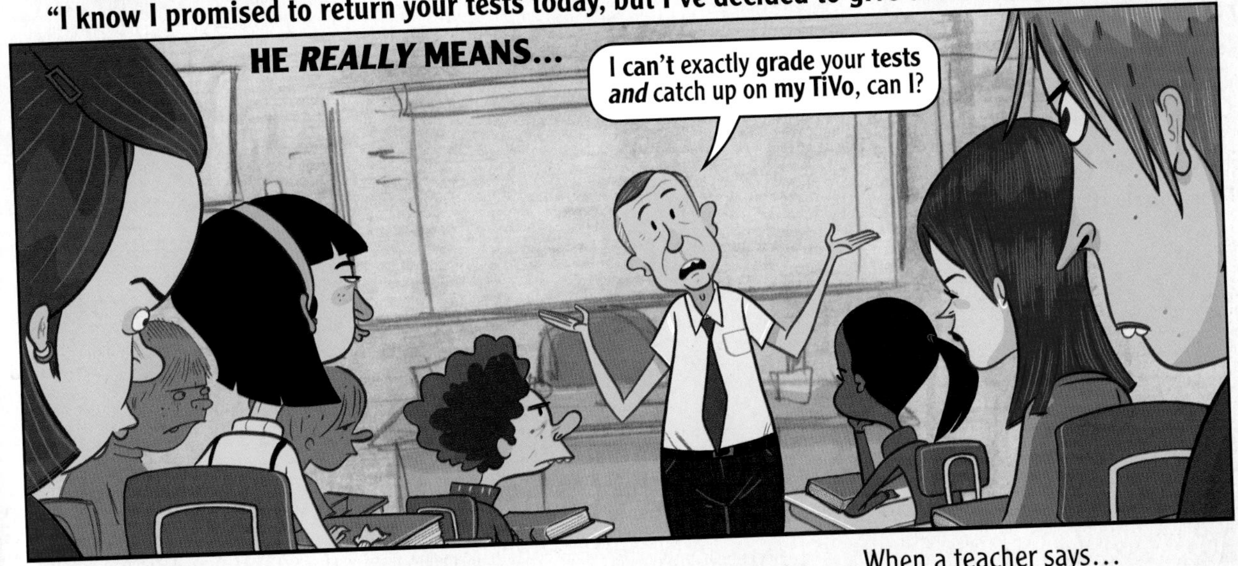
HE *REALLY* MEANS…
I can't exactly grade your tests *and* catch up on my TiVo, can I?

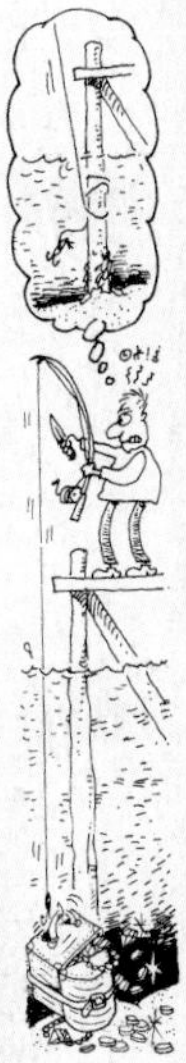

When a teacher says…
"I don't usually do this, but I'm going to let you re-take the final."

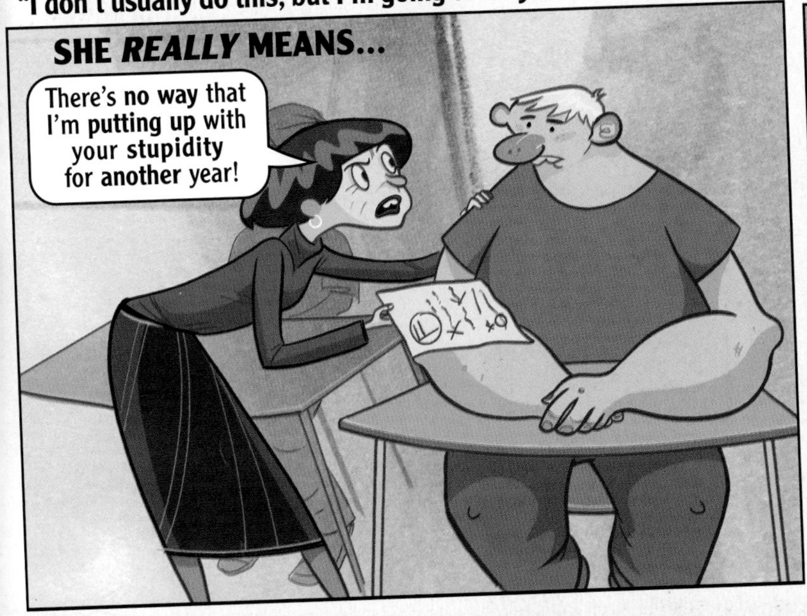
SHE *REALLY* MEANS…
There's no way that I'm putting up with your stupidity for another year!

When a teacher says…
"I'm sorry, but the rules are the rules."

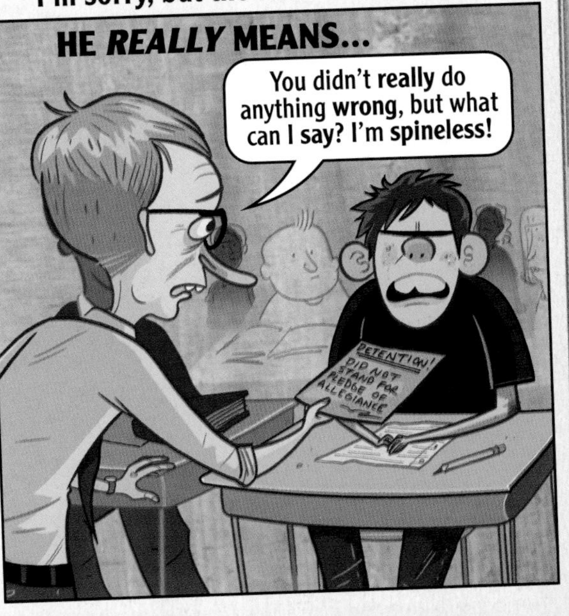
HE *REALLY* MEANS…
You didn't really do anything wrong, but what can I say? I'm spineless!
DETENTION!
DID NOT STAND FOR PLEDGE OF ALLEGIANCE

MOCKTOBER 31ST DEPT.

Candy! Costumes! Parties! Halloween must be the greatest holiday of the year, right? Wrong! Halloween has a disguise all its own — underneath the mask of fun and frivolity, it's every bit as soul-crushing and annoying as Arbor Day! It's true! So don't fill up on candy — make sure you leave some room for...

THE 18 WORST THINGS ABOUT

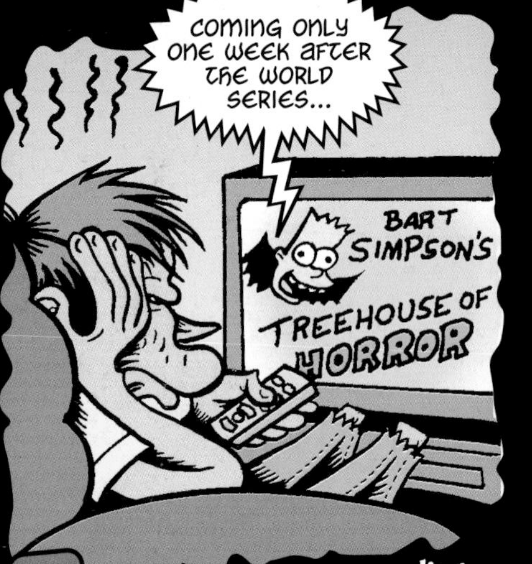

COMING ONLY ONE WEEK AFTER THE WORLD SERIES...
BART SIMPSON'S TREEHOUSE OF HORROR

1 Because of the never-ending baseball playoffs, having to wait until November for *The Simpsons* Halloween episode.

2 Morons who think they're the wittiest people who ever lived by noting that a vampire costume "sucks."

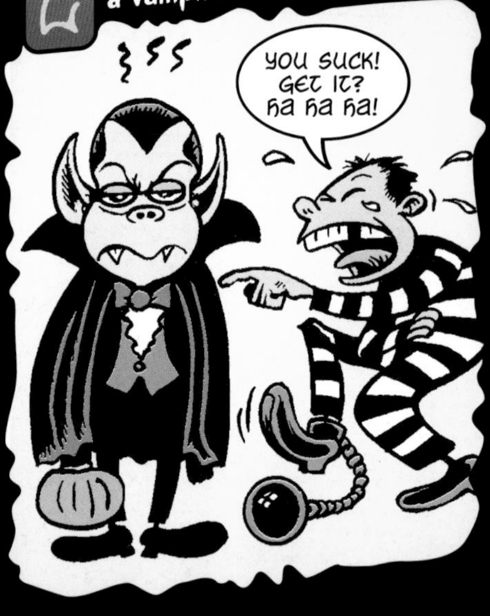

YOU SUCK! GET IT? HA HA HA!

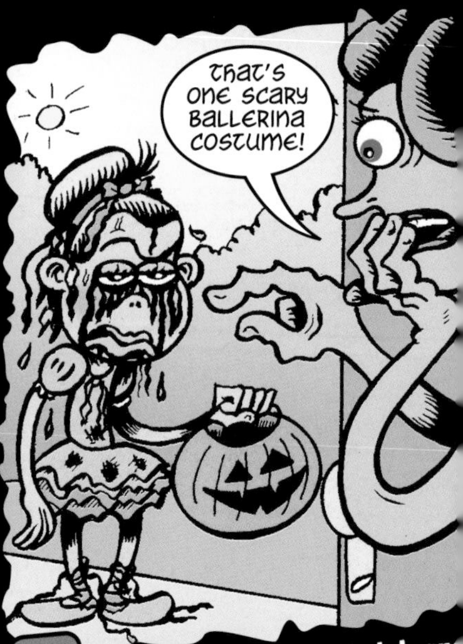

THAT'S ONE SCARY BALLERINA COSTUME!

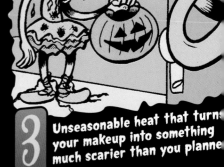

3 Unseasonable heat that turns your makeup into something much scarier than you planne

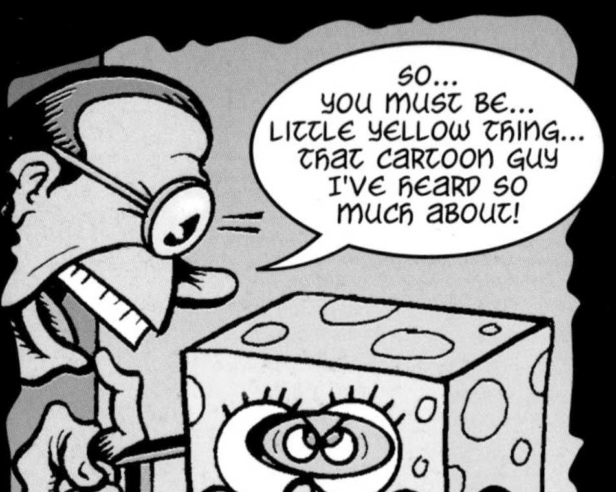

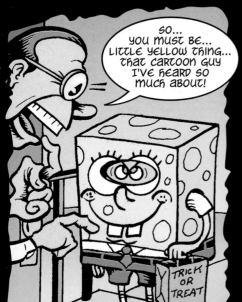

SO... YOU MUST BE... LITTLE YELLOW THING... THAT CARTOON GUY I'VE HEARD SO MUCH ABOUT!
TRICK OR TREAT

7 Out-of-touch adults who don't have a clue what character you're dressed as.

8 Overprotective parents who do everything short of an x-ray search before they'll let their kids so much as unwrap a candy.

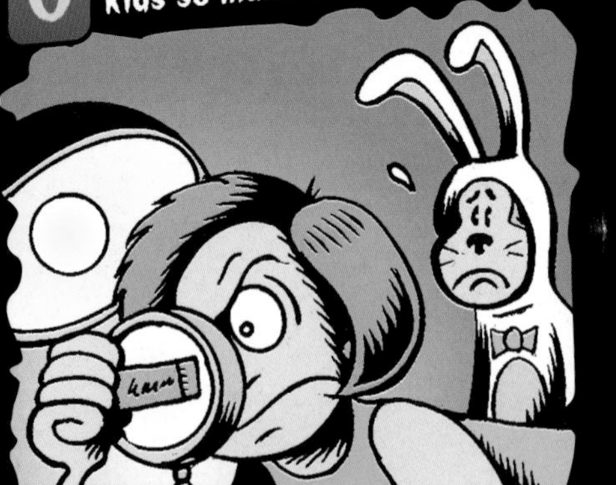

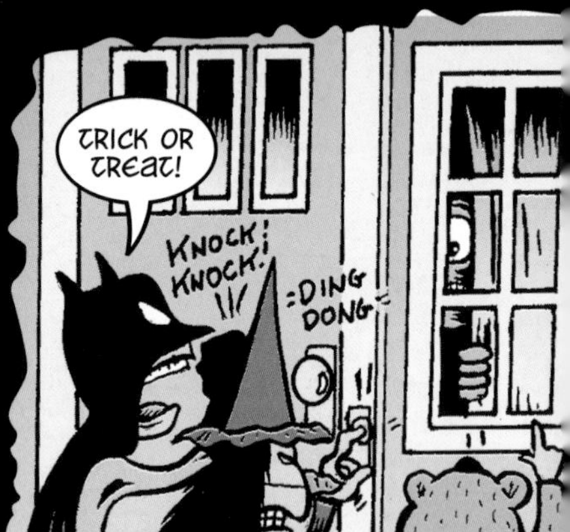

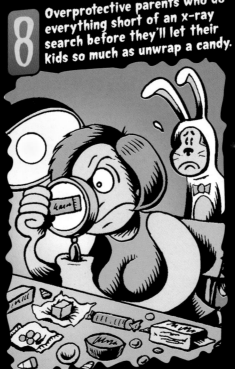

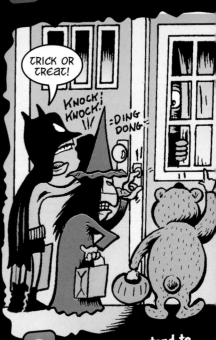

TRICK OR TREAT!
KNOCK! KNOCK!
DING DONG

9 People who pretend to not be home, even though you know they are.

HALLOWEEN

WRITER: JEFF KRUSE
ARTIST: PETER BAGGE

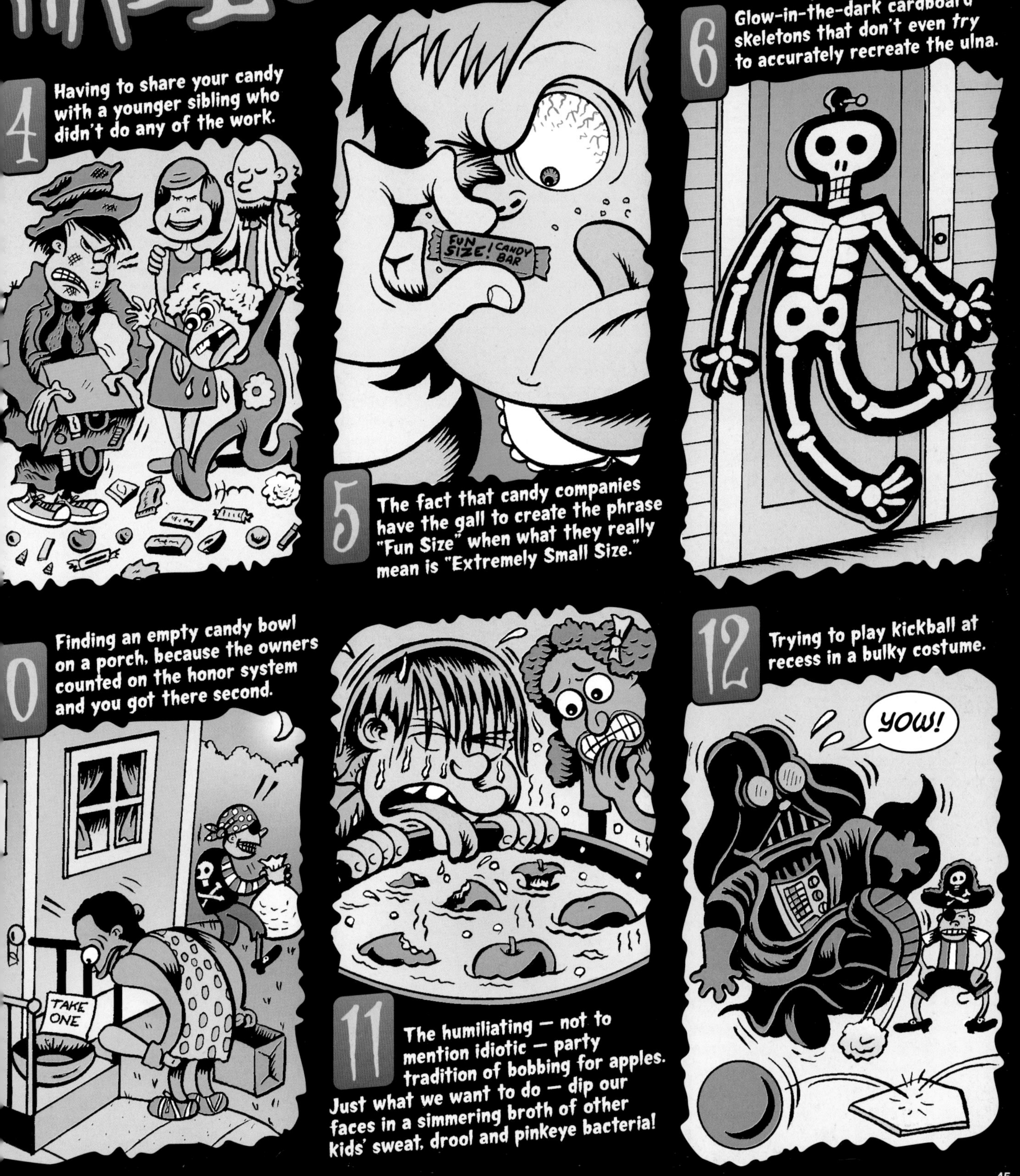
4
Having to share your candy with a younger sibling who didn't do any of the work.
FUN SIZE! CANDY BAR
5
The fact that candy companies have the gall to create the phrase "Fun Size" when what they really mean is "Extremely Small Size."
6
Glow-in-the-dark cardboard skeletons that don't even *try* to accurately recreate the ulna.
0
Finding an empty candy bowl on a porch, because the owners counted on the honor system and you got there second.
TAKE ONE
11
The humiliating — not to mention idiotic — party tradition of bobbing for apples. Just what we want to do — dip our faces in a simmering broth of other kids' sweat, drool and pinkeye bacteria!
12
Trying to play kickball at recess in a bulky costume.
YOW!

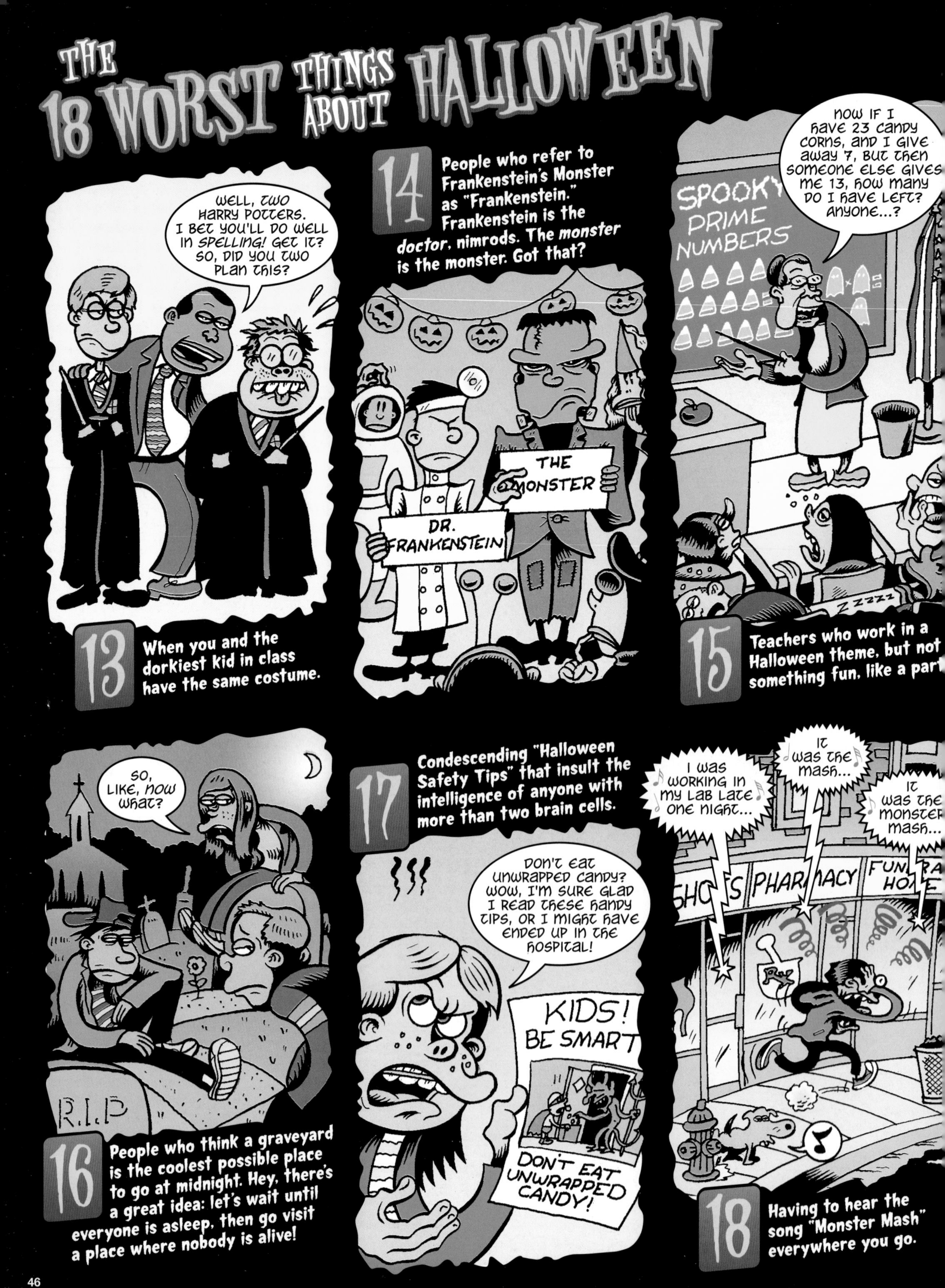

THE 18 WORST THINGS ABOUT HALLOWEEN
WELL, TWO HARRY POTTERS. I BET YOU'LL DO WELL IN SPELLING! GET IT? SO, DID YOU TWO PLAN THIS?
13 When you and the dorkiest kid in class have the same costume.
14 People who refer to Frankenstein's Monster as "Frankenstein." Frankenstein is the doctor, nimrods. The monster is the monster. Got that?
THE MONSTER
DR. FRANKENSTEIN
SPOOKY PRIME NUMBERS
NOW IF I HAVE 23 CANDY CORNS, AND I GIVE AWAY 7, BUT THEN SOMEONE ELSE GIVES ME 13, HOW MANY DO I HAVE LEFT? ANYONE...?
ZZZZZ
15 Teachers who work in a Halloween theme, but not something fun, like a part
SO, LIKE, NOW WHAT?
R.I.P
16 People who think a graveyard is the coolest possible place to go at midnight. Hey, there's a great idea: let's wait until everyone is asleep, then go visit a place where nobody is alive!
17 Condescending "Halloween Safety Tips" that insult the intelligence of anyone with more than two brain cells.
DON'T EAT UNWRAPPED CANDY? WOW, I'M SURE GLAD I READ THESE HANDY TIPS, OR I MIGHT HAVE ENDED UP IN THE HOSPITAL!
KIDS! BE SMART
DON'T EAT UNWRAPPED CANDY!
I WAS WORKING IN MY LAB LATE ONE NIGHT...
IT WAS THE MASH...
IT WAS THE MONSTER MASH...
18 Having to hear the song "Monster Mash" everywhere you go.

THE LEAGUE OF REJECTED SUPERHEROES

What makes a good superhero? Strength? Honor? Bravery? Yes...that about sums it up! (Well, that was certainly easy!) But what makes a really bad superhero? (Other than Ben Affleck portraying him...) That's a little bit harder to figure out — which is why we got help from some of comics' biggest names (who obviously don't care *who* they work for) to illustrate...

WRITER: JEFF KRUSE

INEBRION

THE SUPERHERO WHO CAN'T STAY SOBER

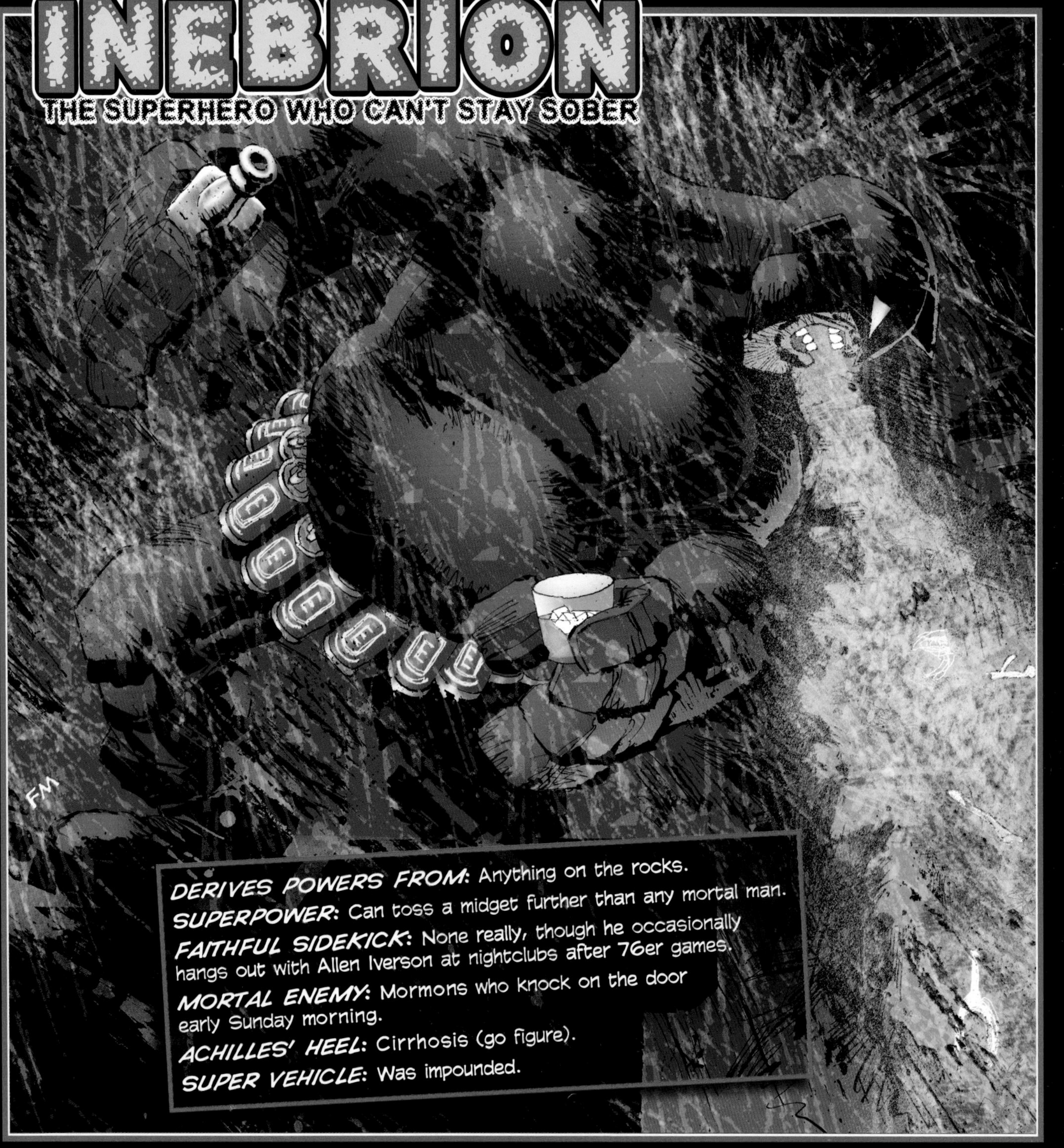

DERIVES POWERS FROM: Anything on the rocks.

SUPERPOWER: Can toss a midget further than any mortal man.

FAITHFUL SIDEKICK: None really, though he occasionally hangs out with Allen Iverson at nightclubs after 76er games.

MORTAL ENEMY: Mormons who knock on the door early Sunday morning.

ACHILLES' HEEL: Cirrhosis (go figure).

SUPER VEHICLE: Was impounded.

ARTIST: FRANK MILLER COLORIST: WILDSTORM

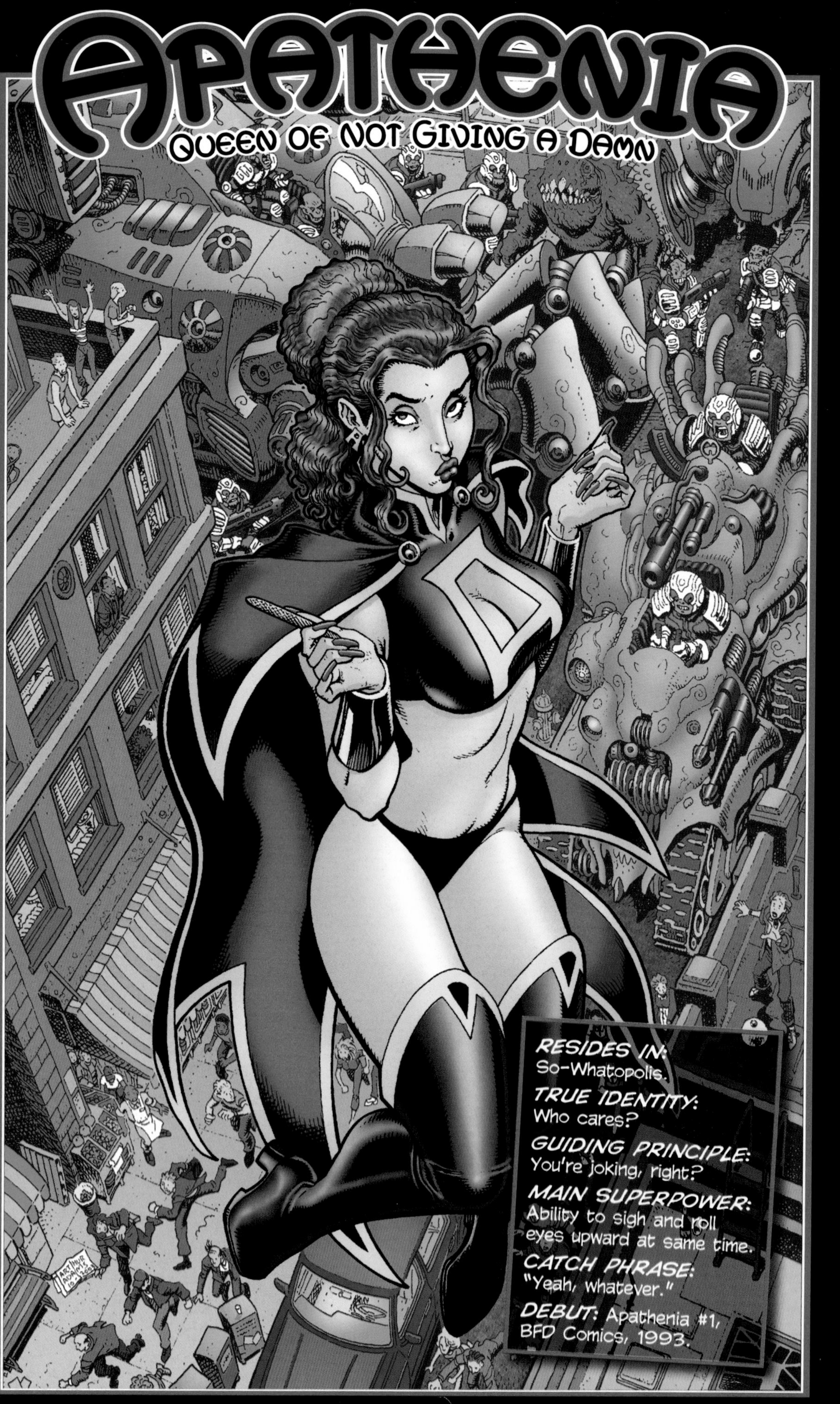
APATHENIA
QUEEN OF NOT GIVING A DAMN
RESIDES IN: So-Whatopolis.
TRUE IDENTITY: Who cares?
GUIDING PRINCIPLE: You're joking, right?
MAIN SUPERPOWER: Ability to sigh and roll eyes upward at same time.
CATCH PHRASE: "Yeah, whatever."
DEBUT: Apathenia #1, BFD Comics, 1993.

ARTIST: ARTHUR ADAMS COLORIST: WILDSTORM

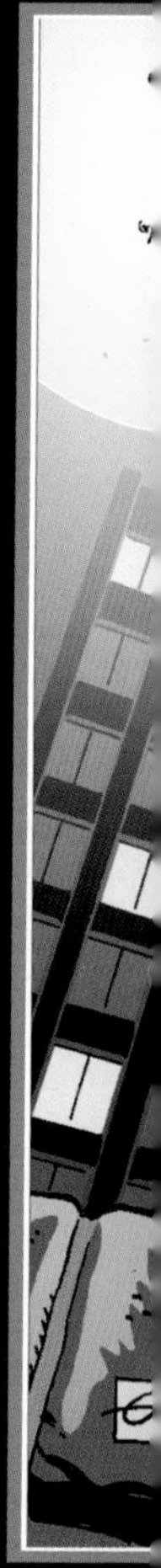

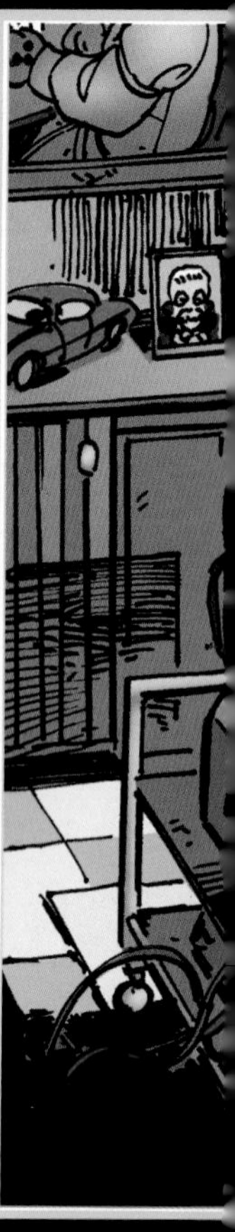

the Entomologist

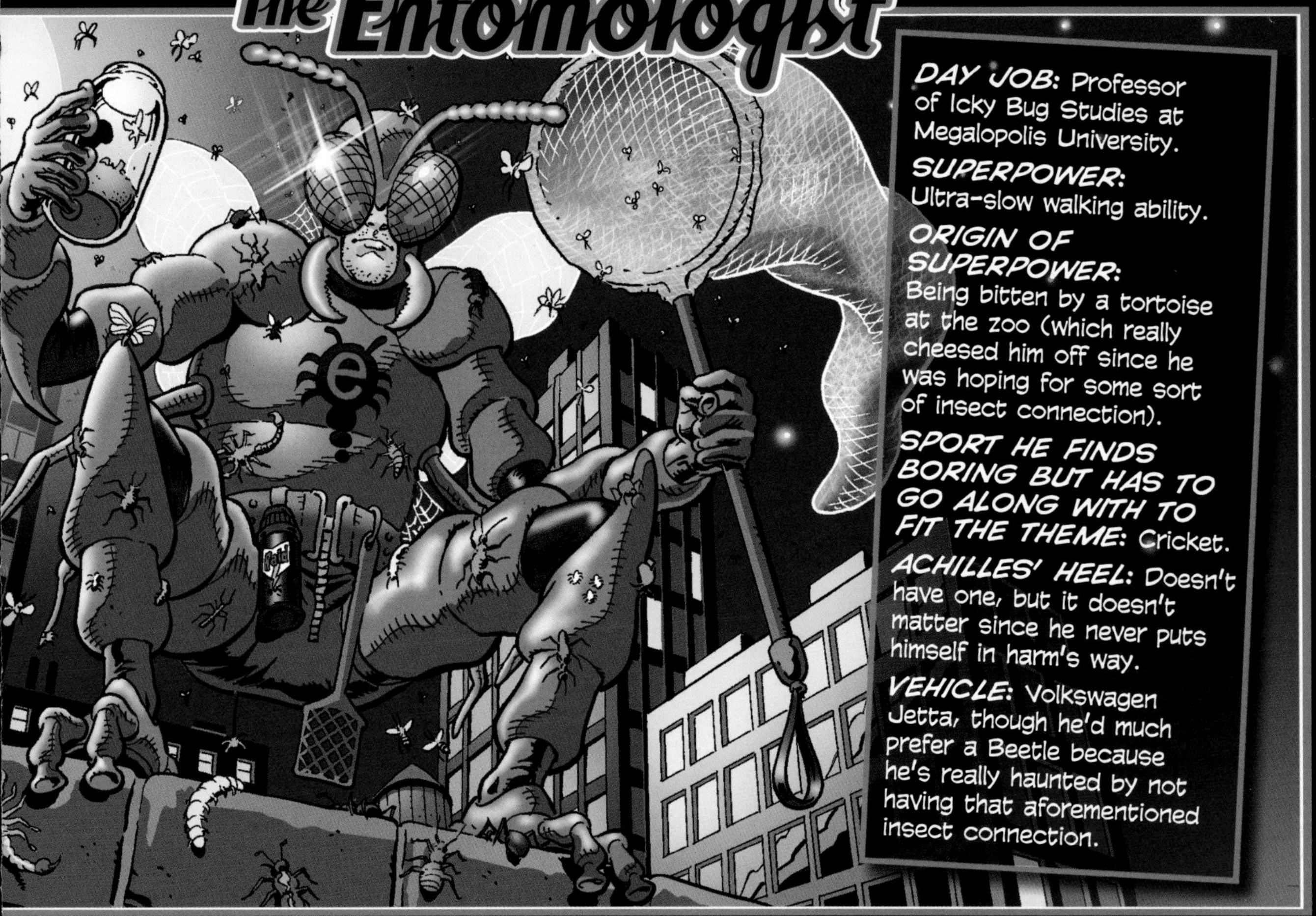
DAY JOB: Professor of Icky Bug Studies at Megalopolis University.
SUPERPOWER: Ultra-slow walking ability.
ORIGIN OF SUPERPOWER: Being bitten by a tortoise at the zoo (which really cheesed him off since he was hoping for some sort of insect connection).
SPORT HE FINDS BORING BUT HAS TO GO ALONG WITH TO FIT THE THEME: Cricket.
ACHILLES' HEEL: Doesn't have one, but it doesn't matter since he never puts himself in harm's way.
VEHICLE: Volkswagen Jetta, though he'd much prefer a Beetle because he's really haunted by not having that aforementioned insect connection.

ARTIST: DAVE GIBBONS COLORIST: WILDSTORM

mediocre man

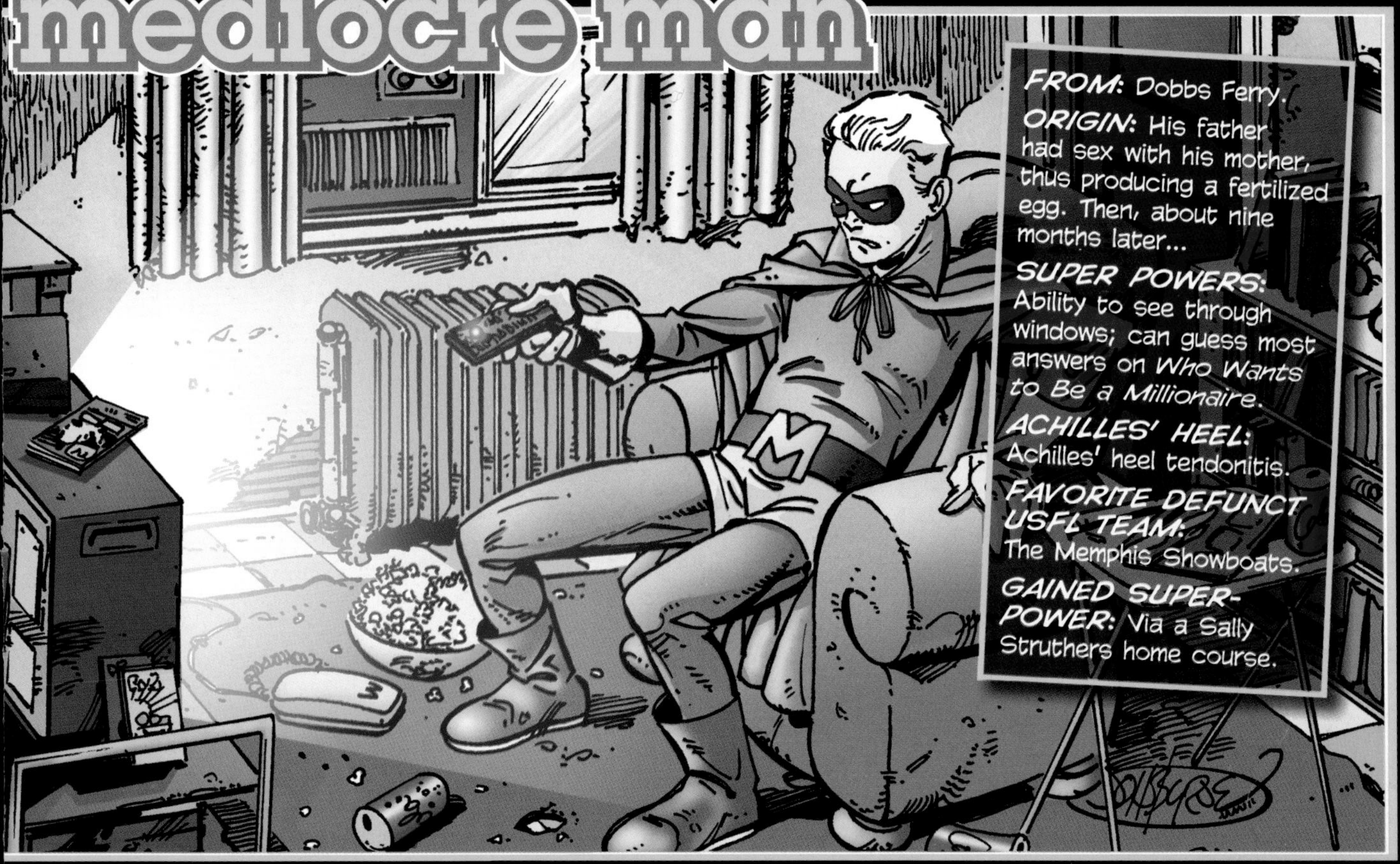
FROM: Dobbs Ferry.
ORIGIN: His father had sex with his mother, thus producing a fertilized egg. Then, about nine months later...
SUPER POWERS: Ability to see through windows; can guess most answers on *Who Wants to Be a Millionaire*.
ACHILLES' HEEL: Achilles' heel tendonitis.
FAVORITE DEFUNCT USFL TEAM: The Memphis Showboats.
GAINED SUPER-POWER: Via a Sally Struthers home course.

ARTIST: JOHN BYRNE COLORIST: WILDSTORM

SLOGGTOR OF GLOBBZORR

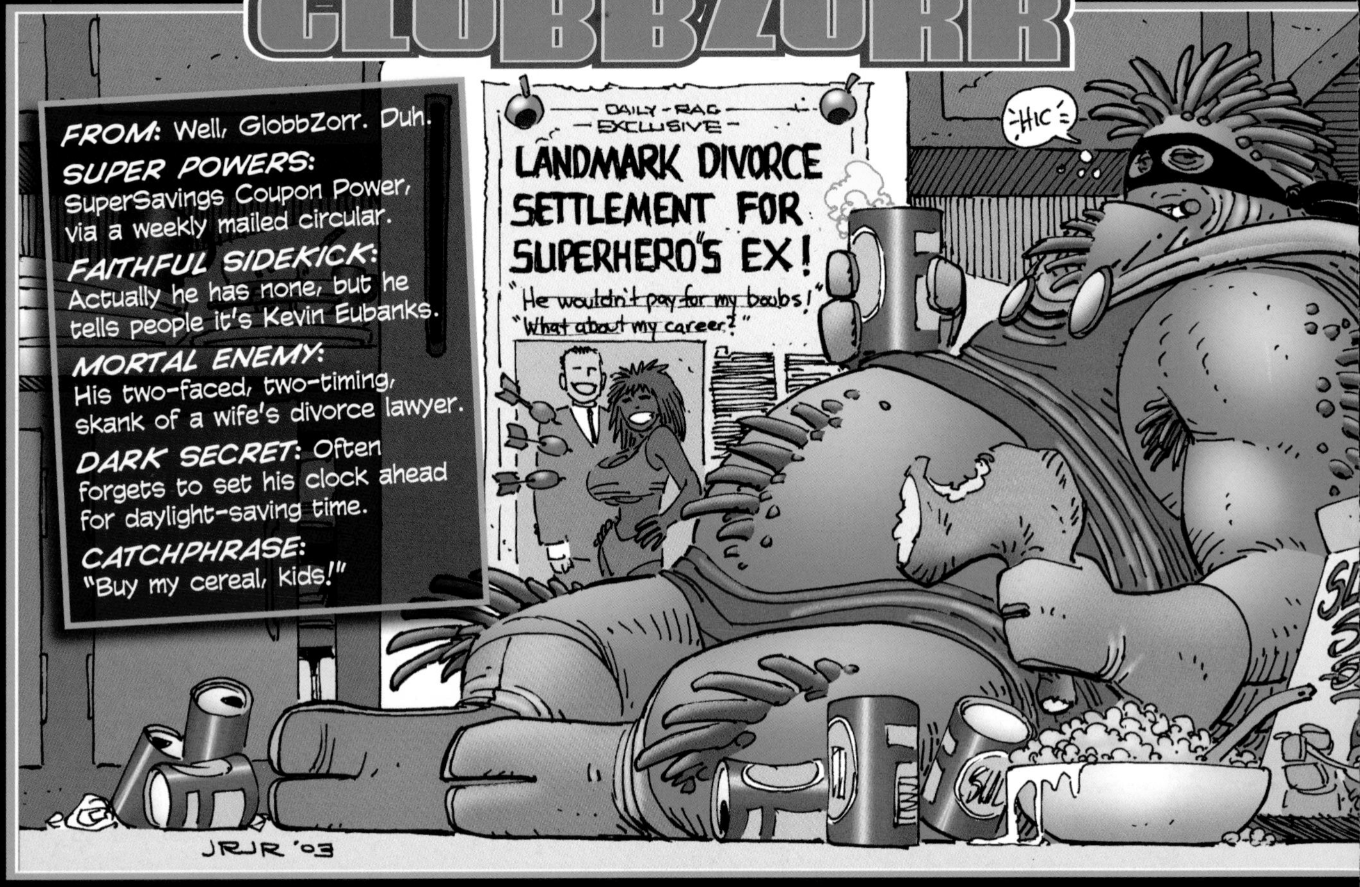
FROM: Well, GlobbZorr. Duh.
SUPER POWERS: SuperSavings Coupon Power, via a weekly mailed circular.
FAITHFUL SIDEKICK: Actually he has none, but he tells people it's Kevin Eubanks.
MORTAL ENEMY: His two-faced, two-timing, skank of a wife's divorce lawyer.
DARK SECRET: Often forgets to set his clock ahead for daylight-saving time.
CATCHPHRASE: "Buy my cereal, kids!"
DAILY RAG EXCLUSIVE
LANDMARK DIVORCE SETTLEMENT FOR SUPERHERO'S EX!
"He wouldn't pay for my boobs!"
"What about my career?"
HIC
JRJR '03

VOCABULON

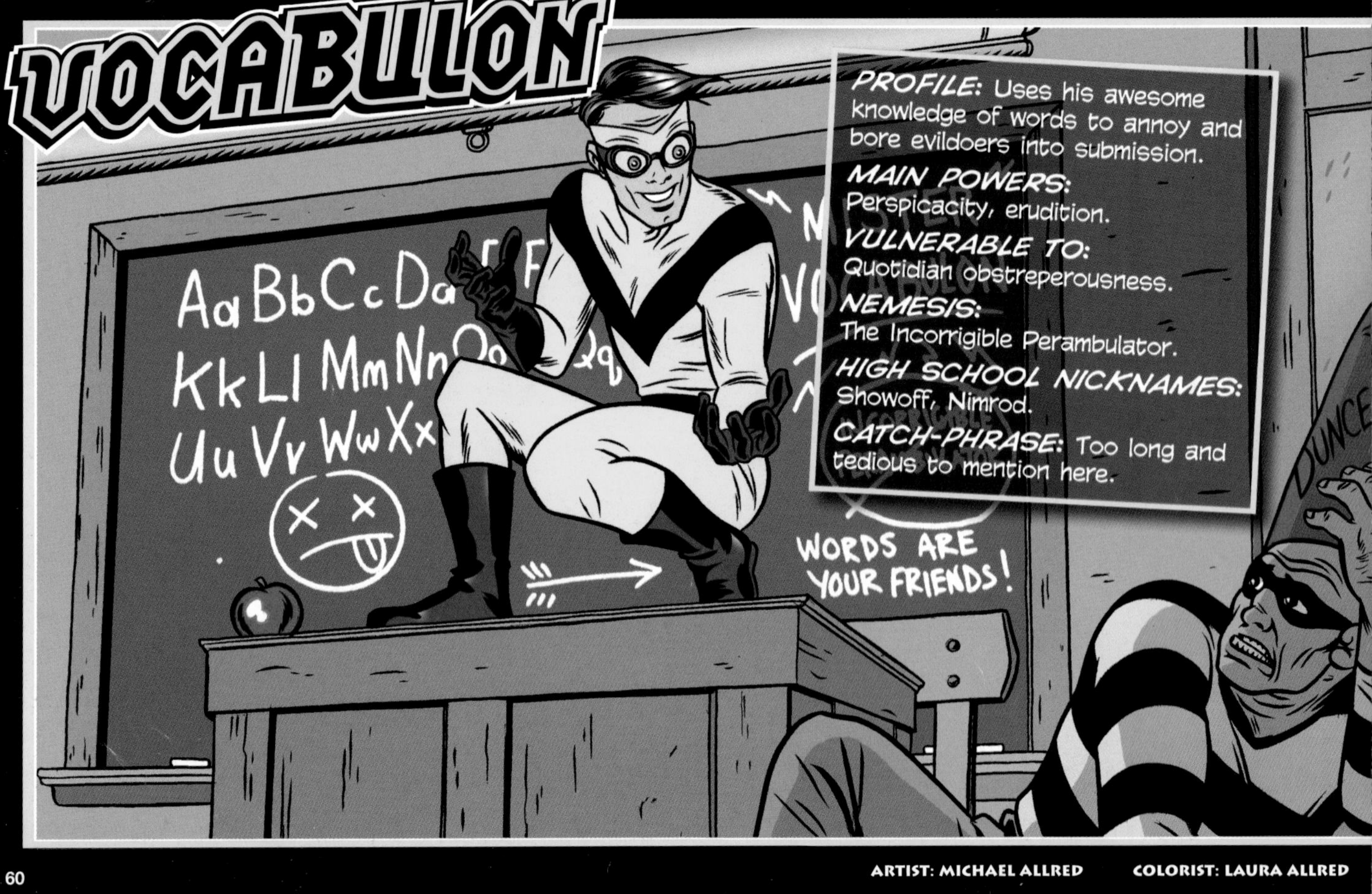
PROFILE: Uses his awesome knowledge of words to annoy and bore evildoers into submission.
MAIN POWERS: Perspicacity, erudition.
VULNERABLE TO: Quotidian obstreperousness.
NEMESIS: The Incorrigible Perambulator.
HIGH SCHOOL NICKNAMES: Showoff, Nimrod.
CATCH-PHRASE: Too long and tedious to mention here.
Aa Bb Cc Dd
Kk Ll Mm Nn Oo
Uu Vv Ww Xx
WORDS ARE YOUR FRIENDS!
DUNCE

ARTIST: MICHAEL ALLRED COLORIST: LAURA ALLRED

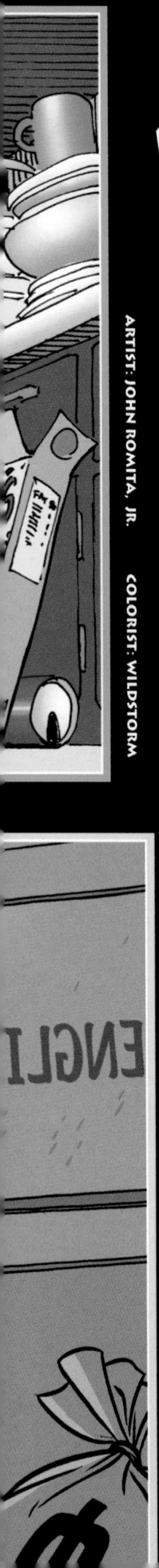

ARTIST: JOHN ROMITA, JR. COLORIST: WILDSTORM

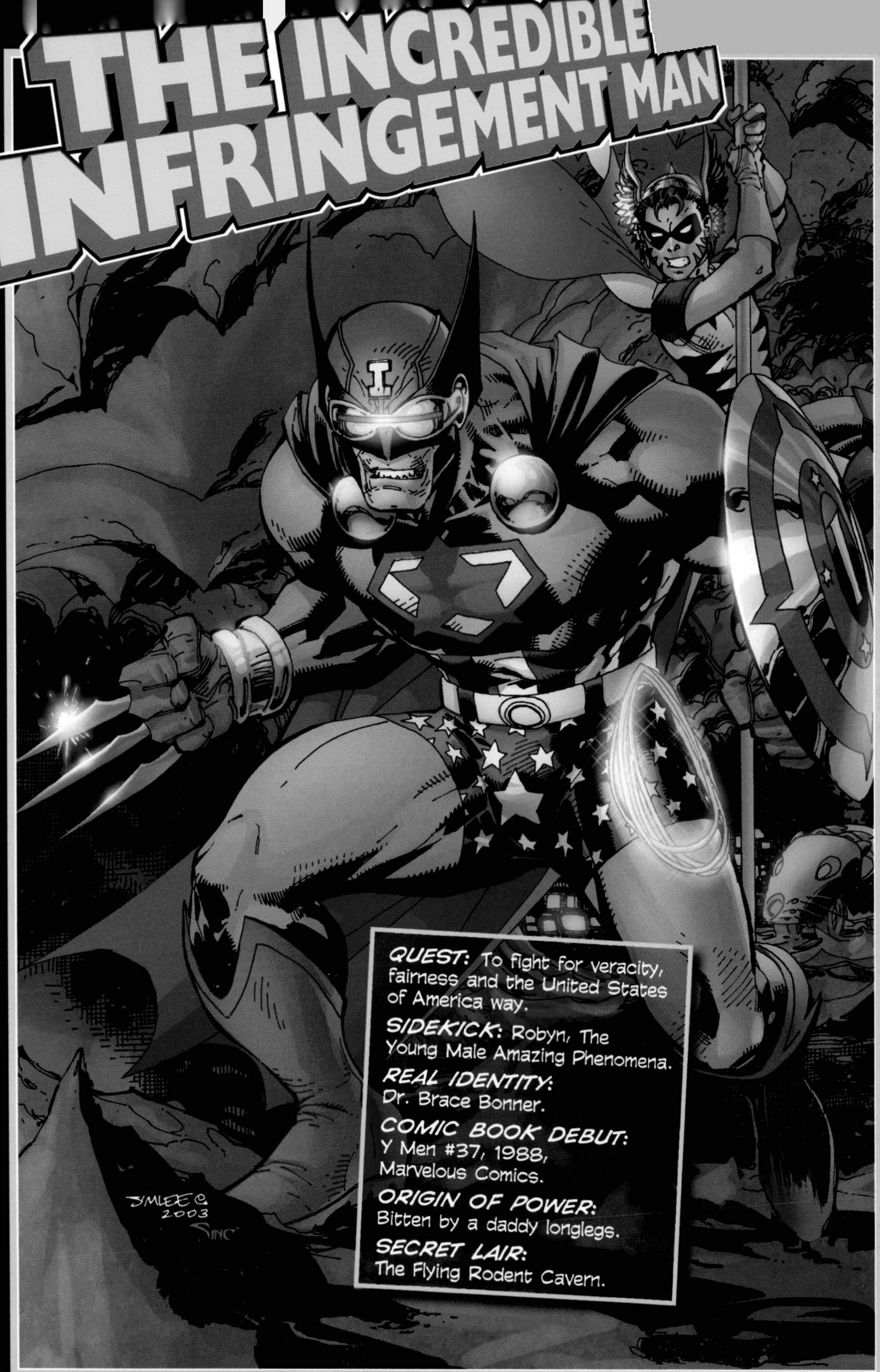

THE INCREDIBLE INFRINGEMENT MAN
QUEST: To fight for veracity, fairness and the United States of America way.
SIDEKICK: Robyn, The Young Male Amazing Phenomena.
REAL IDENTITY: Dr. Brace Bonner.
COMIC BOOK DEBUT: Y Men #37, 1988, Marvelous Comics.
ORIGIN OF POWER: Bitten by a daddy longlegs.
SECRET LAIR: The Flying Rodent Cavern.

ALL JAFFEE DEPT.

GOOD LORD! IT'S YET ANOTHER RIDICULOUS EPISODE OF...

SNAPPY ANSWERS TO

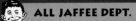

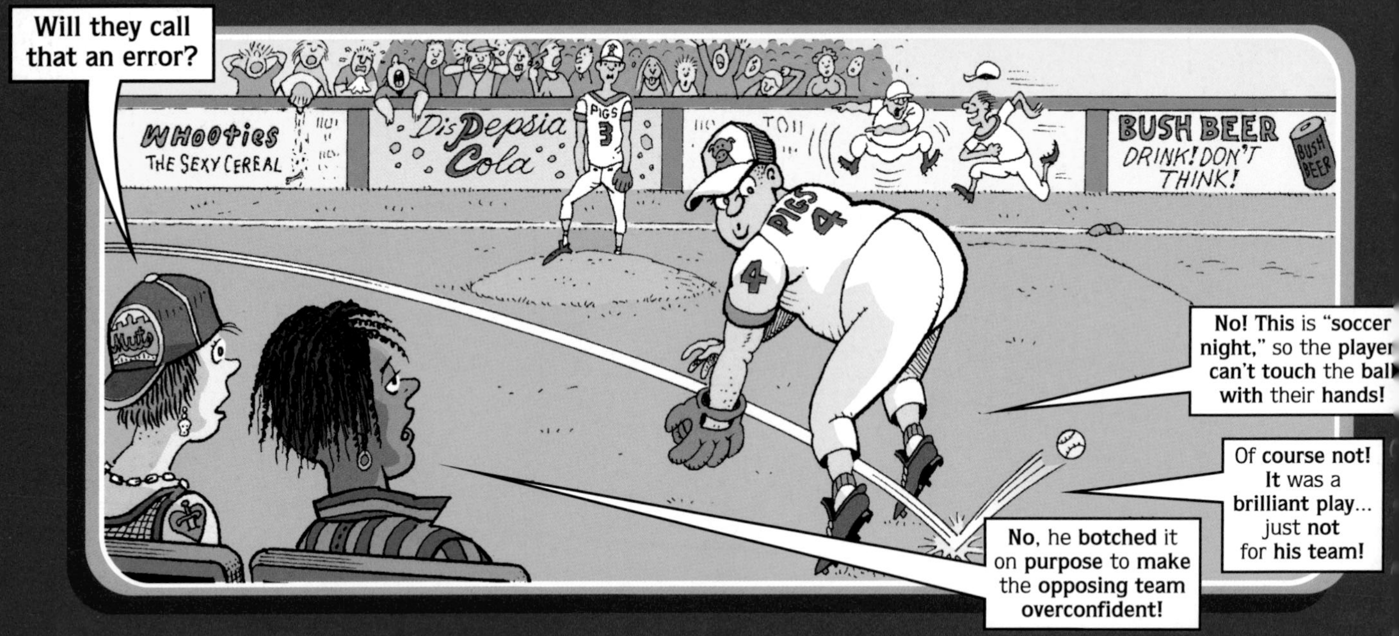
Will they call that an error?
WHOOPIES THE SEXY CEREAL
DisPepsia Cola
PIGS 3
PIGS 4
BUSH BEER DRINK! DON'T THINK!
BUSH BEER
Muts
No! This is "soccer night," so the player can't touch the ball with their hands!
Of course not! It was a brilliant play... just not for his team!
No, he botched it on purpose to make the opposing team overconfident!

ARTIST AND WRITER: AL JAFFEE

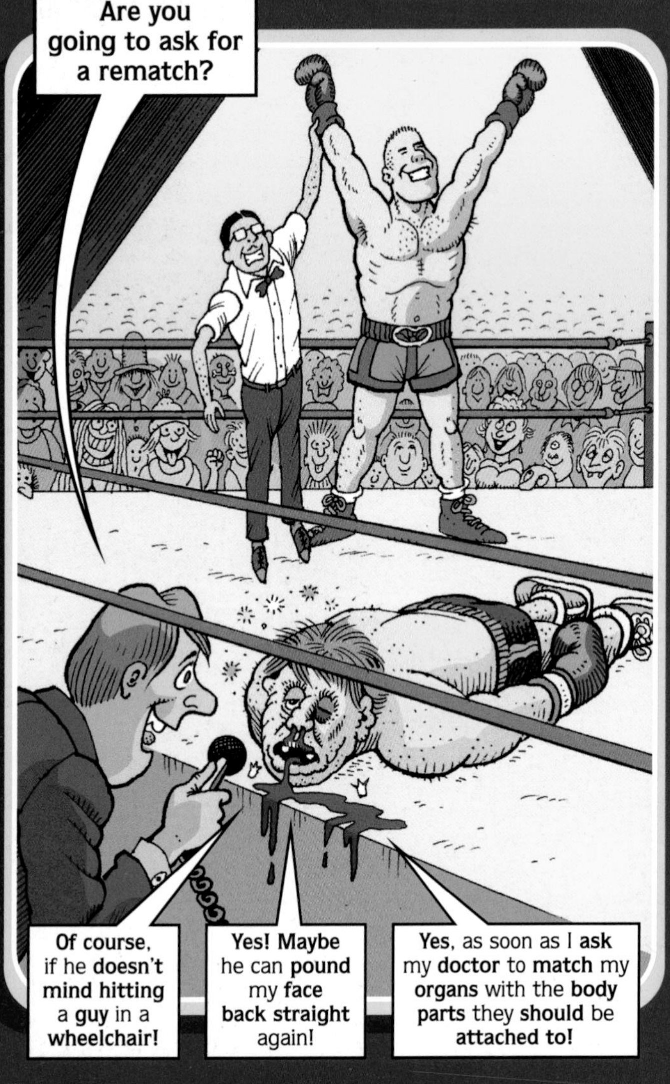
Are you going to ask for a rematch?
Of course, if he doesn't mind hitting a guy in a wheelchair!
Yes! Maybe he can pound my face back straight again!
Yes, as soon as I ask my doctor to match my organs with the body parts they should be attached to!

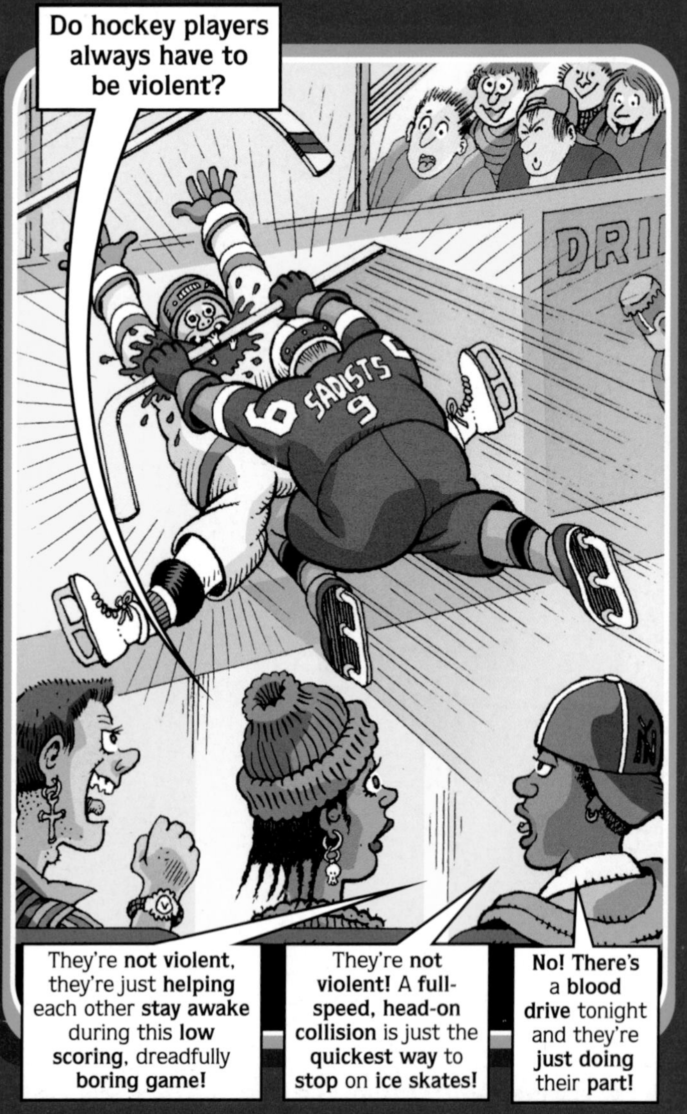
Do hockey players always have to be violent?
SADISTS 9
6
They're not violent, they're just helping each other stay awake during this low scoring, dreadfully boring game!
They're not violent! A full-speed, head-on collision is just the quickest way to stop on ice skates!
No! There's a blood drive tonight and they're just doing their part!

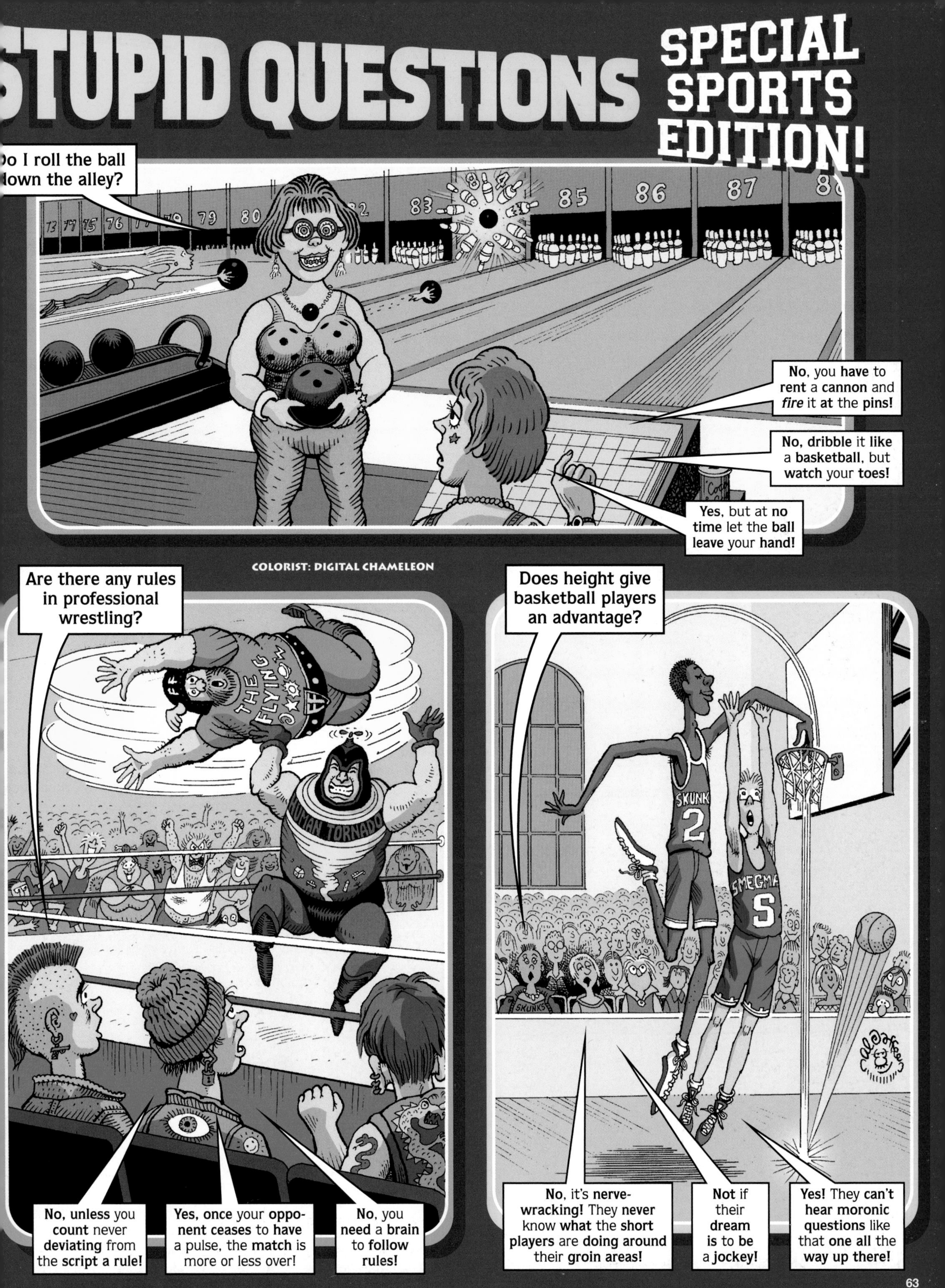

STUPID QUESTIONS
SPECIAL SPORTS EDITION!
Do I roll the ball down the alley?
No, you have to rent a cannon and fire it at the pins!
No, dribble it like a basketball, but watch your toes!
Yes, but at no time let the ball leave your hand!
COLORIST: DIGITAL CHAMELEON
Are there any rules in professional wrestling?
THE FLYING
HUMAN TORNADO
No, unless you count never deviating from the script a rule!
Yes, once your opponent ceases to have a pulse, the match is more or less over!
No, you need a brain to follow rules!
Does height give basketball players an advantage?
SKUNKS 2
SMEGMA 5
No, it's nerve-wracking! They never know what the short players are doing around their groin areas!
Not if their dream is to be a jockey!
Yes! They can't hear moronic questions like that one all the way up there!

Remember when your mom used to put a little note and a treat in with your lunch? (No? What a sad childhood you had!) From a few scribbled lines and your favorite homemade cookies, you knew that she loved you and was thinking of you. (You really missed out, fella.) Yep, you can tell a lot about a mom from what she packs in your lunch. But every brown paper bag tells a different tale — and not all of them are so heartwarming. So to help decipher your mother's personality type based on her midday meal selections, MAD now presents...

LUNCH-PACKING MOM PROFILES

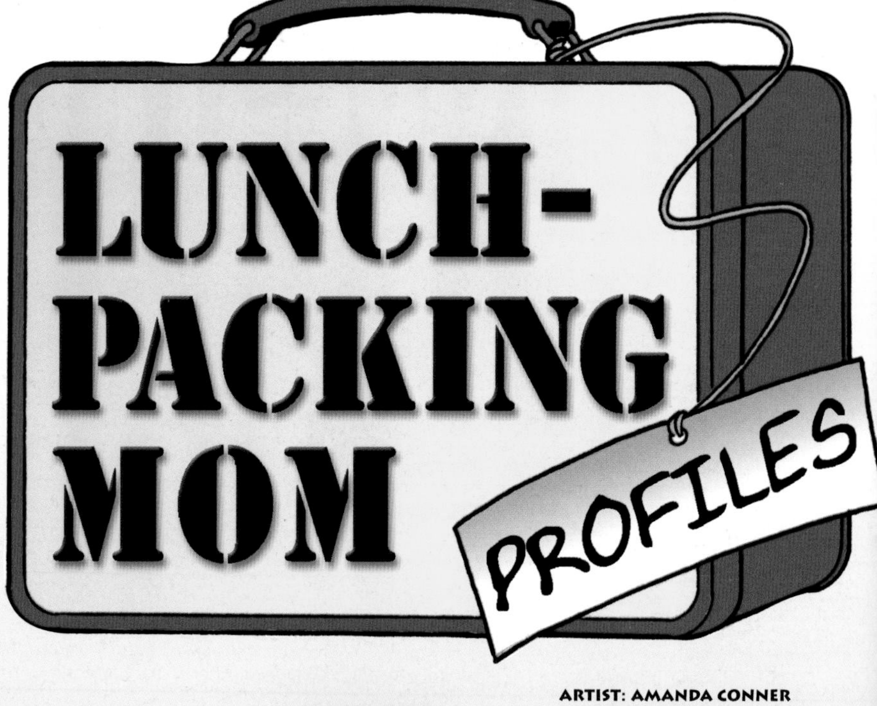

ARTIST: AMANDA CONNER
WRITER: RYAN PAGELOW
COLORIST: WILDSTORM

NEW AGE MOM

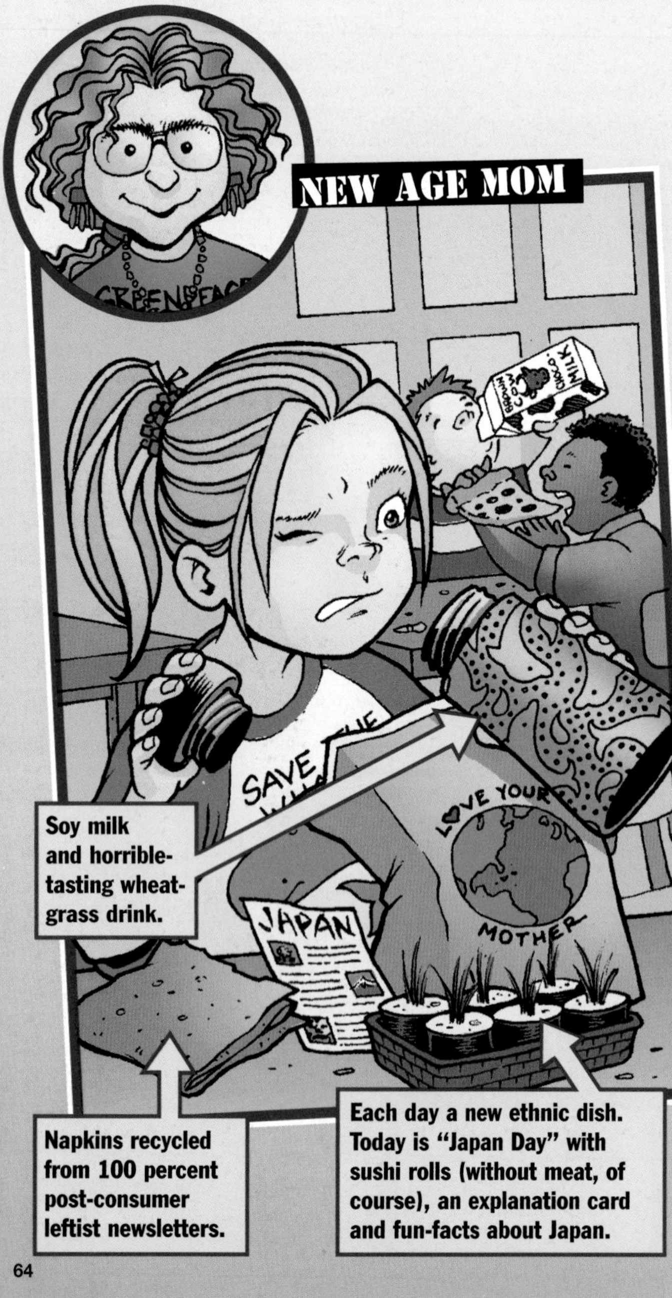
GREENPEACE
CHOCO MILK
SAVE THE
LOVE YOUR MOTHER
JAPAN
Soy milk and horrible-tasting wheat-grass drink.
Napkins recycled from 100 percent post-consumer leftist newsletters.
Each day a new ethnic dish. Today is "Japan Day" with sushi rolls (without meat, of course), an explanation card and fun-facts about Japan.

DIVORCED MOM

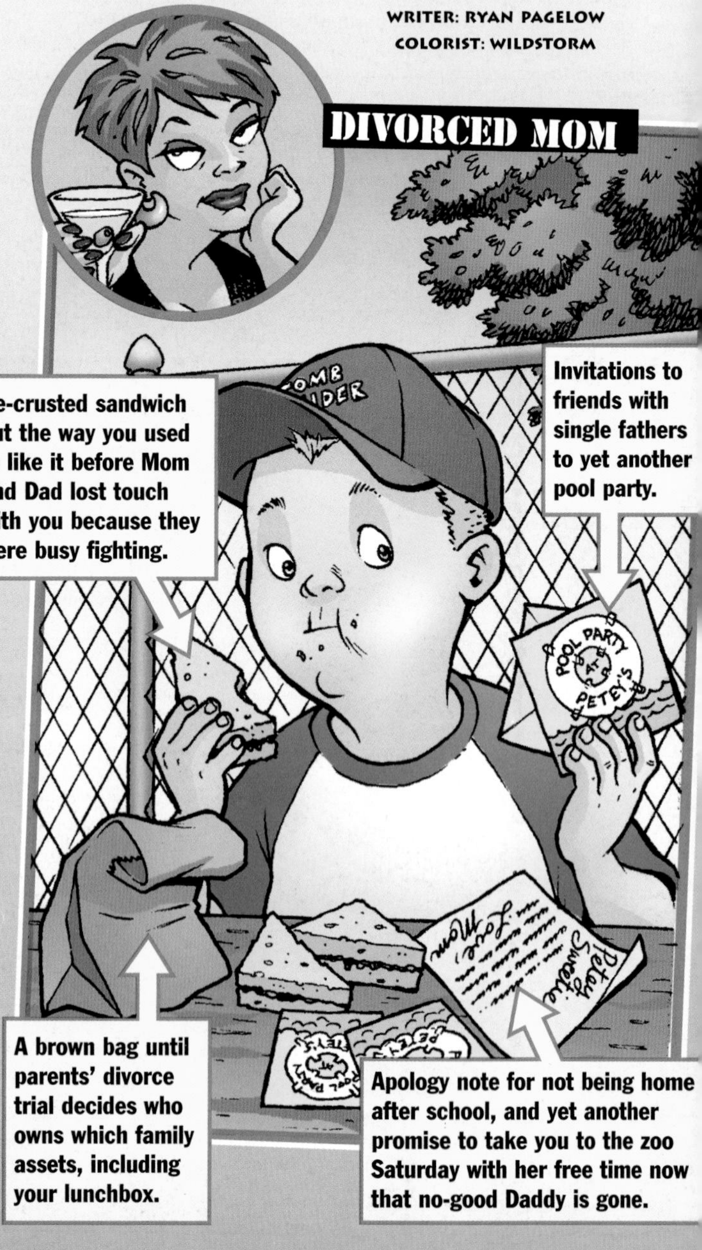
De-crusted sandwich cut the way you used to like it before Mom and Dad lost touch with you because they were busy fighting.
Invitations to friends with single fathers to yet another pool party.
POOL PARTY AT PETEY'S
Petey, Sweetie ... Love, Mom
A brown bag until parents' divorce trial decides who owns which family assets, including your lunchbox.
Apology note for not being home after school, and yet another promise to take you to the zoo Saturday with her free time now that no-good Daddy is gone.

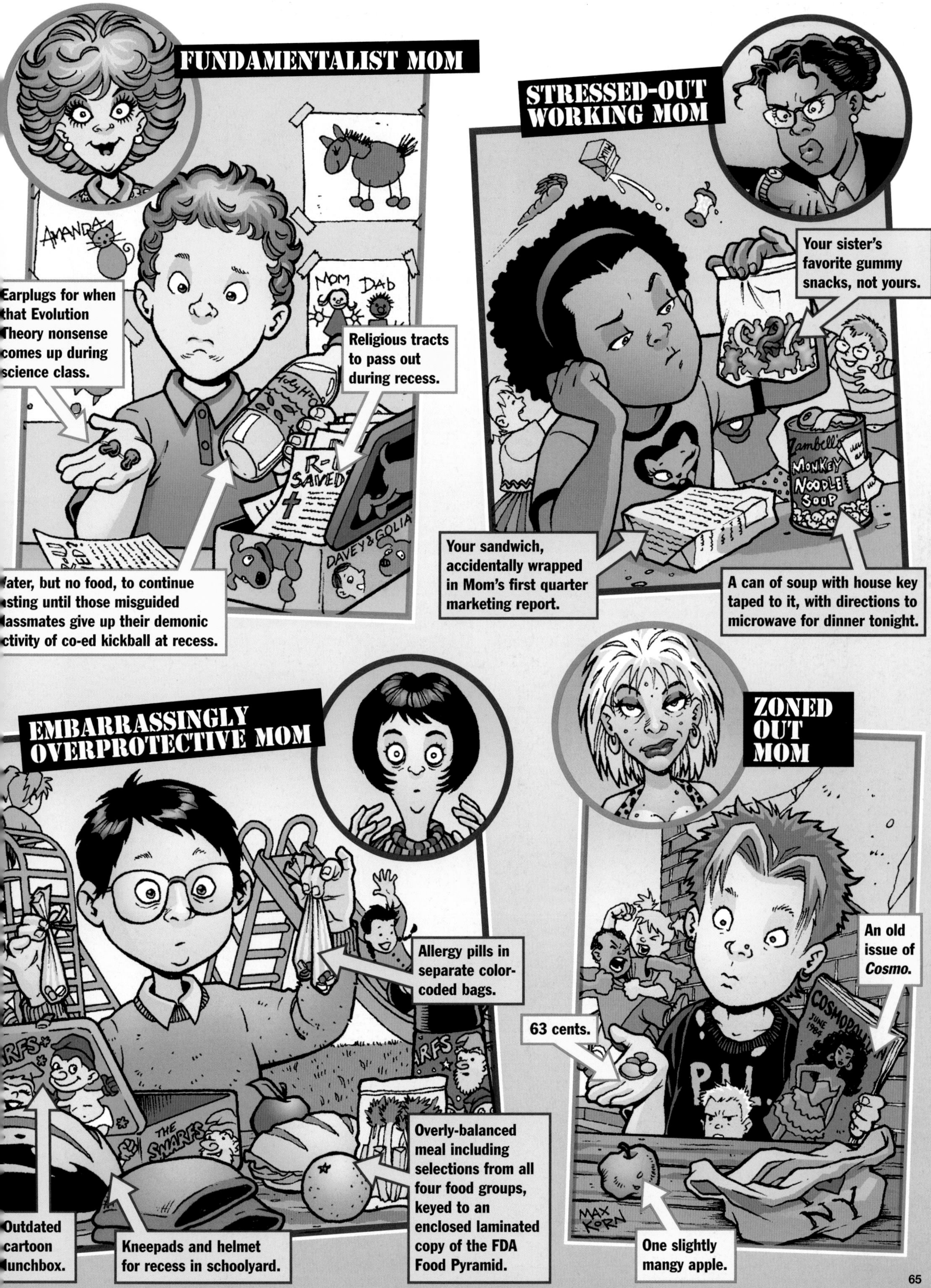
FUNDAMENTALIST MOM
AMANDA
MOM DAD
Earplugs for when
that Evolution
Theory nonsense
comes up during
science class.
Religious tracts
to pass out
during recess.
R-U SAVED
DAVEY & GOLIA
ater, but no food, to continue
asting until those misguided
lassmates give up their demonic
ctivity of co-ed kickball at recess.
STRESSED-OUT
WORKING MOM
Your sister's
favorite gummy
snacks, not yours.
Zambelli's
MONKEY
NOODLE
SOUP
Your sandwich,
accidentally wrapped
in Mom's first quarter
marketing report.
A can of soup with house key
taped to it, with directions to
microwave for dinner tonight.
EMBARRASSINGLY
OVERPROTECTIVE MOM
Allergy pills in
separate color-
coded bags.
THE SNARFS
Overly-balanced
meal including
selections from all
four food groups,
keyed to an
enclosed laminated
copy of the FDA
Food Pyramid.
Outdated
cartoon
unchbox.
Kneepads and helmet
for recess in schoolyard.
ZONED
OUT
MOM
An old
issue of
Cosmo.
COSMOPOLITAN
JUNE 1984
63 cents.
One slightly
mangy apple.
MAX KORN

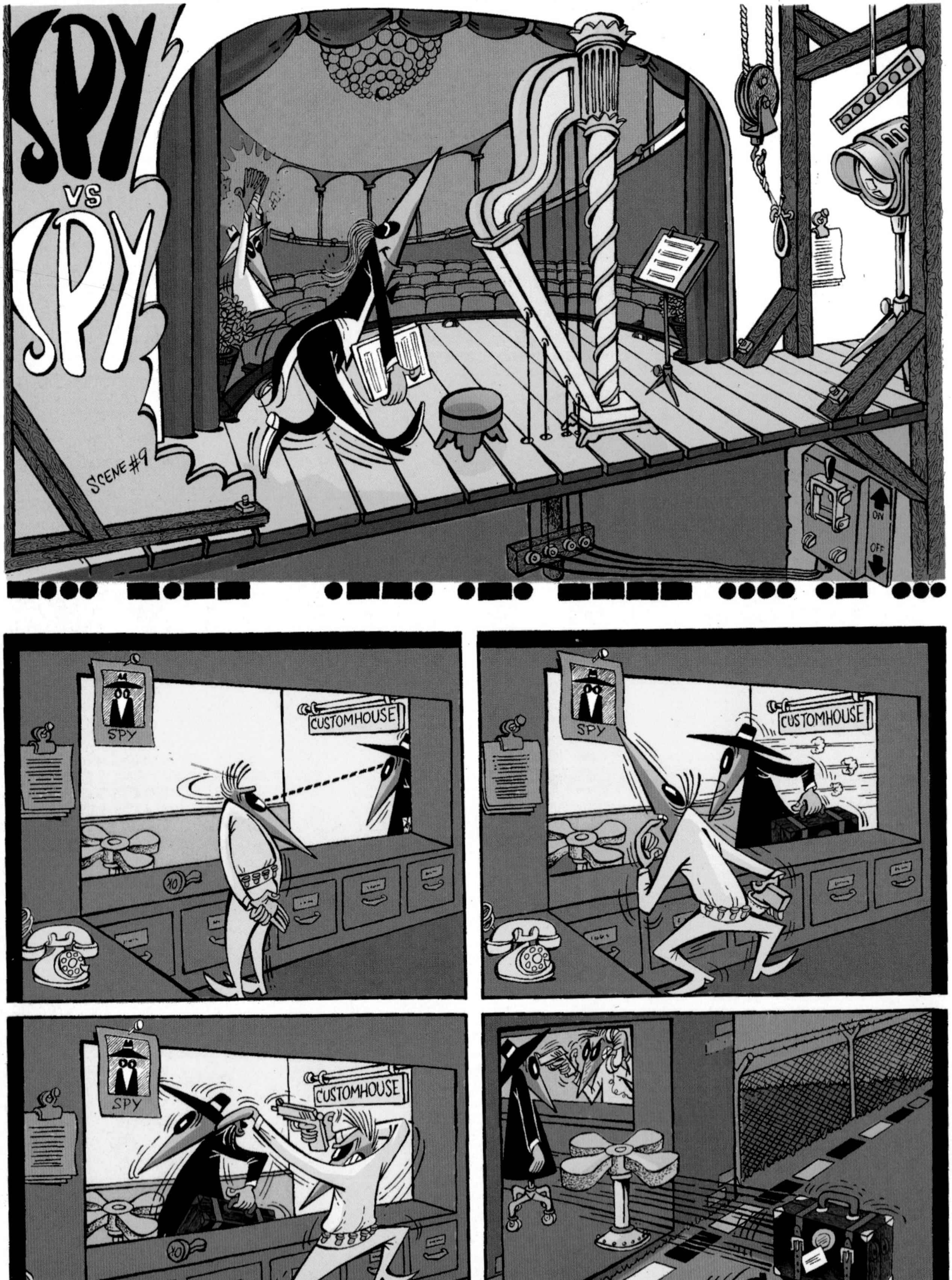
SPY
vs
SPY
SCENE #9
ON
OFF
SPY
CUSTOMHOUSE
OK
SPY
CUSTOMHOUSE
SPY
CUSTOMHOUSE
OK
Prohias

WRITER AND ARTIST: ANTONIO PROHIAS

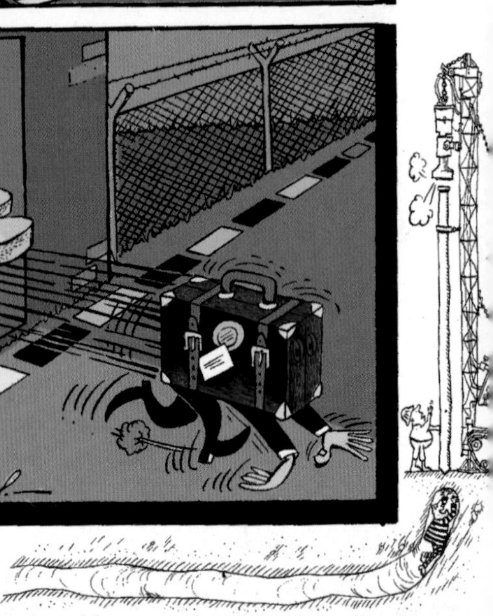

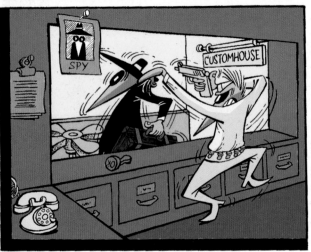

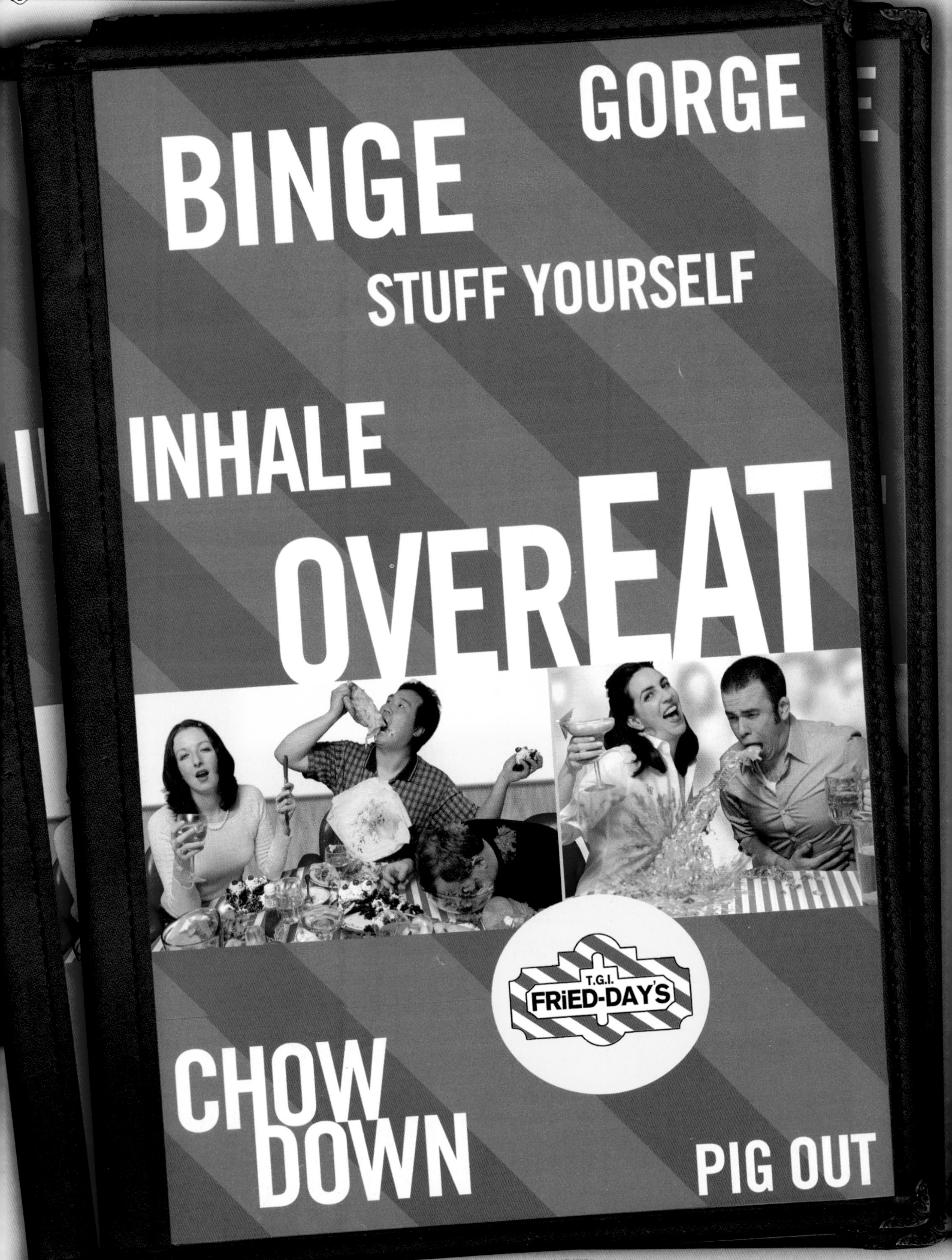
GORGE
BINGE
STUFF YOURSELF
INHALE
OVEREAT
T.G.I.
FRiED-DAY'S
CHOW DOWN
PIG OUT

WRITER: DAVE CROATTO PHOTOGRAPHER: IRVING SCHILD

APPETIZERS

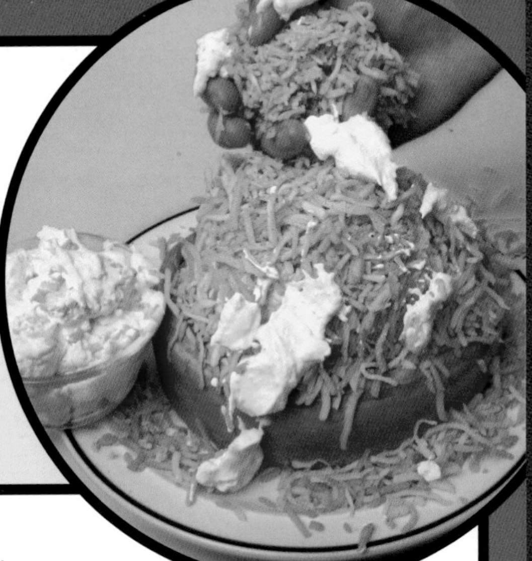

Veggie Sampler

These are NOT your mother's vegetables! Zucchini, cauliflower, mushrooms and jalapeño peppers fried in corn oil, then cornbread-battered and deep-fried AGAIN to a golden brown! Topped with oozing, melted Pepper Jack and served with our Southwestern sour cream dippin' sauce! Garden fresh and delicious! Eating right never tasted so good!

THE CHEESE BOWL

Our legendary giant bowl of 17 different shredded cheeses! Cheddar, American, Swiss, Muenster, Mozzarella, Provolone, Bleu Cheese, Monterey Jack, Brie, Bra, Ricotta, Greve, Herve, Jarlsberg, Penbryn, Tupi, Roquefort! Fun by the fistful! Served in a hollowed-out wheel of Gouda with our famous Mayo cheese-chunk dunkin' sauce!

The Explosi-onion

Our trademark, genetically-engineered onion — 2 lbs. of beer-battered, deep-fried deliciousness!

(Warning: The Explosi-onion is not for everyone. If you are pregnant, suffer from asthma or have high blood pressure, do not order the Explosi-onion. The most common side effects of consuming the Explosi-onion were nausea, chest pains, irregular breathing, loose/oily stools, dizziness and cramping. Check with your doctor to see if The Explosi-onion is right for you.)

The Fried-Day's Ample Sample®

Can't decide which appetizer you want to fill up on? You don't have to! Now you can eat your way through the endless 20-minute wait for your entrée! Includes our Mexican Pizza Chokers, Beer-Battered Tater Skin Kurlers, a Mini Veggie Sampler, Southwestern Chicken Seizures, Great Szechwan Burrito Bites and a half-dozen randomly selected boneless meat products, all served with 15 different Dippin' and Drizzlin' Sauces! There's no reason to be even remotely hungry by the time your meal arrives!

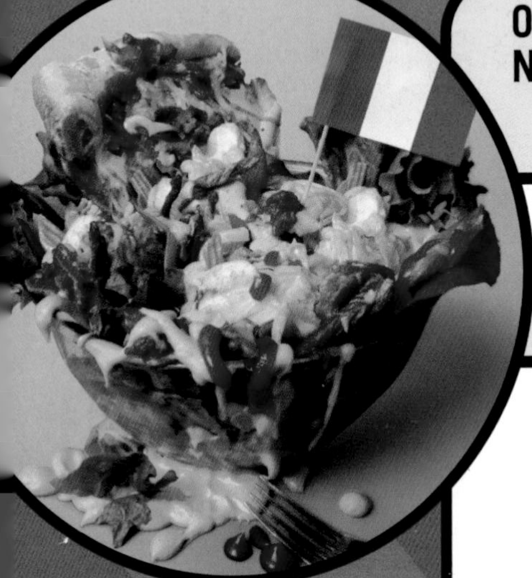

On a diet, but still insist on eating at Fried-Day's?
Not a problem with our…

HEALTHY CHOICE SALADS

The Bacon Burger Garden Salad — Deliciously outrageous!

PIZZA SUPREME SALAD-O ITALIANO — Outrageously delicious!

Death by Chocolate — the Salad

Boneless Buffalo Chicken Wing Salad w/Curly Fries Garnish

"My Favorites" Salad — We've created a salad that features more of what you love best, with none of the lettuce or other vegetables to get in the way! Extra croutons, extra bacon bits, more cheese chunks and your choice of TWO dressings! Add popcorn-fried chicken or shrimp for just $2.50 more!

Ask about our

★ KIDZ MENU!

As featured in the Presidential Council's Report on Child Obesity!

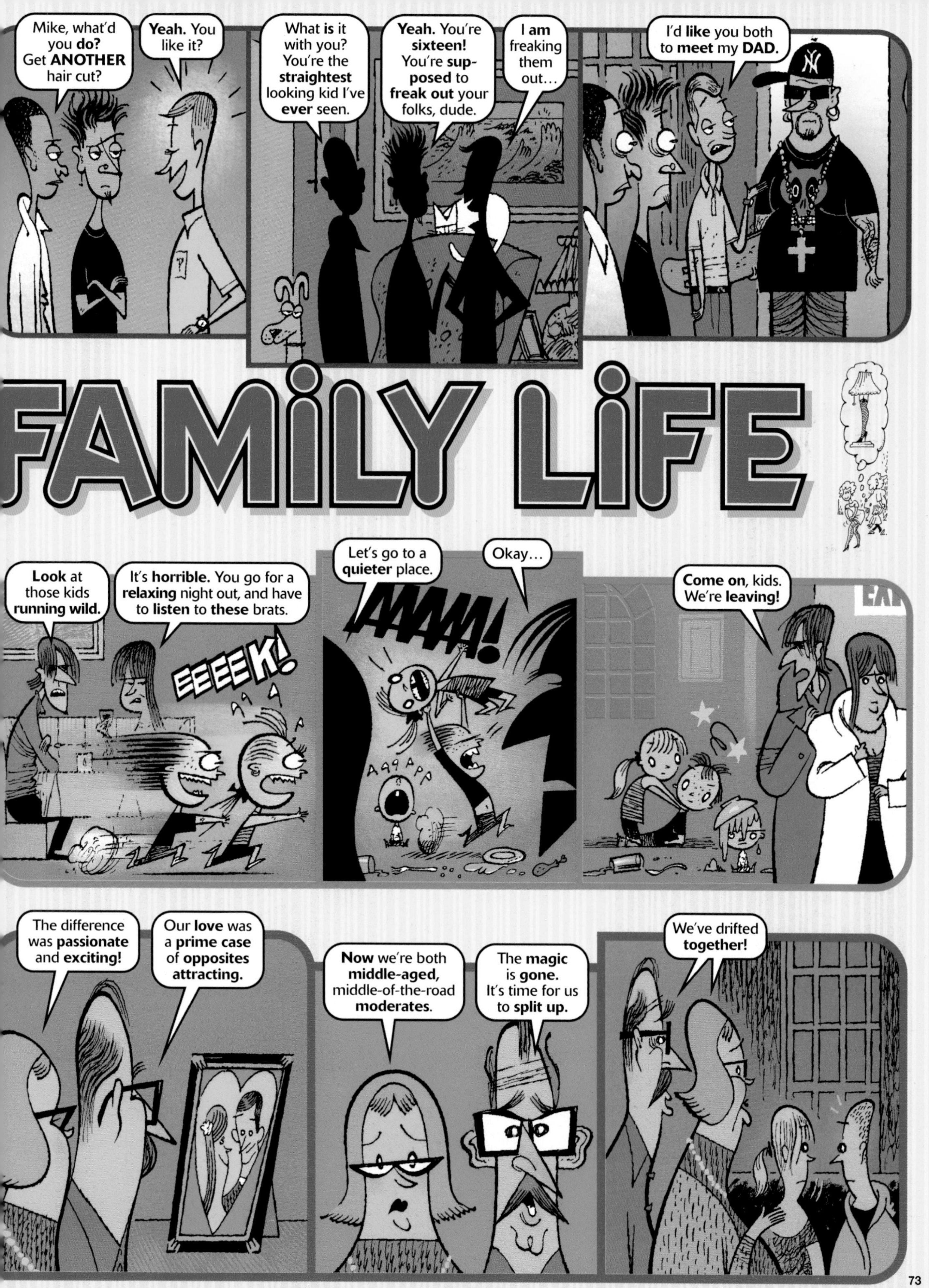
Mike, what'd you do? Get ANOTHER hair cut?
Yeah. You like it?
What is it with you? You're the straightest looking kid I've ever seen.
Yeah. You're sixteen! You're supposed to freak out your folks, dude.
I am freaking them out…
I'd like you both to meet my DAD.
FAMILY LIFE
Look at those kids running wild.
It's horrible. You go for a relaxing night out, and have to listen to these brats.
EEEEK!
Let's go to a quieter place.
Okay…
Come on, kids. We're leaving!
The difference was passionate and exciting!
Our love was a prime case of opposites attracting.
Now we're both middle-aged, middle-of-the-road moderates.
The magic is gone. It's time for us to split up.
We've drifted together!

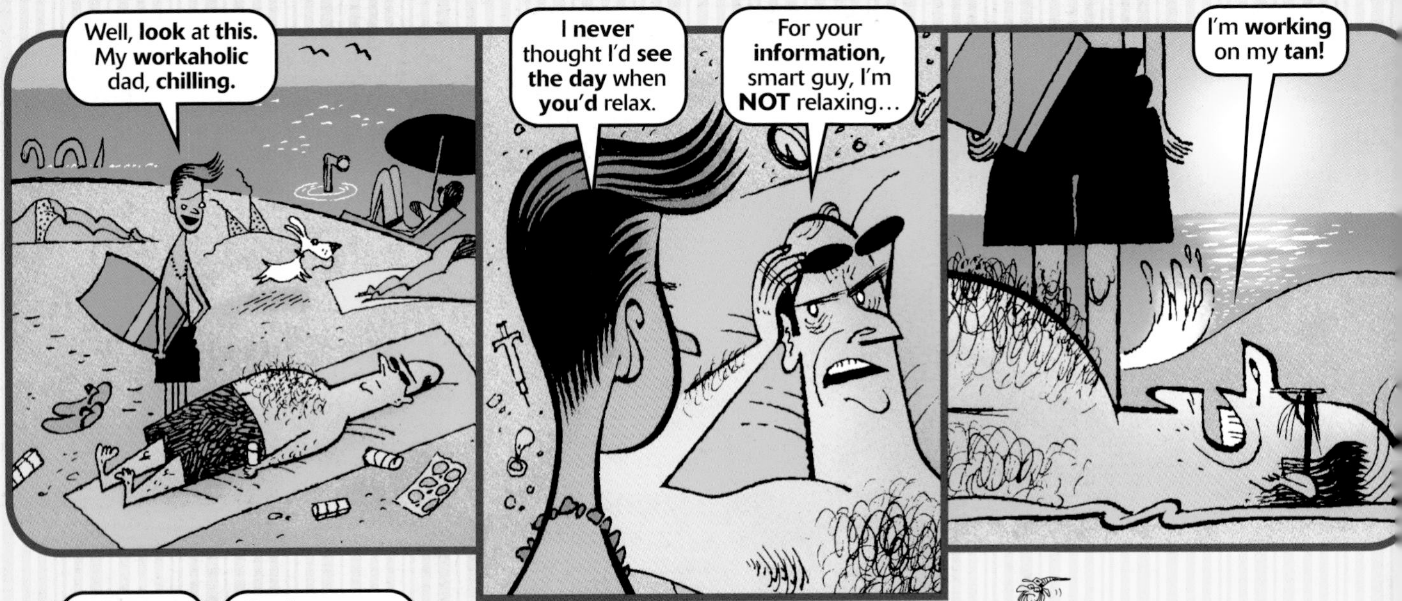
Well, look at this. My workaholic dad, chilling.
I never thought I'd see the day when you'd relax.
For your information, smart guy, I'm NOT relaxing…
I'm working on my tan!

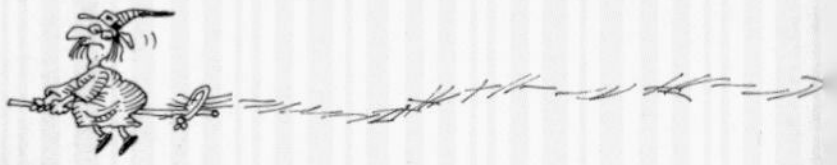

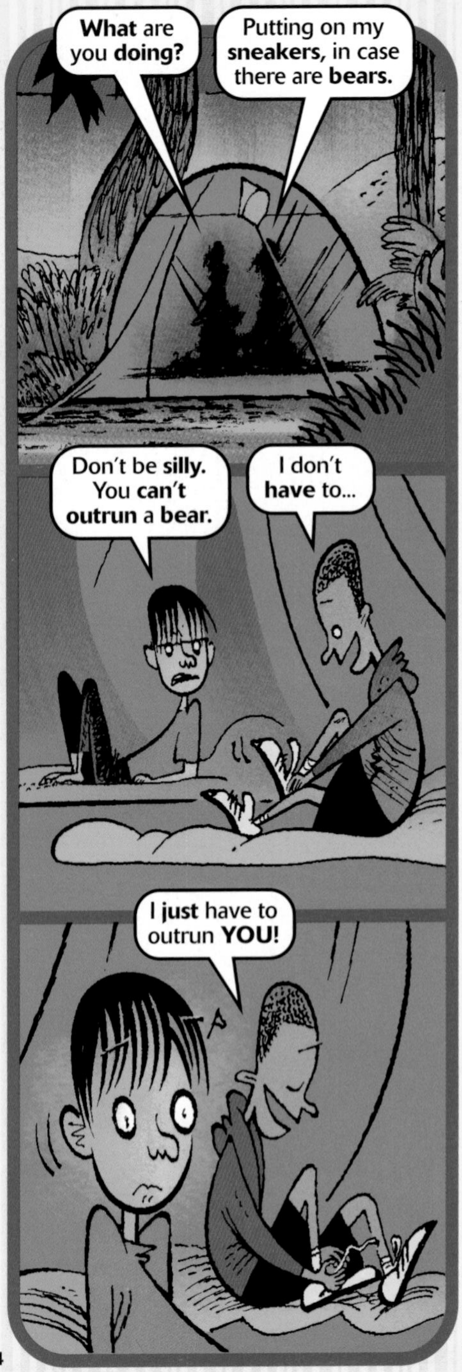
What are you doing?
Putting on my sneakers, in case there are bears.
Don't be silly. You can't outrun a bear.
I don't have to...
I just have to outrun YOU!

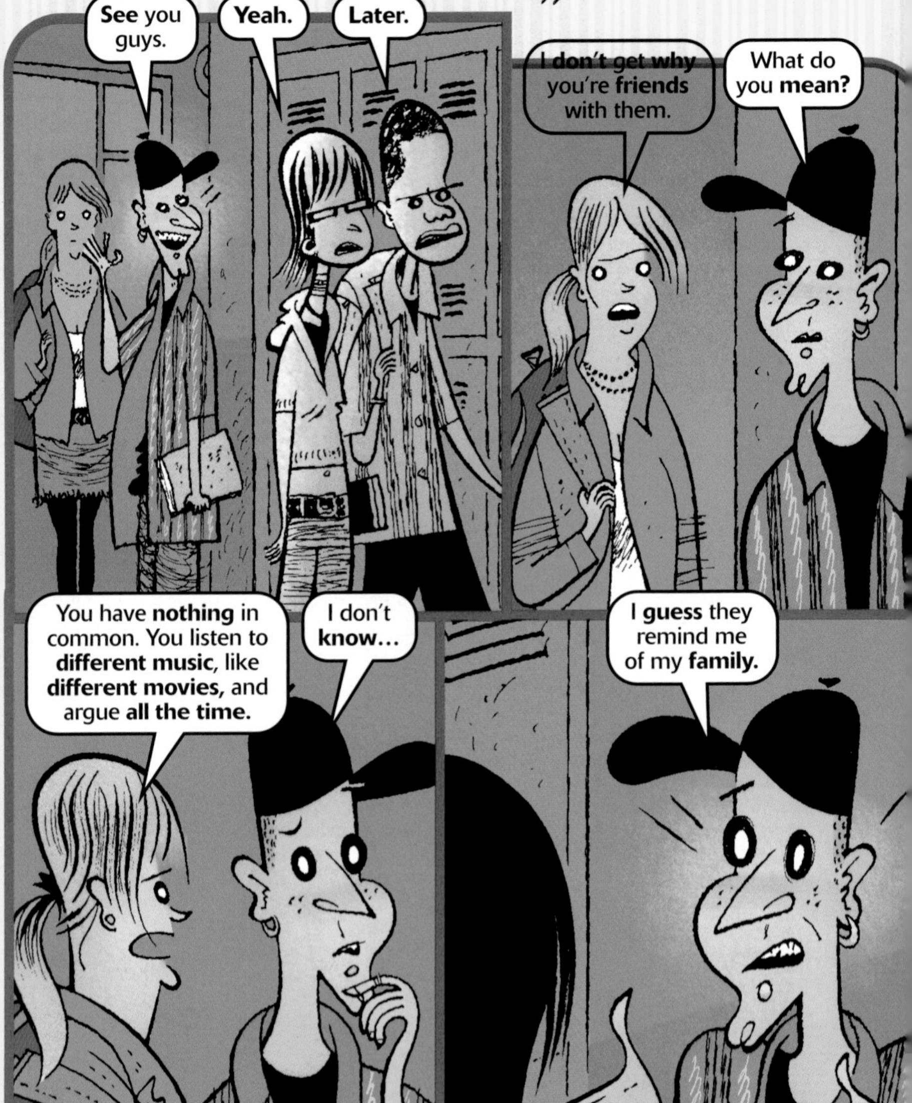
See you guys.
Yeah.
Later.
I don't get why you're friends with them.
What do you mean?
You have nothing in common. You listen to different music, like different movies, and argue all the time.
I don't know…
I guess they remind me of my family.

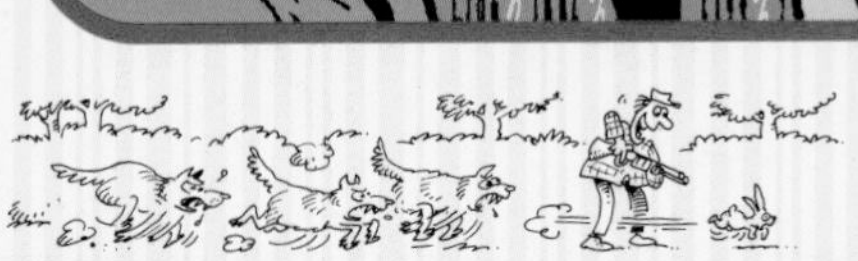

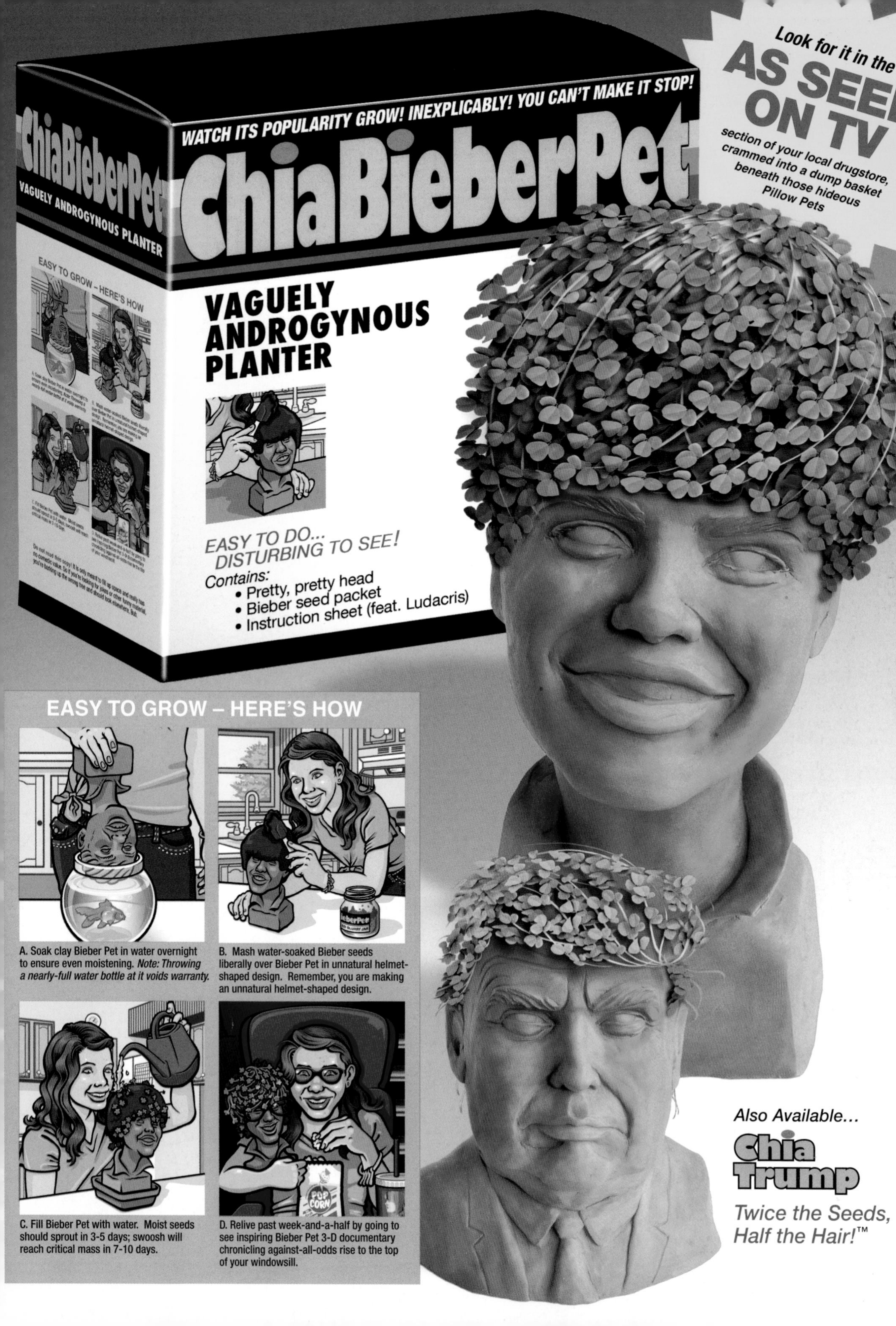
WATCH ITS POPULARITY GROW! INEXPLICABLY! YOU CAN'T MAKE IT STOP!
ChiaBieberPet
ChiaBieberPet
VAGUELY ANDROGYNOUS PLANTER
EASY TO GROW – HERE'S HOW
VAGUELY ANDROGYNOUS PLANTER
EASY TO DO... DISTURBING TO SEE!
Contains:
• Pretty, pretty head
• Bieber seed packet
• Instruction sheet (feat. Ludacris)
Look for it in the AS SEEN ON TV section of your local drugstore, crammed into a dump basket beneath those hideous Pillow Pets
EASY TO GROW – HERE'S HOW
A. Soak clay Bieber Pet in water overnight to ensure even moistening. Note: Throwing a nearly-full water bottle at it voids warranty.
B. Mash water-soaked Bieber seeds liberally over Bieber Pet in unnatural helmet-shaped design. Remember, you are making an unnatural helmet-shaped design.
C. Fill Bieber Pet with water. Moist seeds should sprout in 3-5 days; swoosh will reach critical mass in 7-10 days.
D. Relive past week-and-a-half by going to see inspiring Bieber Pet 3-D documentary chronicling against-all-odds rise to the top of your windowsill.
POP CORN
Also Available...
Chia Trump
Twice the Seeds, Half the Hair!™

WRITER: SCOTT MAIKO SCULPTOR: LIZ LOMAX ARTIST: TIM SHAMEY

SWIMMING ISN'T EVERYTHING DEPT.

In past issues, he has tackled such sensitive subjects as "When Priests Go Bad" and "When Veterinarians Go Bad." But this time, we think cartoon boy is in over his head. Here's...

JOHN CALDWELL'S WHEN LIFEGUARDS GO BAD

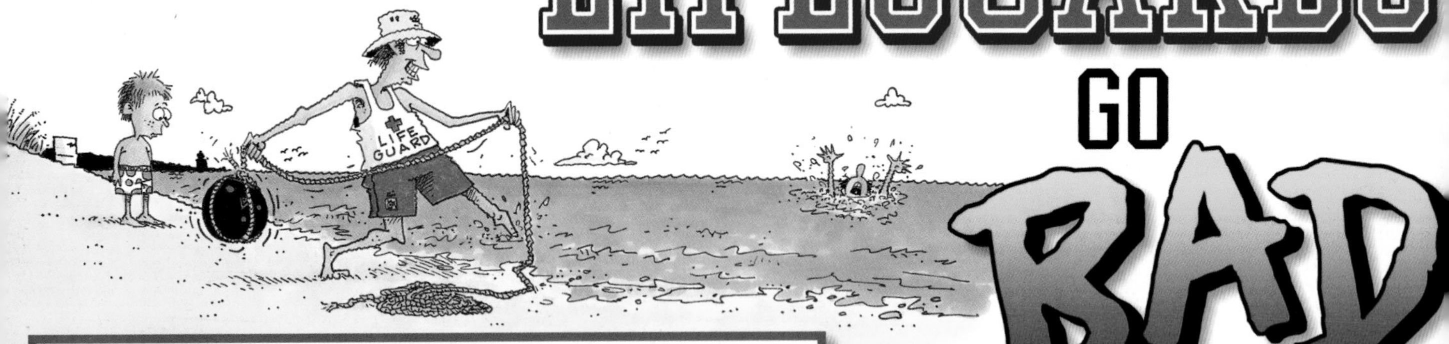

LIFE GUARD

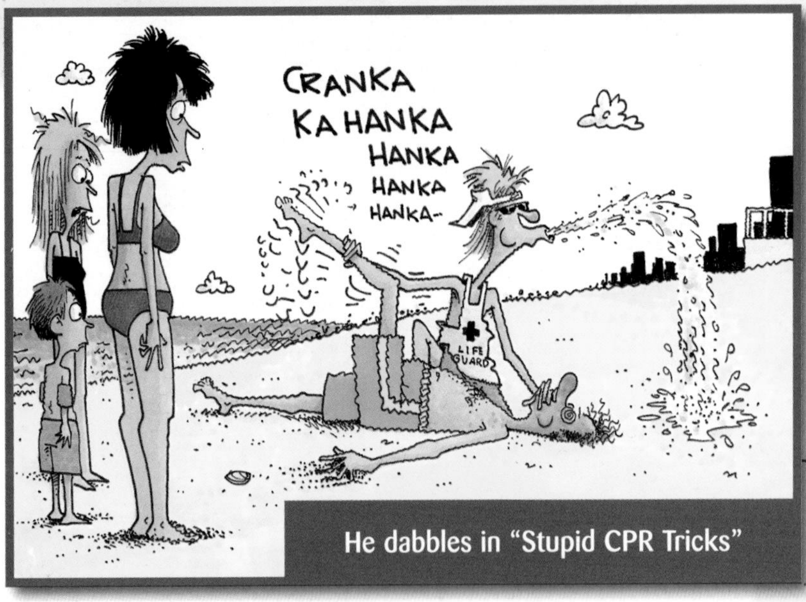

CRANKA
KA HANKA
HANKA
HANKA
HANKA–
LIFE GUARD

He dabbles in "Stupid CPR Tricks"

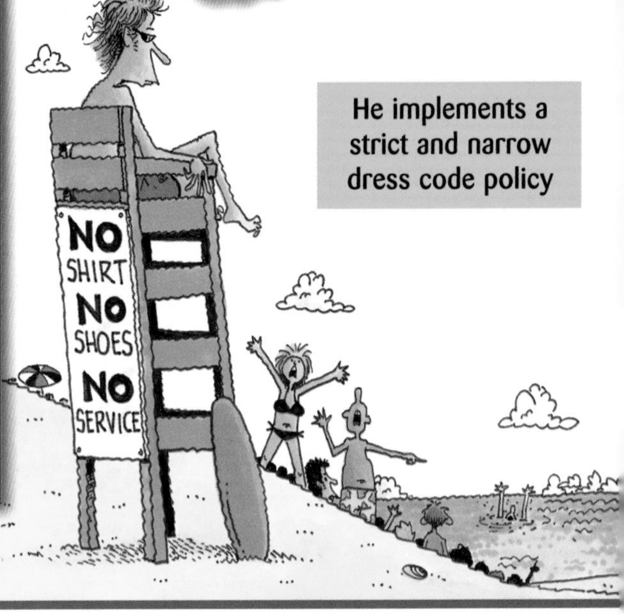

NO SHIRT
NO SHOES
NO SERVICE

He implements a strict and narrow dress code policy

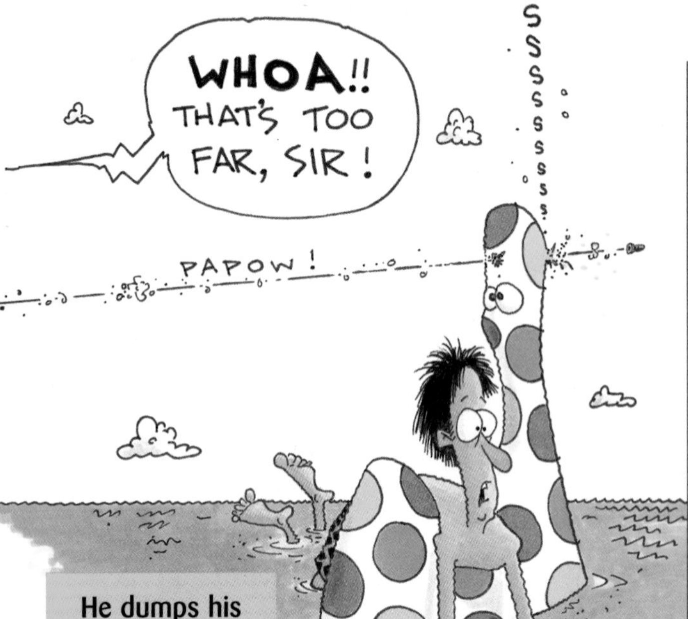

WHOA!! THAT'S TOO FAR, SIR!
PAPOW!
SSSSSSSSSS

He dumps his whistle in favor of firing off a few warning shots

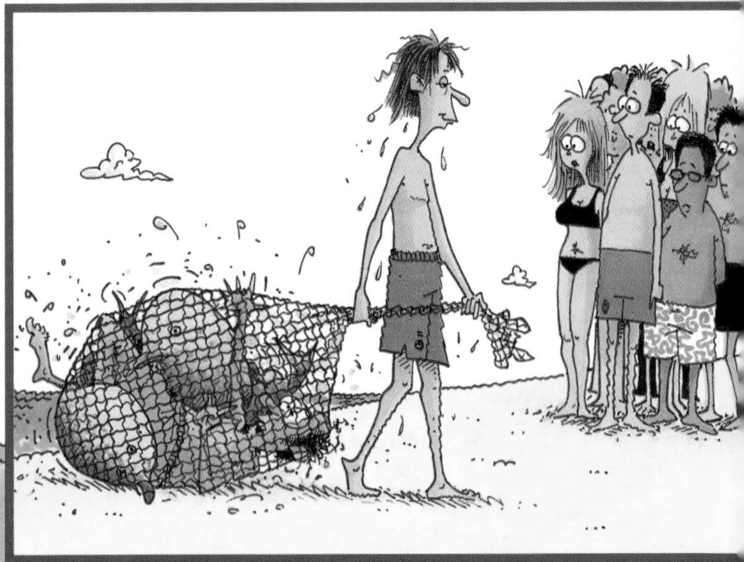

His lifesaving technique is cited by Greenpeace as being somewhat less than dolphin friendly

WRITER AND ARTIST: JOHN CALDWELL

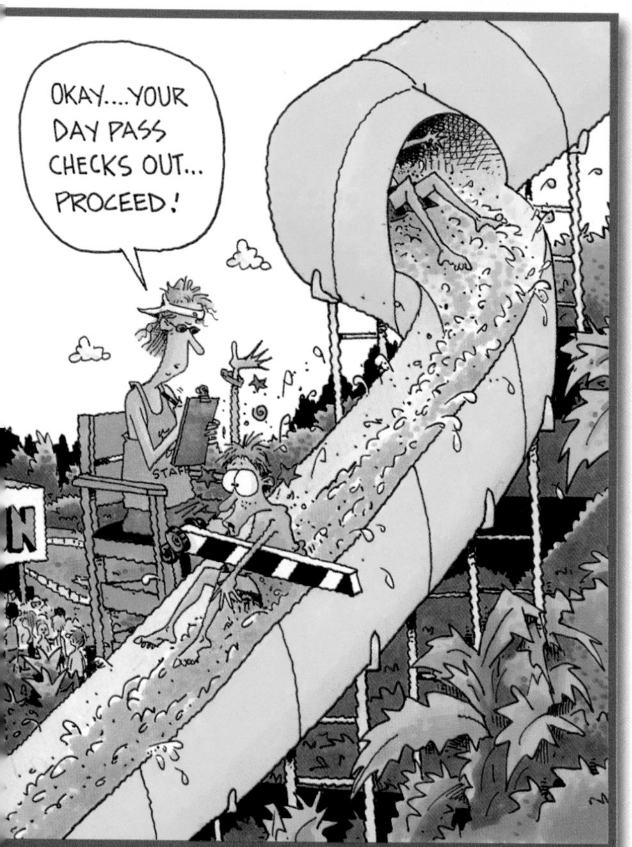
OKAY....YOUR DAY PASS CHECKS OUT... PROCEED!
STAFF

Sets up random, annoying and sometimes painful waterslide checkpoints

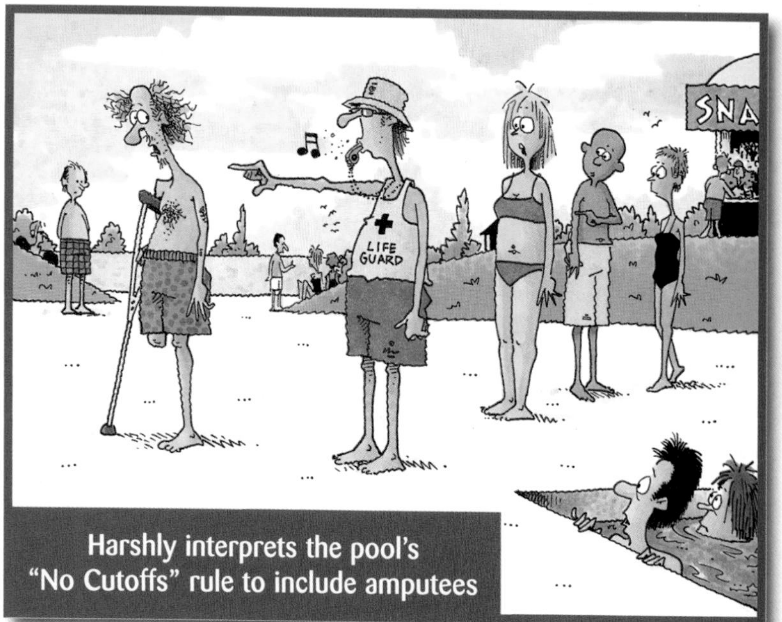
SNA
LIFE GUARD

Harshly interprets the pool's "No Cutoffs" rule to include amputees

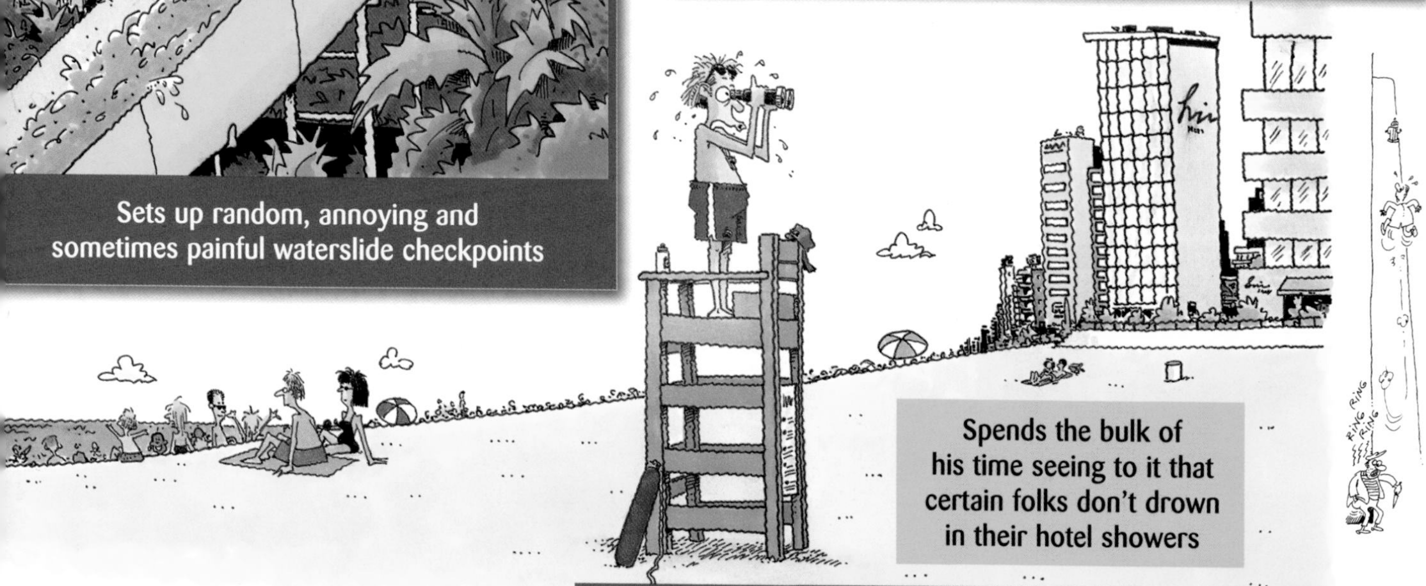
RING
RING
RING

Spends the bulk of his time seeing to it that certain folks don't drown in their hotel showers

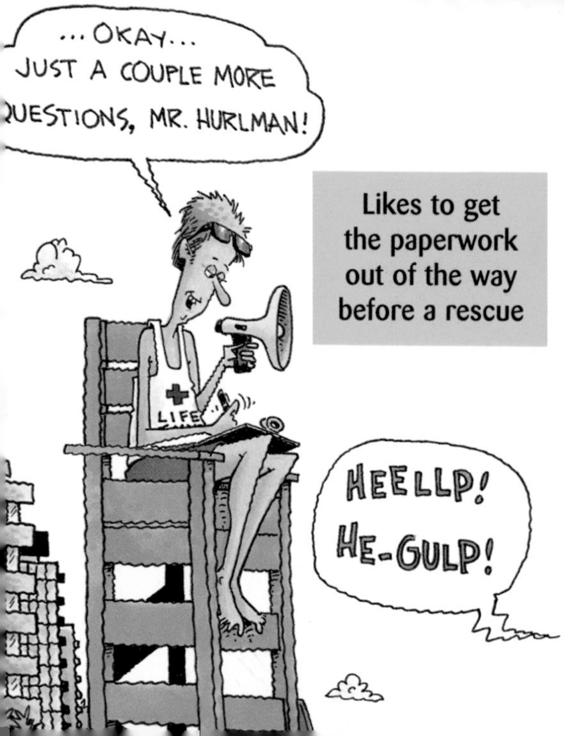
... OKAY...
JUST A COUPLE MORE
QUESTIONS, MR. HURLMAN!
LIFE
HEELLP!
HE-GULP!

Likes to get the paperwork out of the way before a rescue

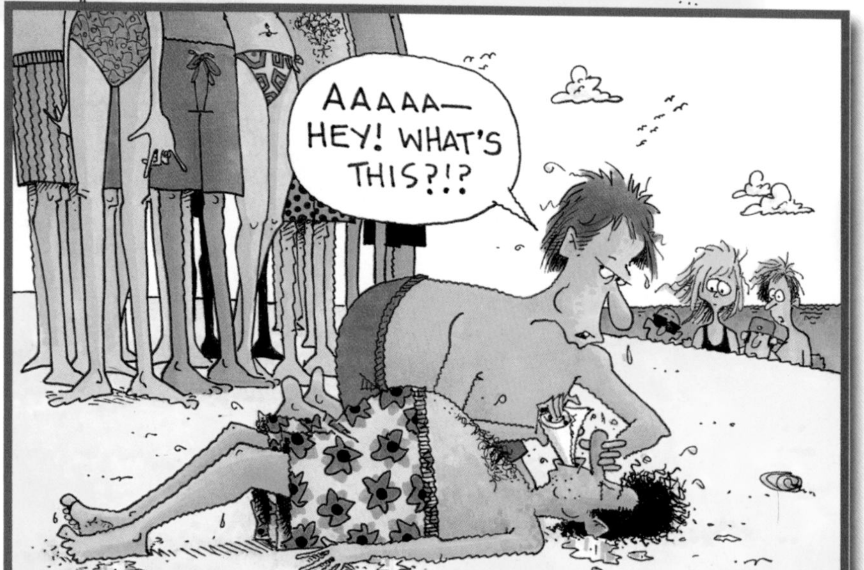
AAAAA—
HEY! WHAT'S
THIS?!?

To be on the "safe" side, he's always ready to plant a suicide note in order to keep his accidental drowning numbers low

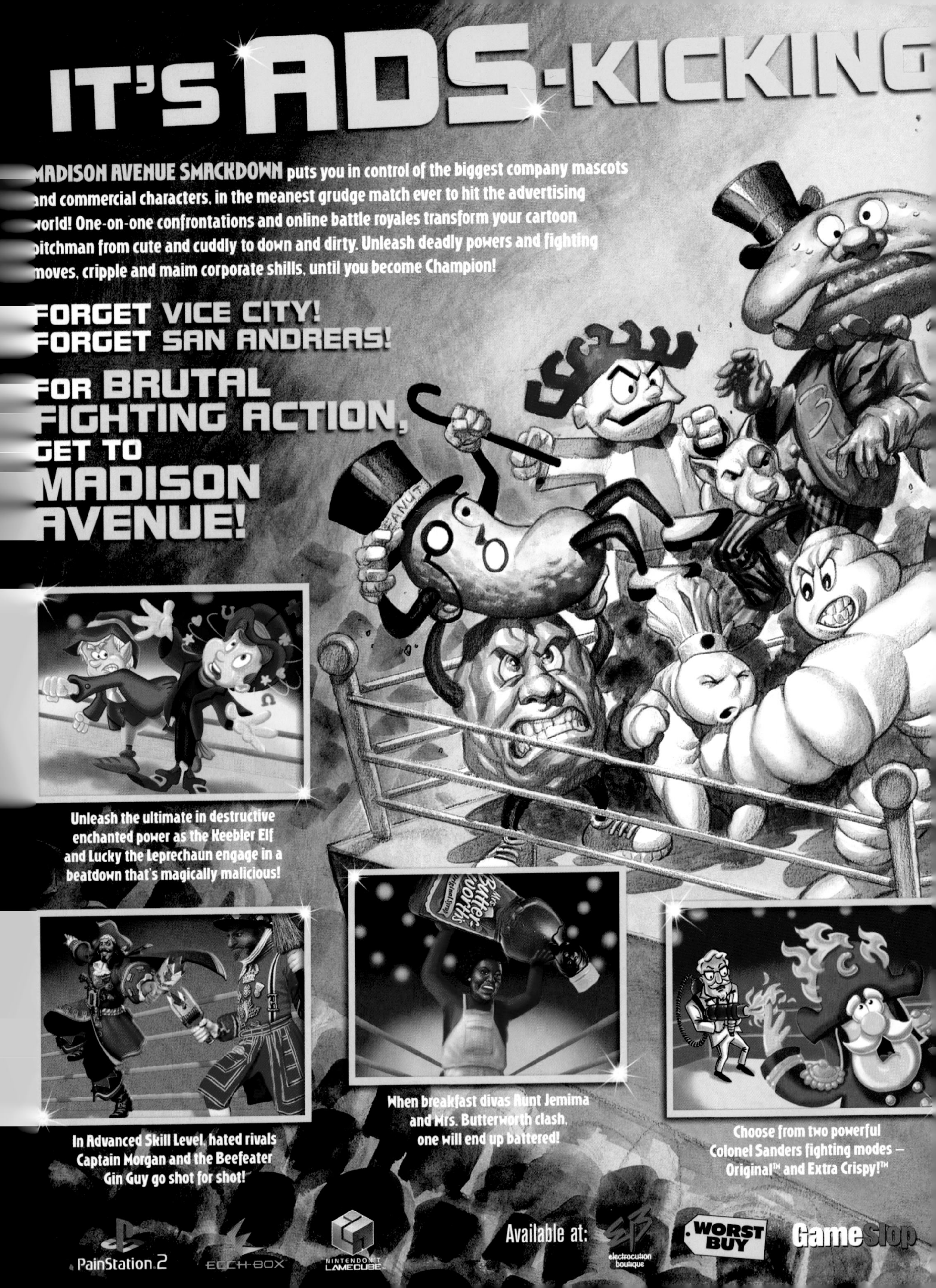
IT'S ADS-KICKING
MADISON AVENUE SMACKDOWN puts you in control of the biggest company mascots and commercial characters, in the meanest grudge match ever to hit the advertising world! One-on-one confrontations and online battle royales transform your cartoon pitchman from cute and cuddly to down and dirty. Unleash deadly powers and fighting moves, cripple and maim corporate shills, until you become Champion!
FORGET VICE CITY!
FORGET SAN ANDREAS!
FOR BRUTAL FIGHTING ACTION, GET TO MADISON AVENUE!
Unleash the ultimate in destructive enchanted power as the Keebler Elf and Lucky the Leprechaun engage in a beatdown that's magically malicious!
In Advanced Skill Level, hated rivals Captain Morgan and the Beefeater Gin Guy go shot for shot!
When breakfast divas Aunt Jemima and Mrs. Butterworth clash, one will end up battered!
Choose from two powerful Colonel Sanders fighting modes — Original™ and Extra Crispy!™
PainStation 2
ECCH-BOX
NINTENDON'T LAMECUBE
Available at:
electrocution boutique
WORST BUY
GameSlop

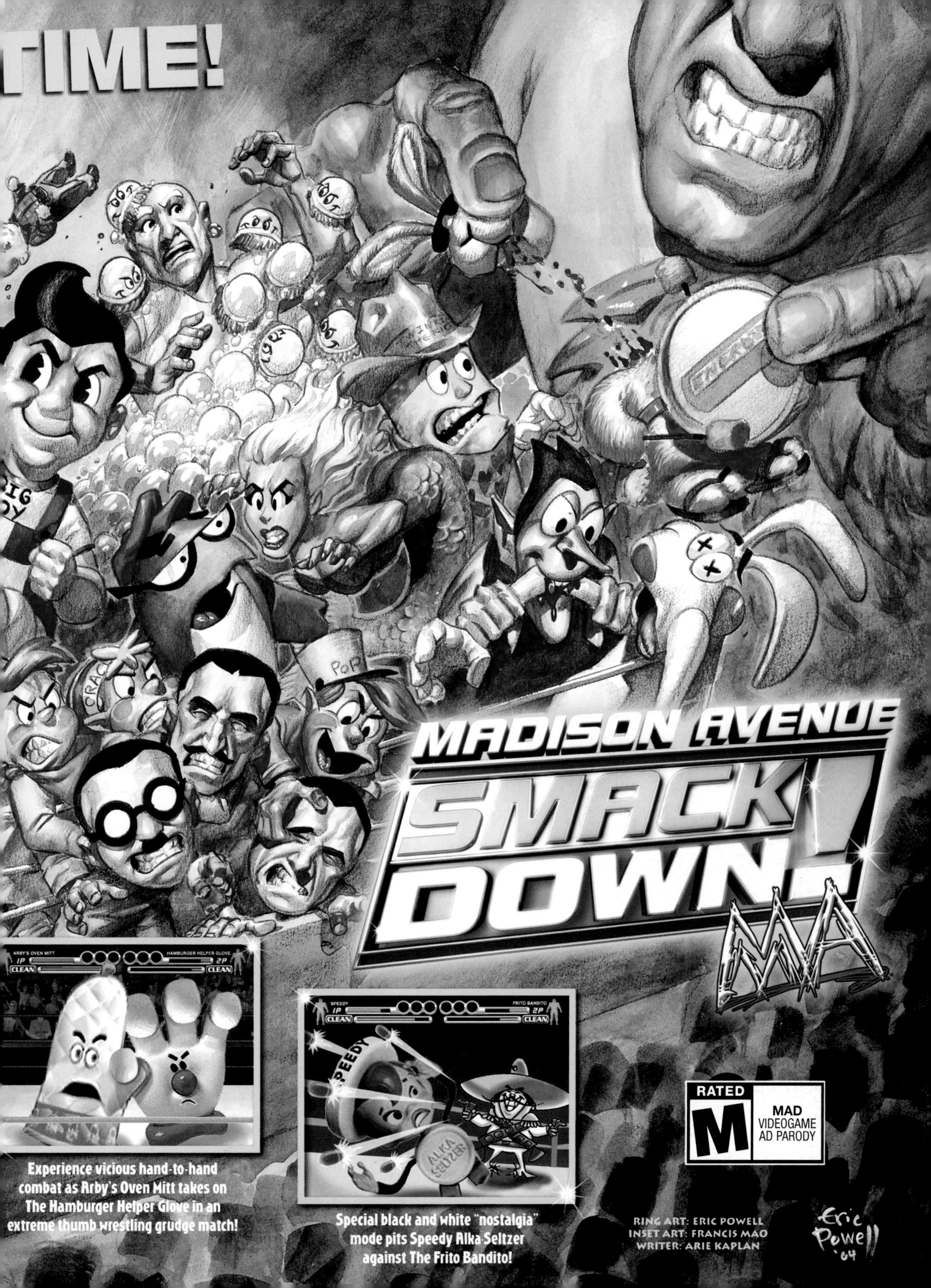
TIME!
MADISON AVENUE
SMACK DOWN!
MAD
ARBY'S OVEN MITT
HAMBURGER HELPER GLOVE
1P
2P
CLEAN
CLEAN
Experience vicious hand-to-hand combat as Arby's Oven Mitt takes on The Hamburger Helper Glove in an extreme thumb wrestling grudge match!
SPEEDY
FRITO BANDITO
1P
2P
CLEAN
CLEAN
SPEEDY
ALKA SELTZER
Special black and white "nostalgia" mode pits Speedy Alka-Seltzer against The Frito Bandito!
RATED
M
MAD
VIDEOGAME
AD PARODY
RING ART: ERIC POWELL
INSET ART: FRANCIS MAO
WRITER: ARIE KAPLAN
Eric Powell '04

PEN AND STINK DEPT.

The Comic Club

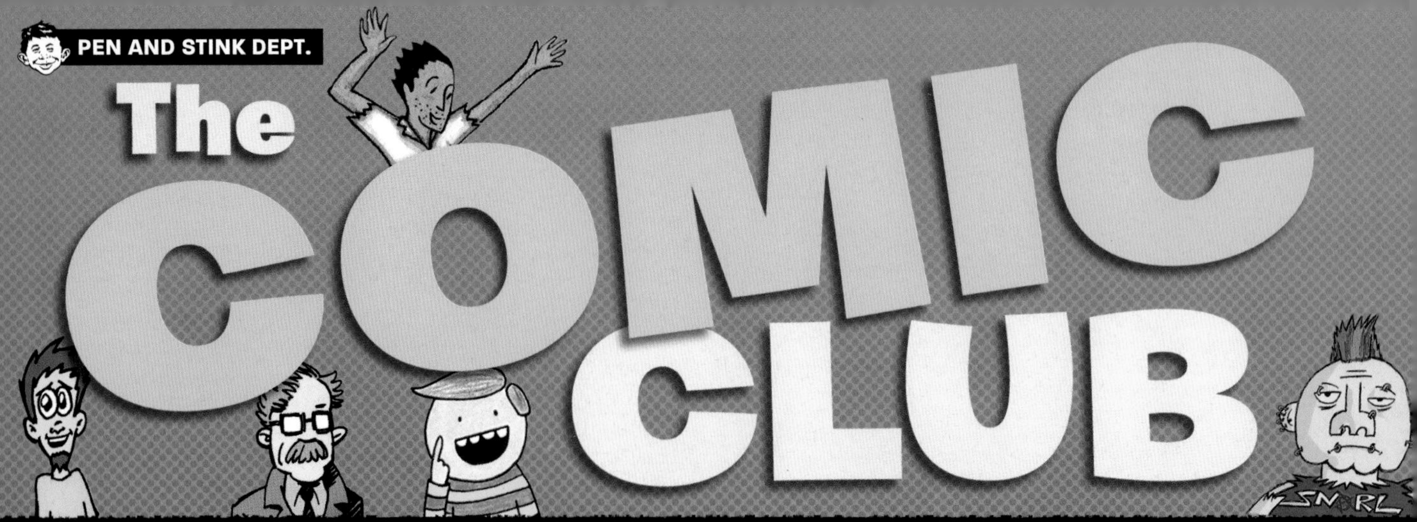

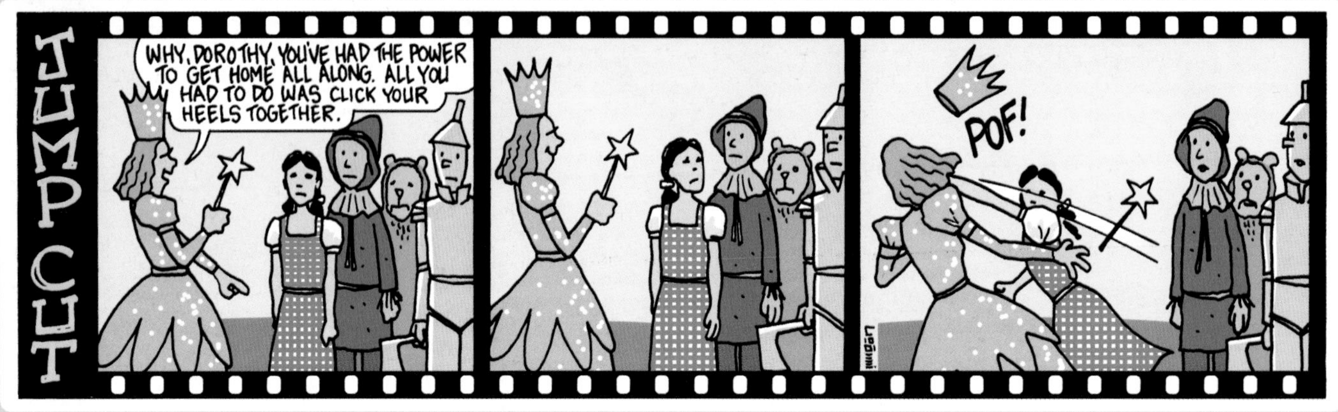
JUMP CUT
WHY, DOROTHY, YOU'VE HAD THE POWER TO GET HOME ALL ALONG. ALL YOU HAD TO DO WAS CLICK YOUR HEELS TOGETHER.
POF!

PAUL GILLIGAN

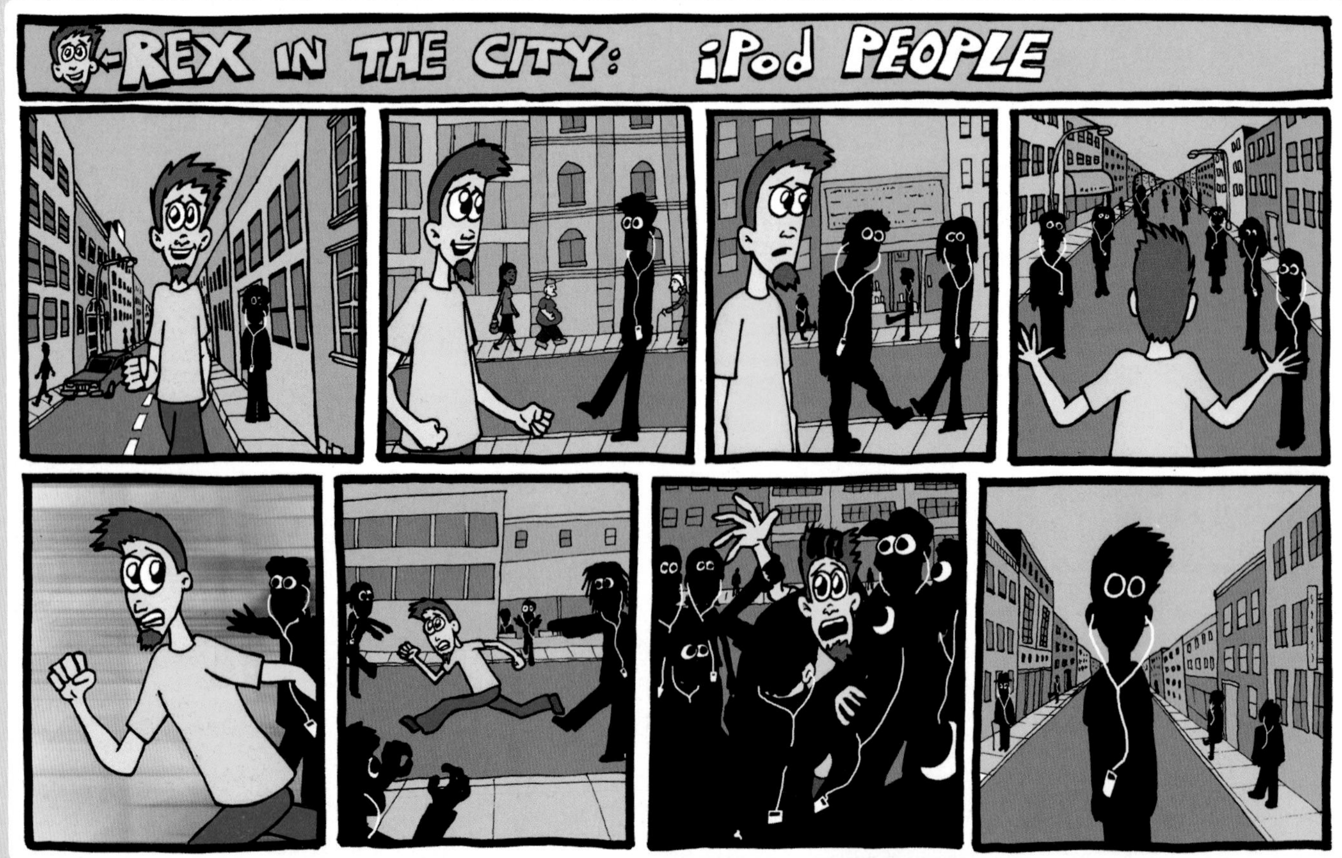
REX IN THE CITY: iPod PEOPLE

DUSTIN GLICK

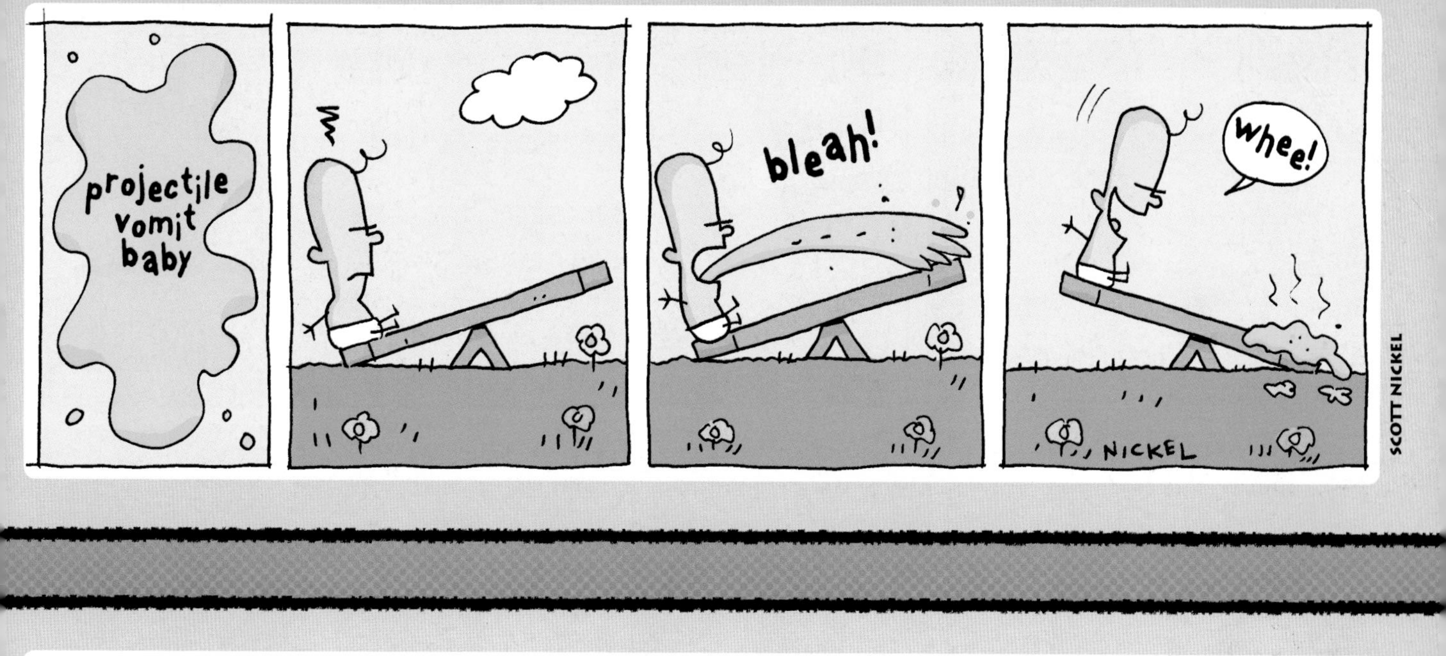
projectile vomit baby
bleah!
whee!
NICKEL

SCOTT NICKEL

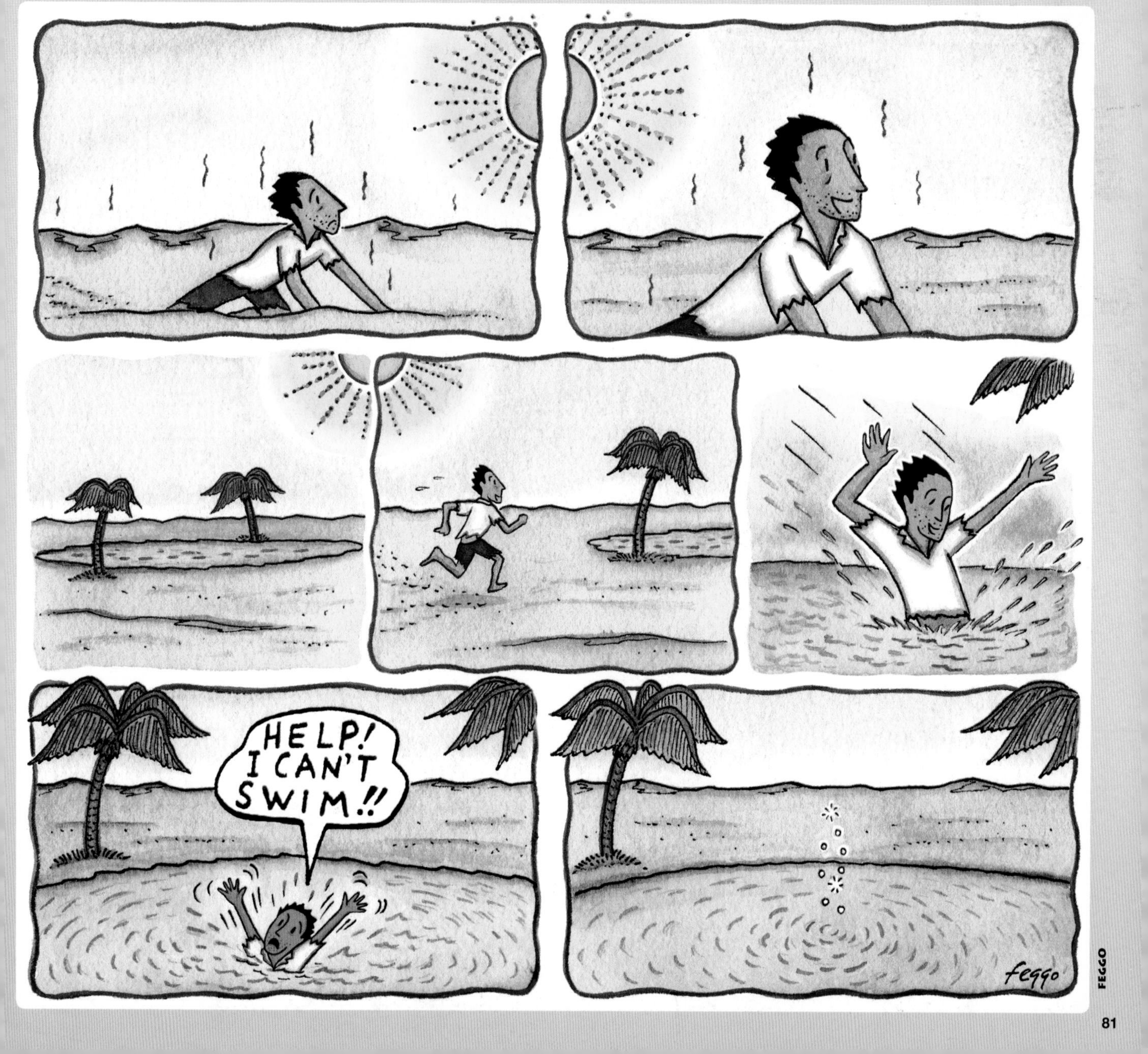
HELP! I CAN'T SWIM!!
feggo

FEGGO

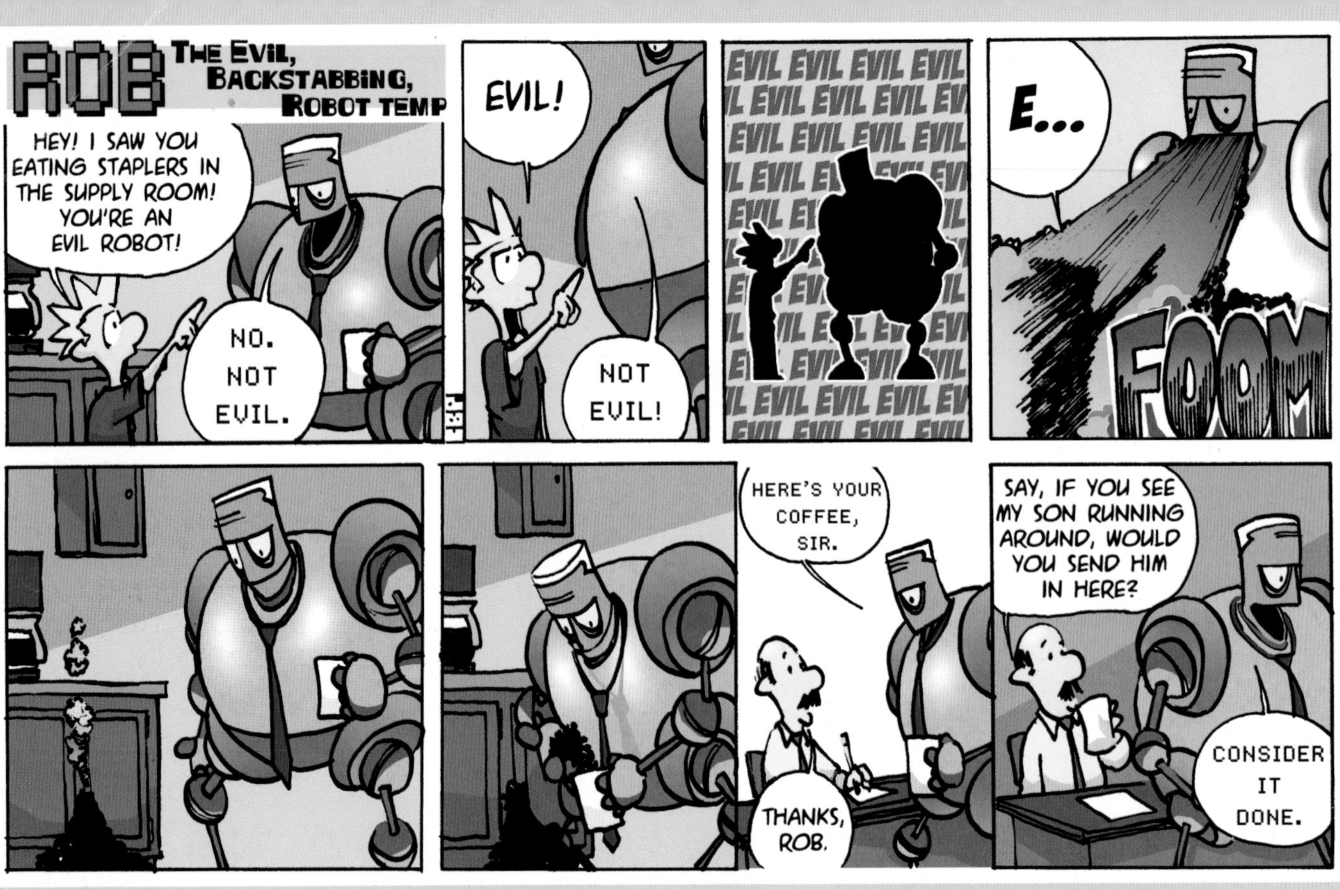
ROB
The Evil, Backstabbing, Robot Temp
HEY! I SAW YOU EATING STAPLERS IN THE SUPPLY ROOM! YOU'RE AN EVIL ROBOT!
NO. NOT EVIL.
EVIL!
NOT EVIL!
EVIL EVIL EVIL EVIL
E...
FOOM
HERE'S YOUR COFFEE, SIR.
THANKS, ROB.
SAY, IF YOU SEE MY SON RUNNING AROUND, WOULD YOU SEND HIM IN HERE?
CONSIDER IT DONE.

COREY PANDOLPH

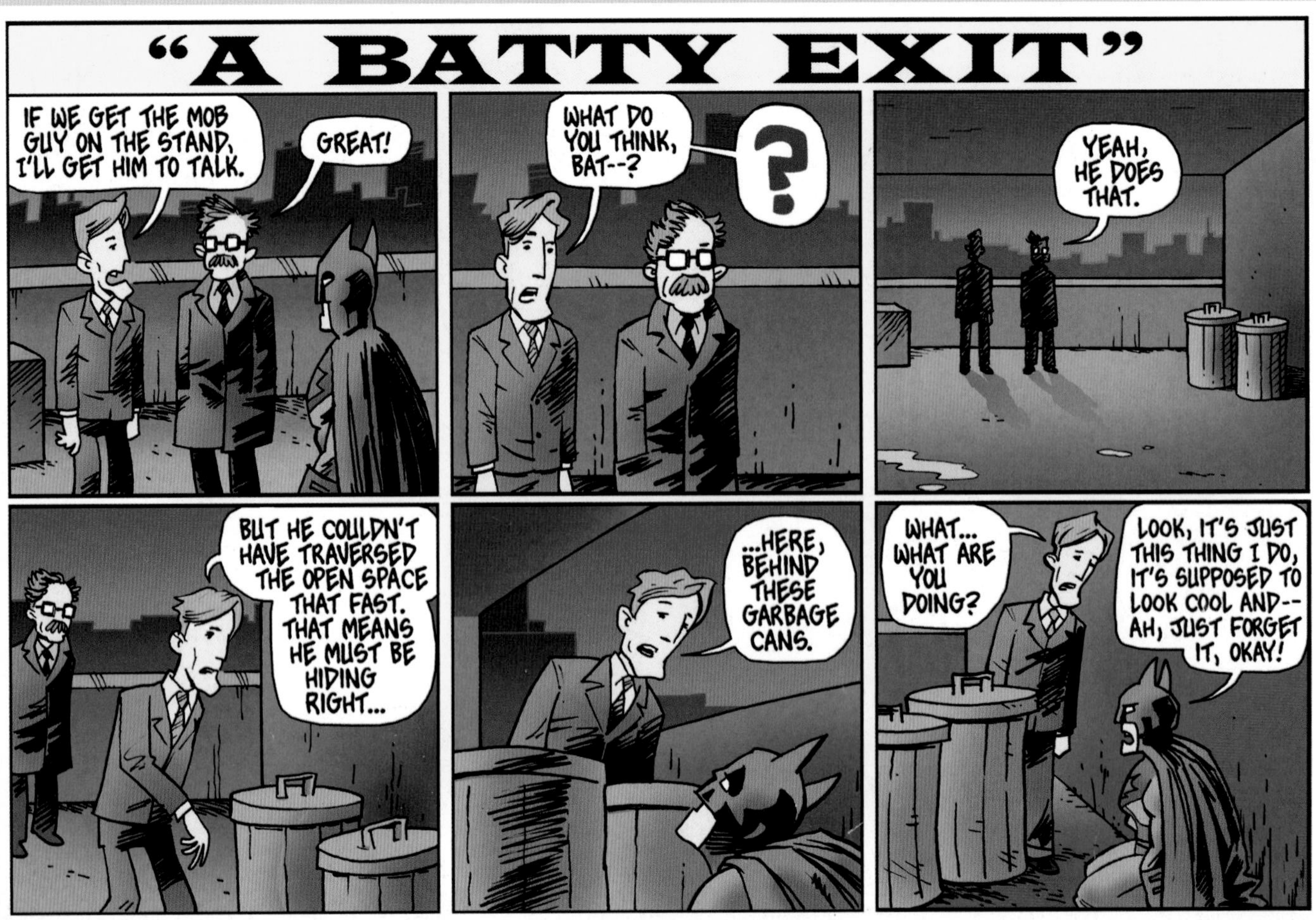
"A BATTY EXIT"
IF WE GET THE MOB GUY ON THE STAND, I'LL GET HIM TO TALK.
GREAT!
WHAT DO YOU THINK, BAT--?
?
YEAH, HE DOES THAT.
BUT HE COULDN'T HAVE TRAVERSED THE OPEN SPACE THAT FAST. THAT MEANS HE MUST BE HIDING RIGHT...
...HERE, BEHIND THESE GARBAGE CANS.
WHAT... WHAT ARE YOU DOING?
LOOK, IT'S JUST THIS THING I DO, IT'S SUPPOSED TO LOOK COOL AND-- AH, JUST FORGET IT, OKAY!

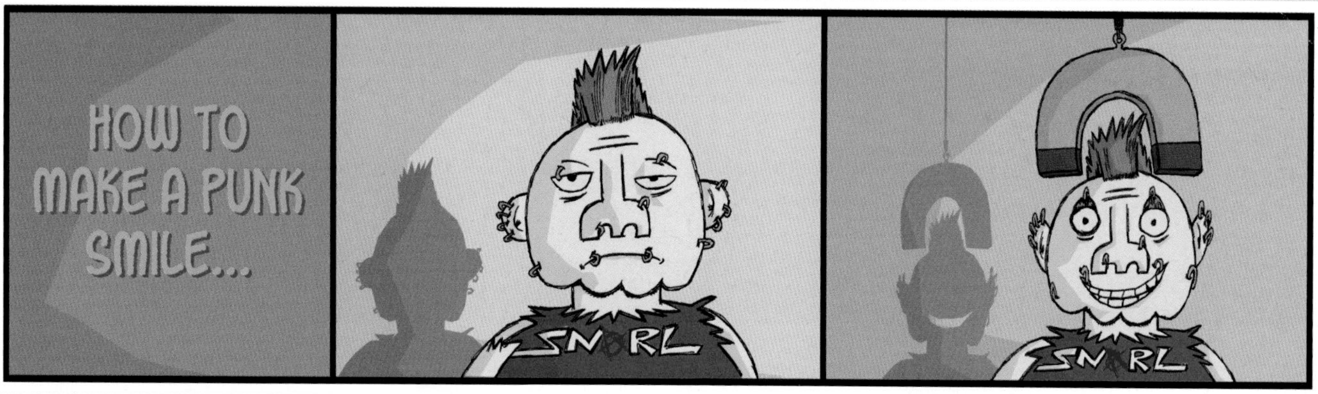

HOW TO MAKE A PUNK SMILE...
SNARL
SNARL

MO WILLEMS

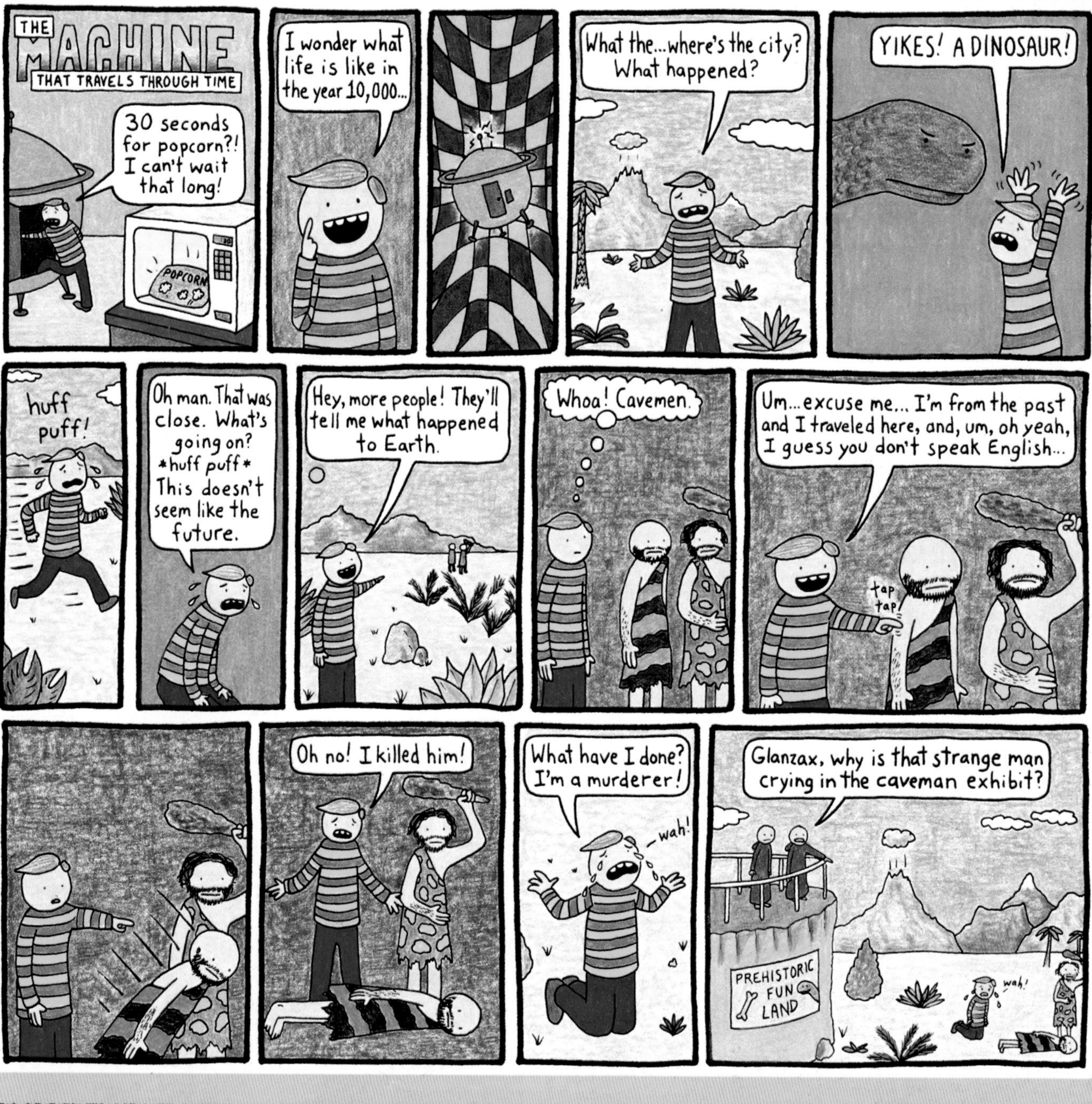

THE MACHINE THAT TRAVELS THROUGH TIME
30 seconds for popcorn?! I can't wait that long!
POPCORN
I wonder what life is like in the year 10,000...
What the...where's the city? What happened?
YIKES! A DINOSAUR!
huff puff!
Oh man. That was close. What's going on? *huff puff* This doesn't seem like the future.
Hey, more people! They'll tell me what happened to Earth.
Whoa! Cavemen.
Um...excuse me... I'm from the past and I traveled here, and, um, oh yeah, I guess you don't speak English...
tap tap
Oh no! I killed him!
What have I done? I'm a murderer!
wah!
Glanzax, why is that strange man crying in the caveman exhibit?
PREHISTORIC FUN LAND
wah!

JOEY ALISON SAYERS

ANY SPORT IN A STORM DEPT.

Before ESPN, we never knew how dull sports could be. Anyone who's ever watched the 24-hour all-sports channel knows that 99% of its programming is about as exciting as watching mold spread! Now, with ESPN2, ESPN Classic (i.e. repeats), ESPN Deportes, ESPN International and ESPNEWS, the ESPN name has become synonymous with super-intense mind-numbing boredom! And the *very* bad news is that the worst is still to come in the form of (GAK!) ESPN 3! (PLEASE! NO MORE! WE BEG OF YOU!!!) So be afraid, be very afraid as we offer...

A SNEAK PEEK AT THE ES

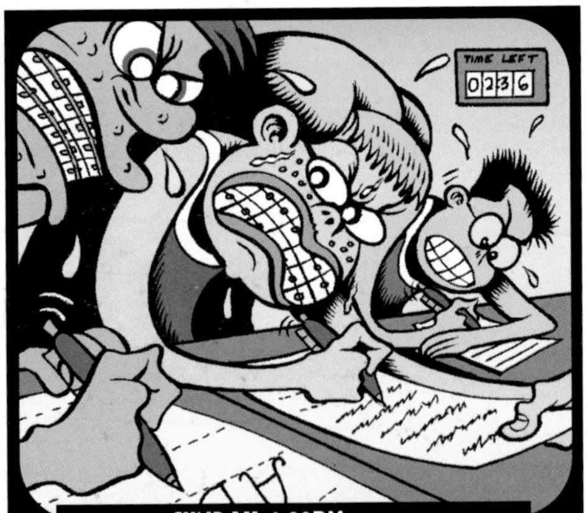
TIME LEFT
0236

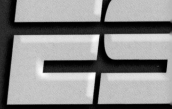

ESPN3 SUNDAY•4:30PM
ULTIMATE PENMANSHIP

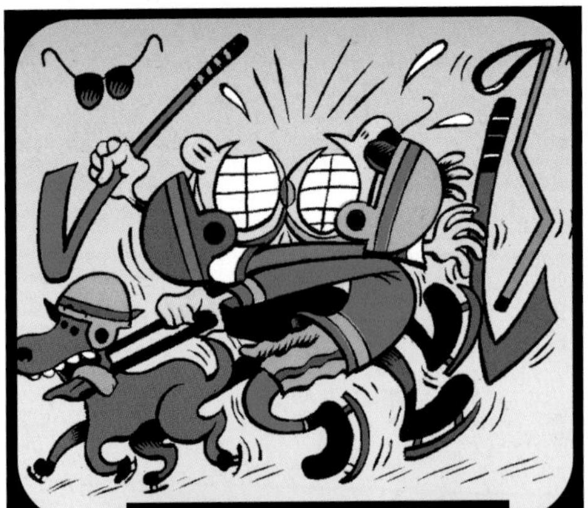

ESPN3 MONDAY•9:00PM
ICE HOCKEY FOR THE BLIND

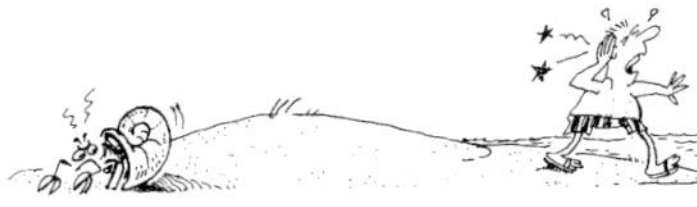

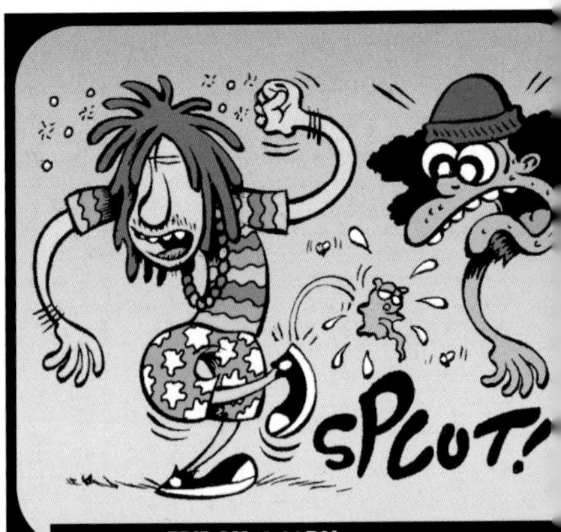
SPLUT!

ESPN3 FRIDAY•2:30PM
FETAL PIG HACKEY SACK

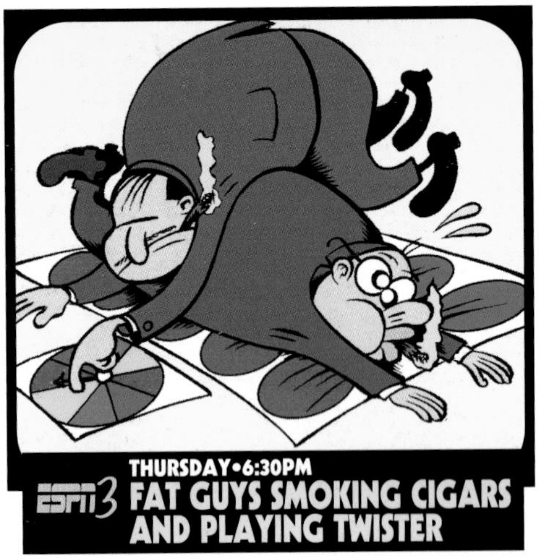

ESPN3 THURSDAY•6:30PM
FAT GUYS SMOKING CIGARS AND PLAYING TWISTER

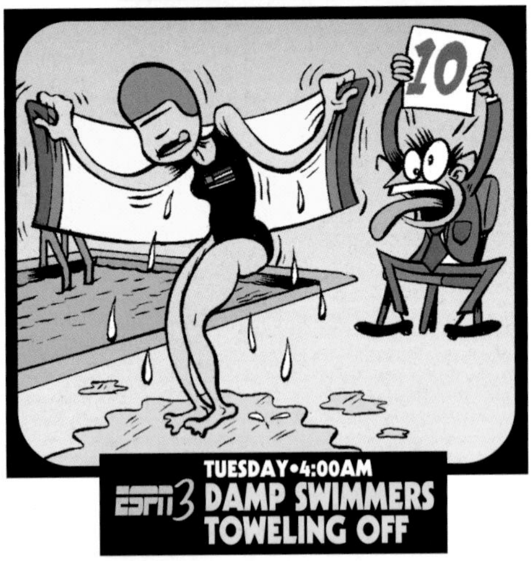
10

ESPN3 TUESDAY•4:00AM
DAMP SWIMMERS TOWELING OFF

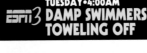

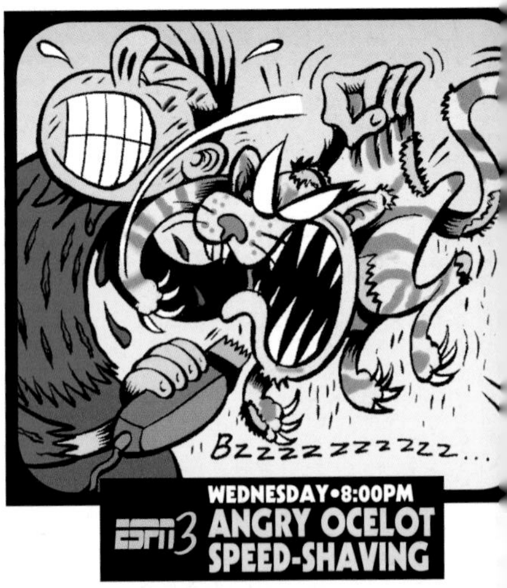
Bzzzzzzzzzz...

ESPN3 WEDNESDAY•8:00PM
ANGRY OCELOT SPEED-SHAVING

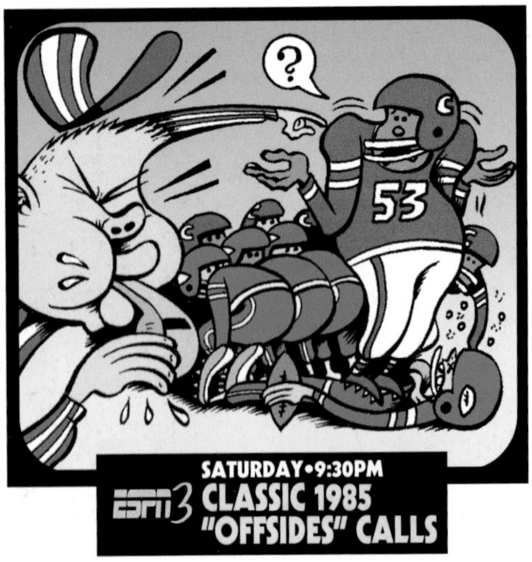
?
53

ESPN3 SATURDAY•9:30PM
CLASSIC 1985 "OFFSIDES" CALLS

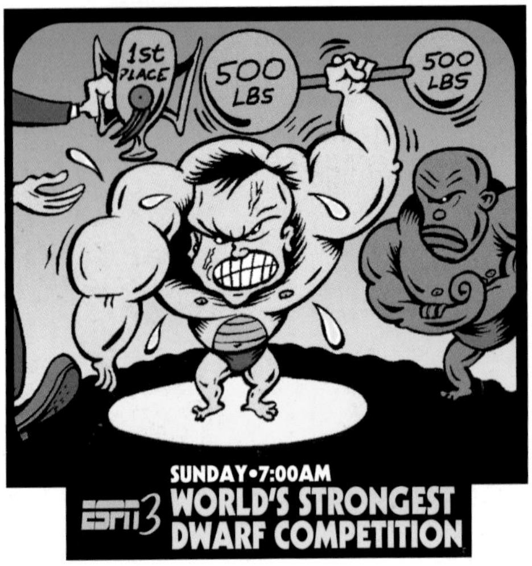
1st PLACE
500 LBS
500 LBS

ESPN3 SUNDAY•7:00AM
WORLD'S STRONGEST DWARF COMPETITION

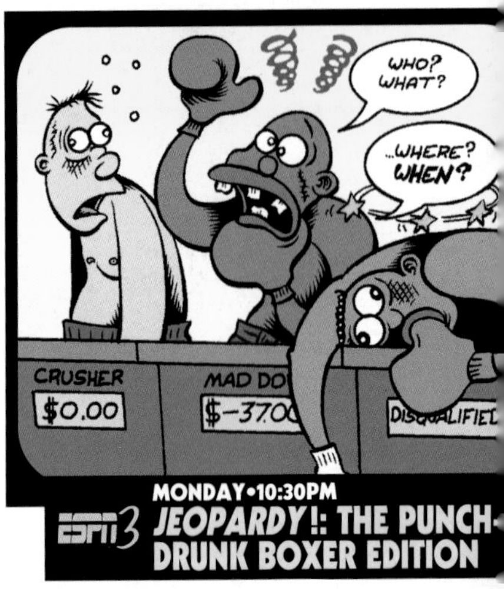
WHO? WHAT?
...WHERE? WHEN?
CRUSHER
$0.00
MAD DO
$-3700
DISQUALIFIED

ESPN3 MONDAY•10:30PM
JEOPARDY!: THE PUNCH-DRUNK BOXER EDITION

ARTIST: PETER BAGGE

WRITER: DESMOND DEVLIN

YouTube...

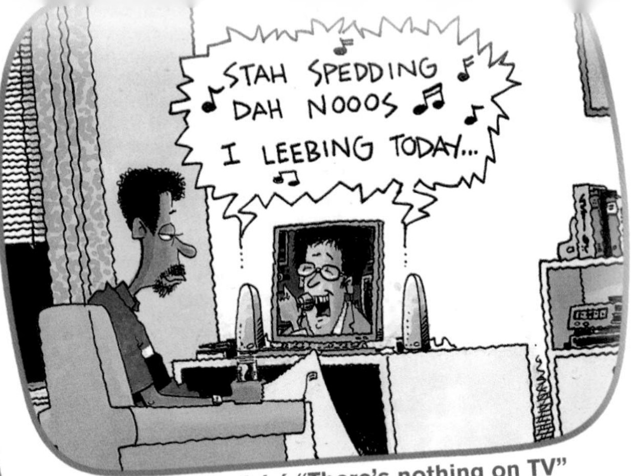
STAH SPEDDING DAH NOOOS I LEEBING TODAY...

...the old cliché "There's nothing on TV" can now be commonly followed up with, "So, I think I'll watch some drunk Korean accountants sing karaoke!"

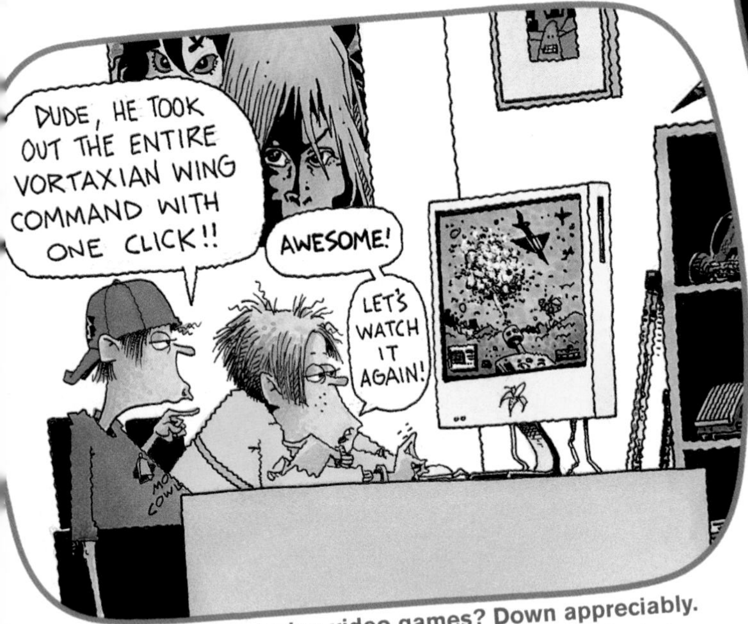
DUDE, HE TOOK OUT THE ENTIRE VORTAXIAN WING COMMAND WITH ONE CLICK!!
AWESOME!
LET'S WATCH IT AGAIN!

...time spent playing video games? Down appreciably. Time spent watching clips of other people playing video games? Through the roof!

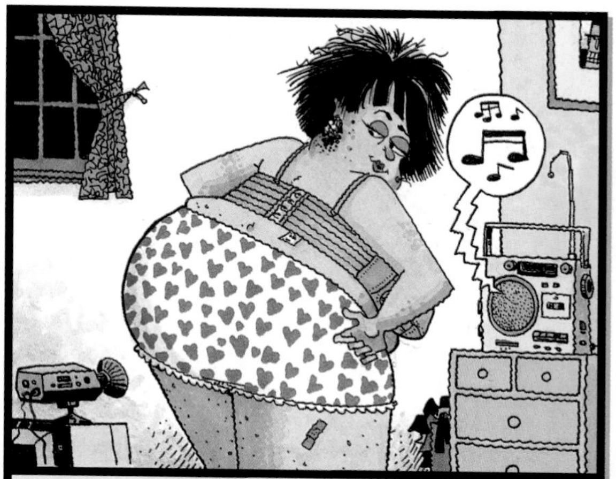

...you are always just a click away from a Slavic rendition of "The Booty Dance"!

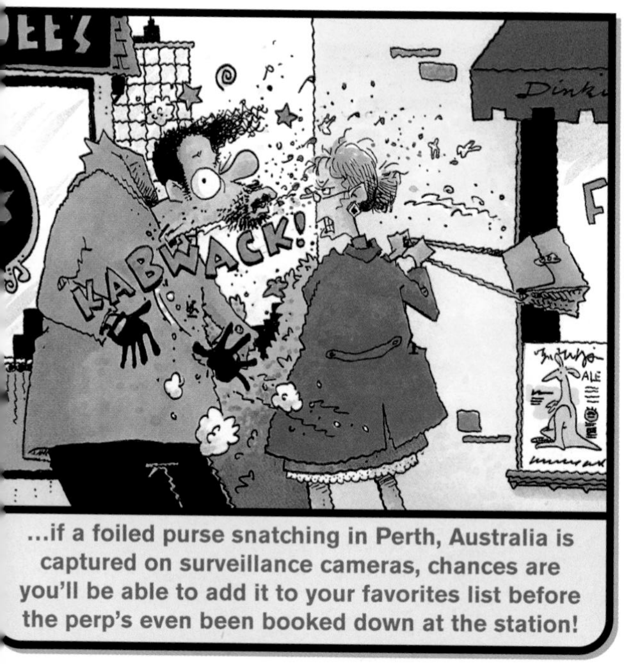
KABWACK!

...if a foiled purse snatching in Perth, Australia is captured on surveillance cameras, chances are you'll be able to add it to your favorites list before the perp's even been booked down at the station!

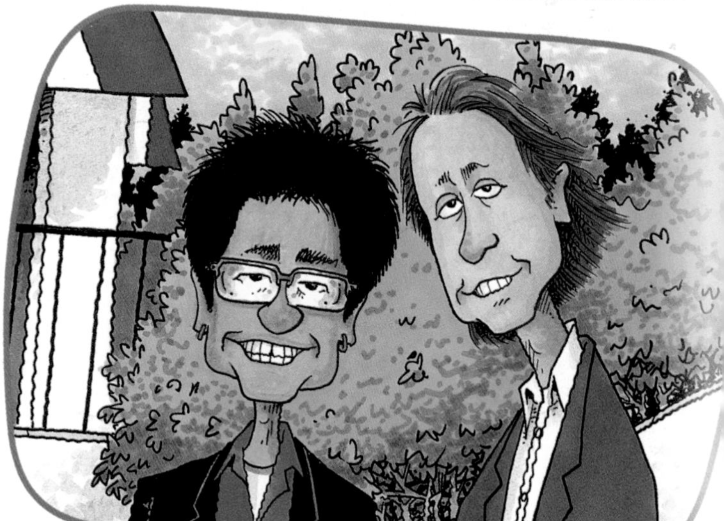

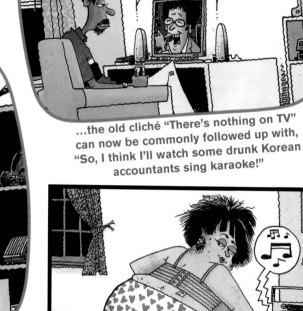

...the guys who started the site are a billion dollars richer after selling to Google, so they finally have the time (and a good excuse) to make one of those pointless, amateurish, shaky image, dorky videos that make up 99% of their site's content!

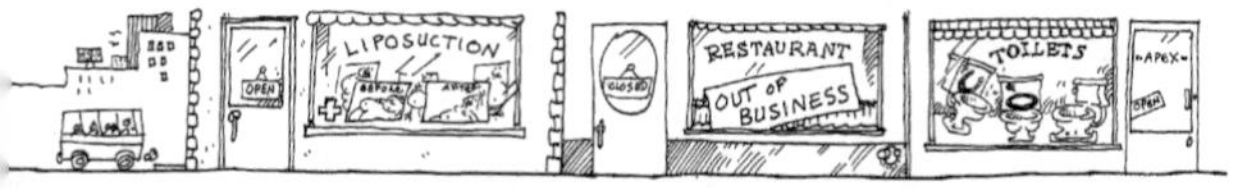
LIPOSUCTION
RESTAURANT
OUT OF BUSINESS
TOILETS

RACE UNDER FIRE DEPT.

Sure, NASCAR may look like a bunch of sun-baked *Cannonball Run* refugees making hard lefts until their gas tanks empty or their bladders get full. But to true fume-huffers, NASCAR isn't just a mind-numbingly repetitive crackerfest — it's a mind-numbingly repetitive crackerfest with rules! (For example, all windshields must be "standard protection laminated glass or hard-coated polycarbonate with a minimum one-quarter inch thickness." Too bad there's not a similar requirement for the thickness of NASCAR fans' skulls!) So now, with the betterment of the, er, "sport" in mind, we not-so-humbly offer...

MAD'S PROPOSED RULE CHANGES FOR THE UPCOMING NASCAR SEASON

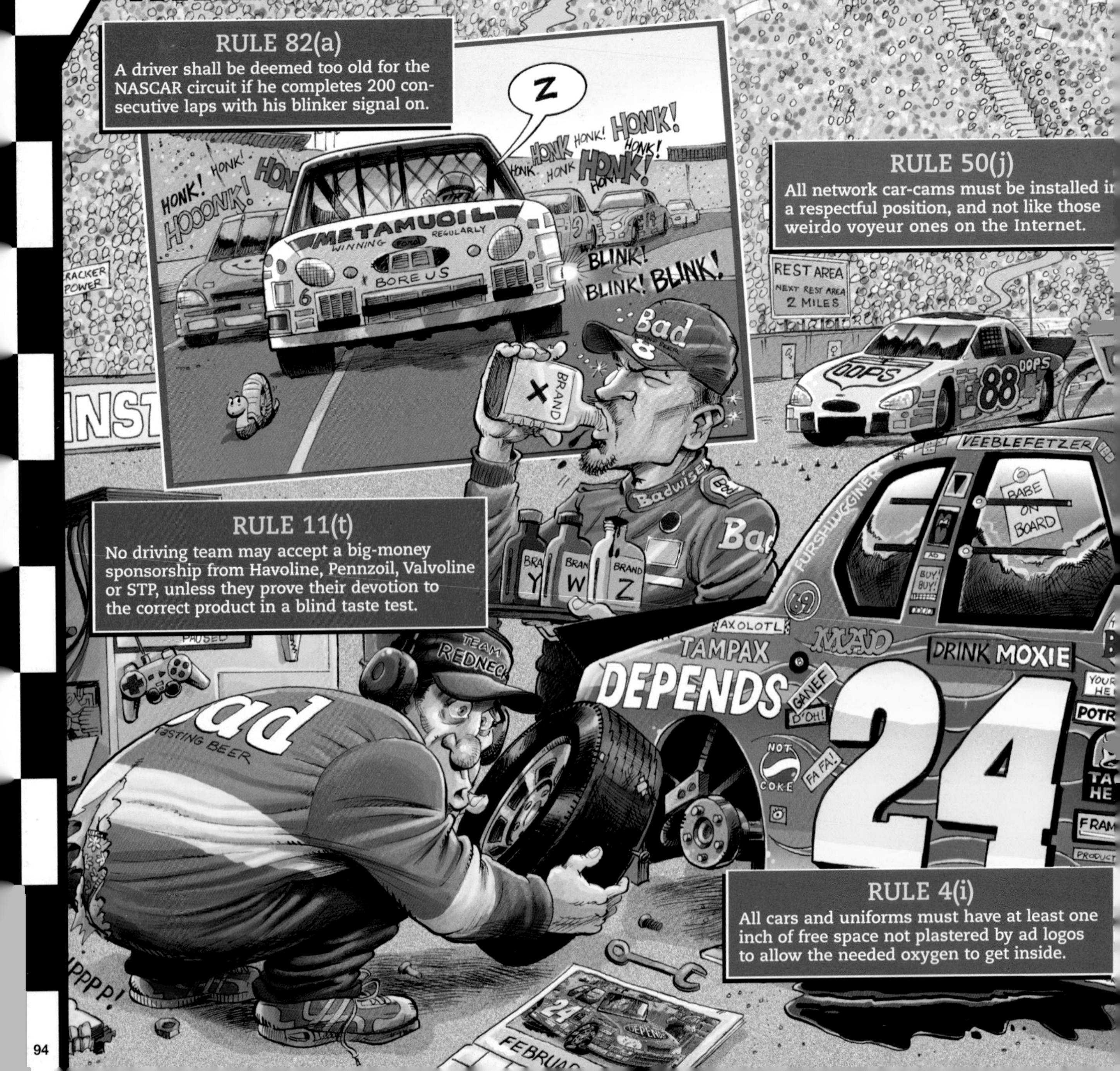
Z
HONK! HONK! HONK! HONK! HONK! HONK!
HONK! HONK! HOOONK!
METAMUOIL
WINNING REGULARLY
BOREUS
BLINK! BLINK! BLINK!
REST AREA
NEXT REST AREA 2 MILES
Bad
BRAND X
BRAND Y
BRAND W
BRAND Z
OOPS
88
VEEBLEFETZER
BABE ON BOARD
FURSHLUGGINER
BUY! BUY!
TEAM REDNECK
AXOLOTL
TAMPAX
DRINK MOXIE
DEPENDS
GANEF
D'OH!
NOT COKE
FA FA!
24
FEBRUA

RULE 82(a)
A driver shall be deemed too old for the NASCAR circuit if he completes 200 consecutive laps with his blinker signal on.

RULE 50(j)
All network car-cams must be installed in a respectful position, and not like those weirdo voyeur ones on the Internet.

RULE 11(t)
No driving team may accept a big-money sponsorship from Havoline, Pennzoil, Valvoline or STP, unless they prove their devotion to the correct product in a blind taste test.

RULE 4(i)
All cars and uniforms must have at least one inch of free space not plastered by ad logos to allow the needed oxygen to get inside.

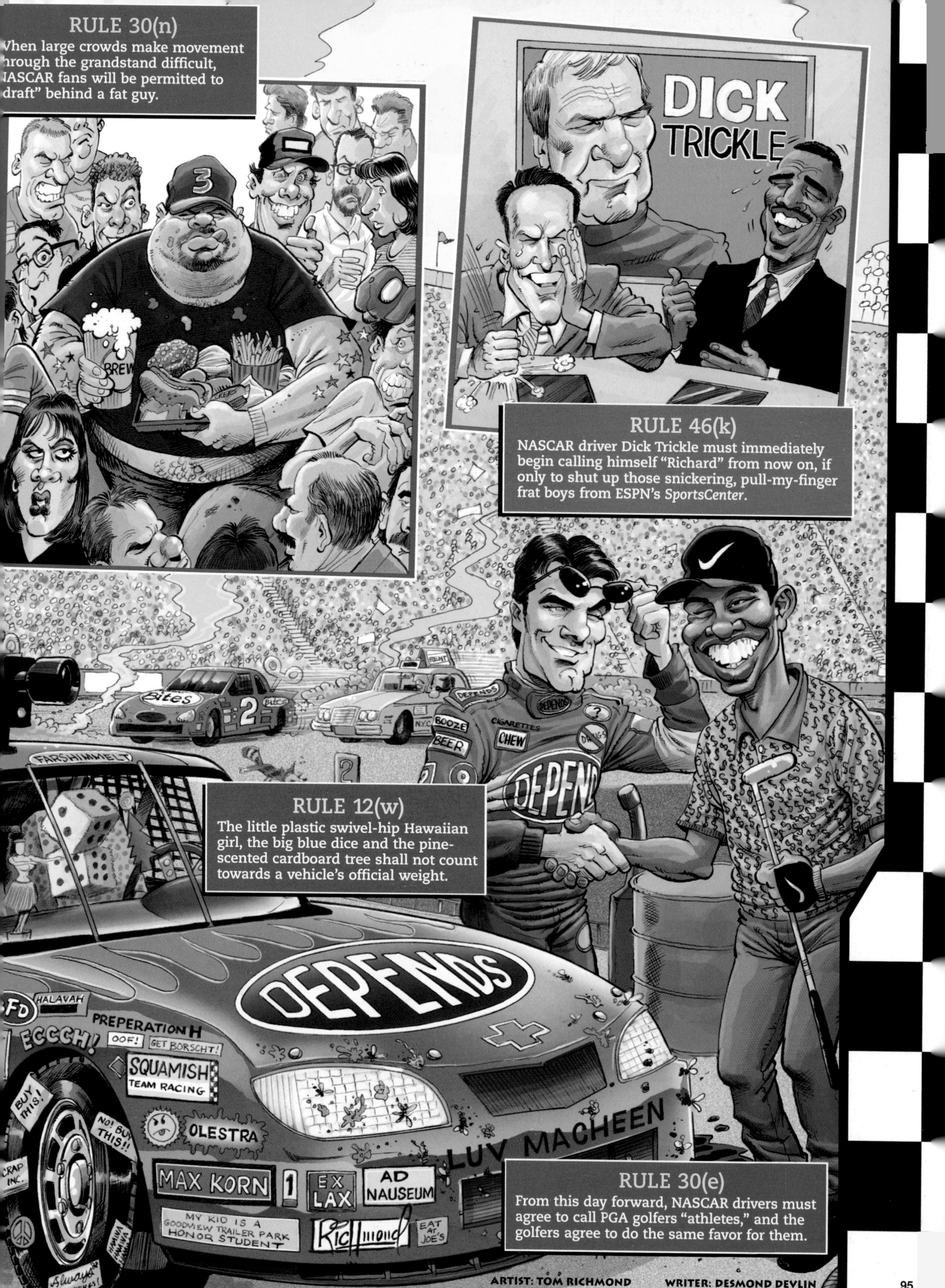
RULE 30(n)
Vhen large crowds make movement hrough the grandstand difficult, ASCAR fans will be permitted to draft" behind a fat guy.
3
BREW
DICK
TRICKLE
RULE 46(k)
NASCAR driver Dick Trickle must immediately begin calling himself "Richard" from now on, if only to shut up those snickering, pull-my-finger frat boys from ESPN's *SportsCenter*.
Bites
2
RENT
NYC
DEPENDS
BOOZE
BEER
CIGARETTES
CHEW
FARSHIMMELT
RULE 12(w)
The little plastic swivel-hip Hawaiian girl, the big blue dice and the pine-scented cardboard tree shall not count towards a vehicle's official weight.
DEPENDS
HALAVAH
PREPERATION H
ECCCH!
OOF!
GET BORSCHT!
SQUAMISH
TEAM RACING
BUY THIS!
NO! BUY THIS!!
OLESTRA
CRAP INC.
MAX KORN
1
EX LAX
AD NAUSEUM
MY KID IS A GOODVIEW TRAILER PARK HONOR STUDENT
EAT AT JOE'S
LUV MACHEEN
Always WITH WINGS!
RULE 30(e)
From this day forward, NASCAR drivers must agree to call PGA golfers "athletes," and the golfers agree to do the same favor for them.

ARTIST: TOM RICHMOND WRITER: DESMOND DEVLIN

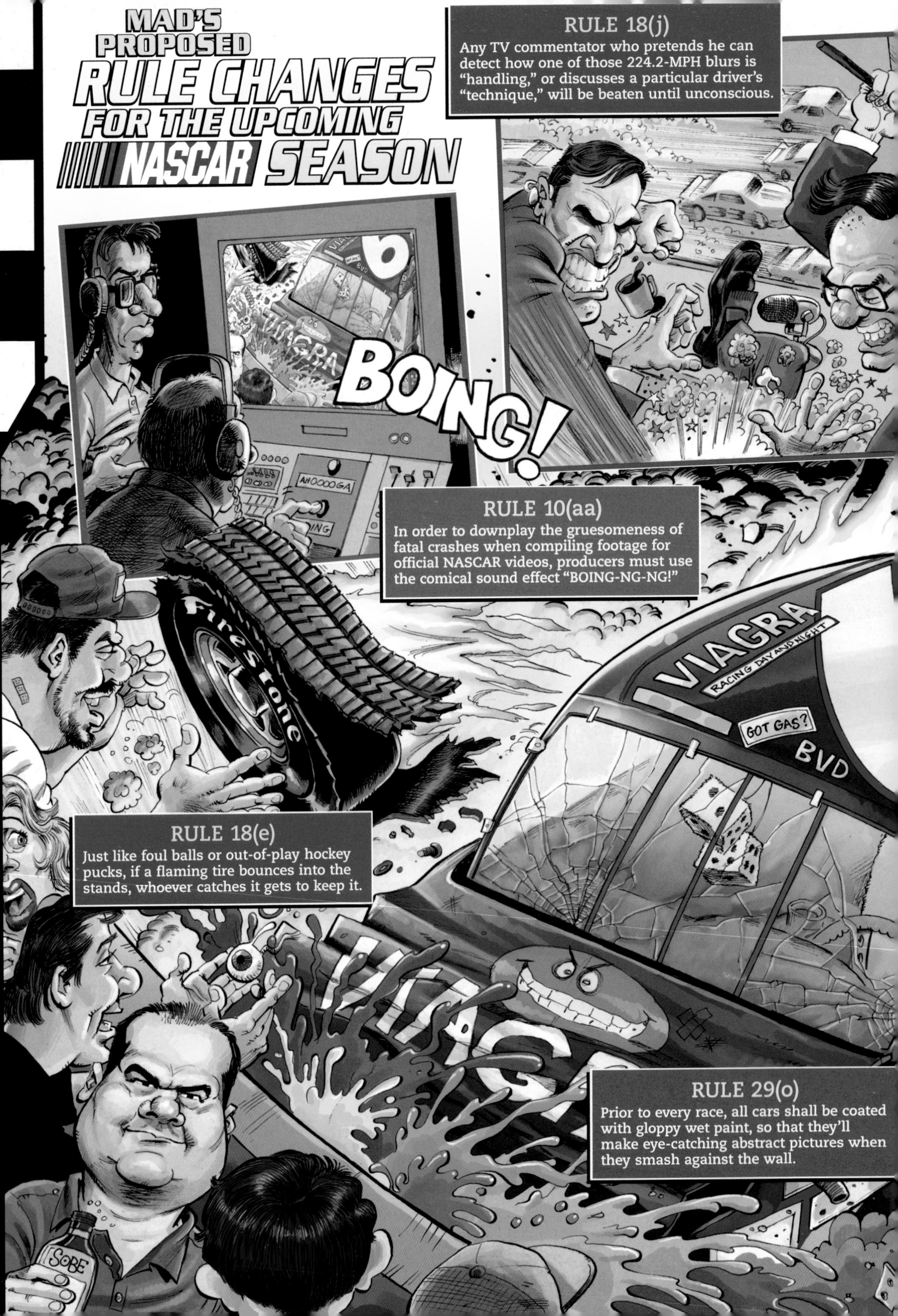
MAD'S PROPOSED
RULE CHANGES
FOR THE UPCOMING
NASCAR SEASON
RULE 18(j)
Any TV commentator who pretends he can detect how one of those 224.2-MPH blurs is "handling," or discusses a particular driver's "technique," will be beaten until unconscious.
VIAGRA
BOING!
AHOOOOGA
RULE 10(aa)
In order to downplay the gruesomeness of fatal crashes when compiling footage for official NASCAR videos, producers must use the comical sound effect "BOING-NG-NG!"
Firestone
VIAGRA
RACING DAY AND NIGHT
GOT GAS?
BVD
RULE 18(e)
Just like foul balls or out-of-play hockey pucks, if a flaming tire bounces into the stands, whoever catches it gets to keep it.
RULE 29(o)
Prior to every race, all cars shall be coated with gloppy wet paint, so that they'll make eye-catching abstract pictures when they smash against the wall.
SOBE

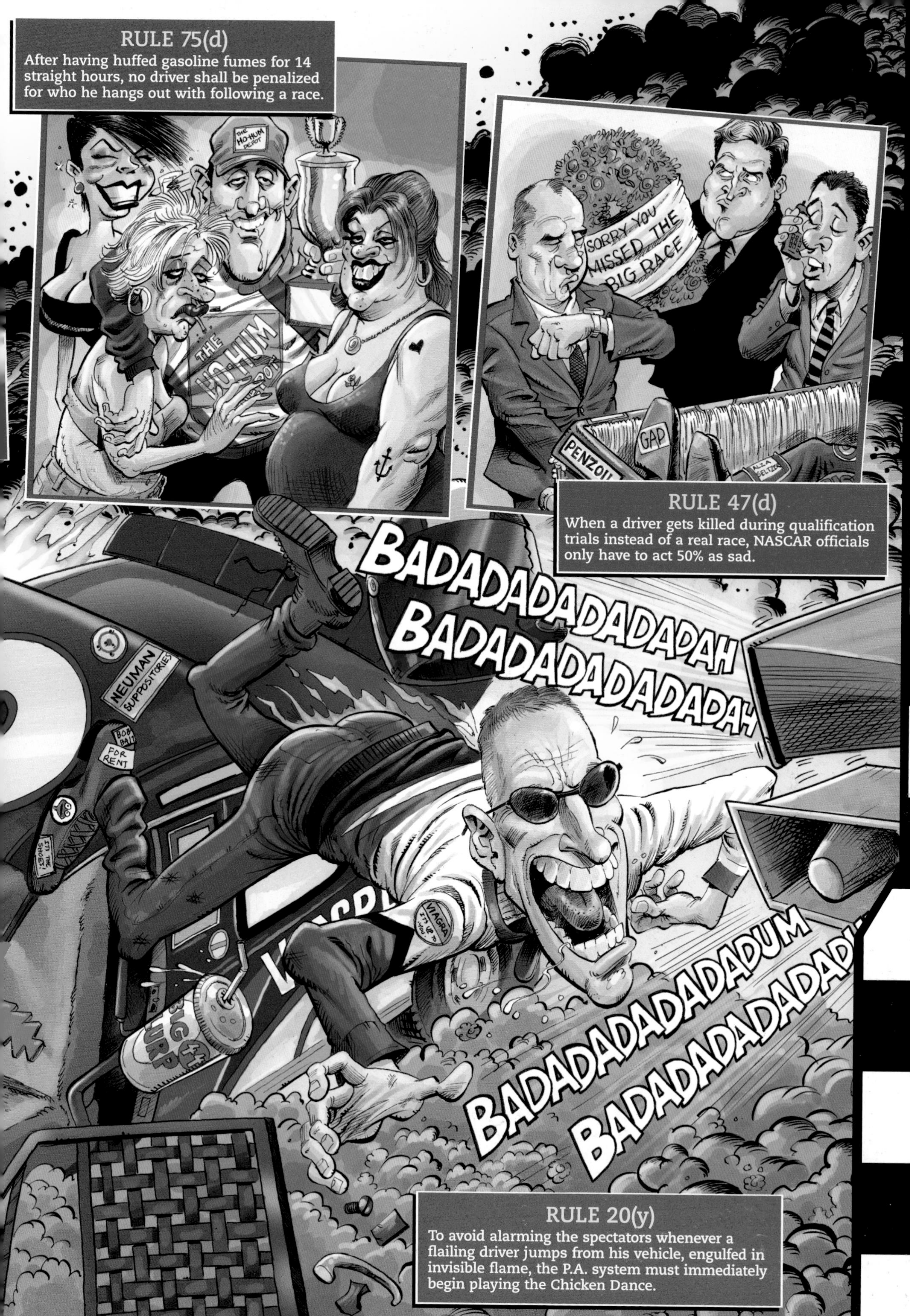
RULE 75(d)
After having huffed gasoline fumes for 14 straight hours, no driver shall be penalized for who he hangs out with following a race.
THE HO-HUM DEPOT
THE HO-HUM DEPOT
SORRY YOU MISSED THE BIG RACE
GAP
PENZOIL
RULE 47(d)
When a driver gets killed during qualification trials instead of a real race, NASCAR officials only have to act 50% as sad.
BADADADADADADADAH
BADADADADADADADAH
NEUMAN SUPPOSITORIES
FOR RENT
VIAGRA
BIG GULP
BADADADADADADUM
BADADADADADADADA
RULE 20(y)
To avoid alarming the spectators whenever a flailing driver jumps from his vehicle, engulfed in invisible flame, the P.A. system must immediately begin playing the Chicken Dance.

The long-anticipated trip to the fun park! The only problem is, you're going to be far too excited to behave in a controlled, thoughtful manner. (In fact, if you're a typical MAD reader, you've *never* behaved in a such a manner! Thankfully, we're here to help you calmly and rationally squeeze every last drop of enjoyment from this hard-won outing with:

MAD'S GUIDE TO

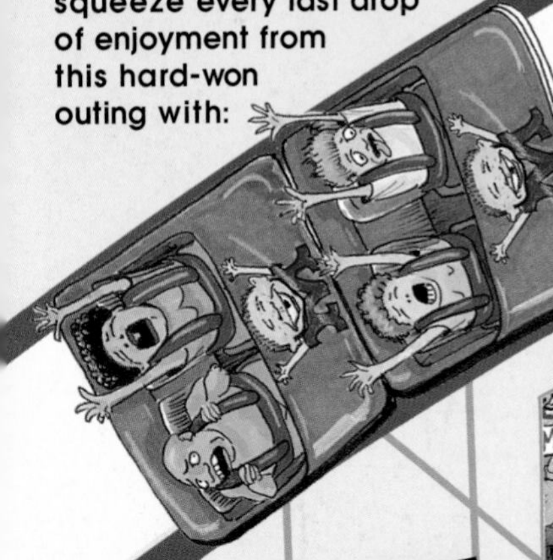

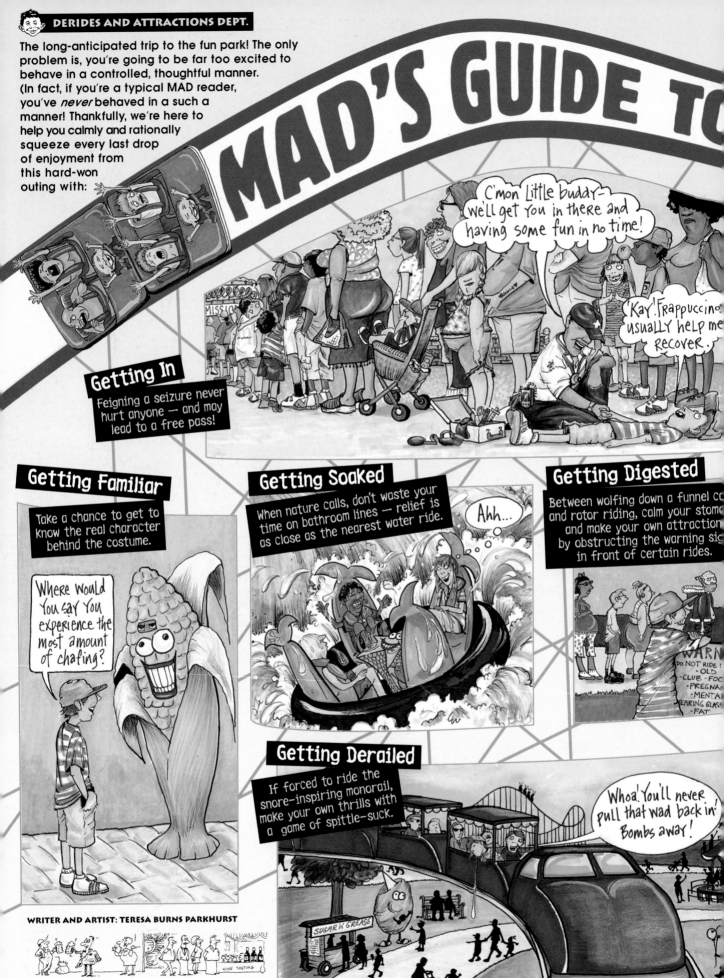

Getting In

Feigning a seizure never hurt anyone — and may lead to a free pass!

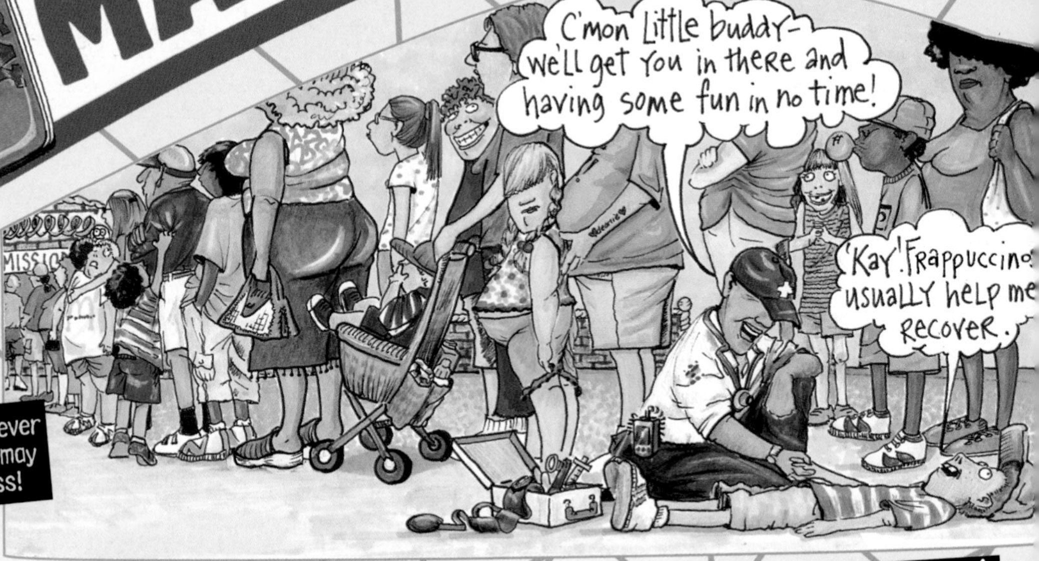
C'mon Little buddy–we'll get you in there and having some fun in no time!
'Kay! Frappuccinos usually help me recover.

Getting Familiar

Take a chance to get to know the real character behind the costume.

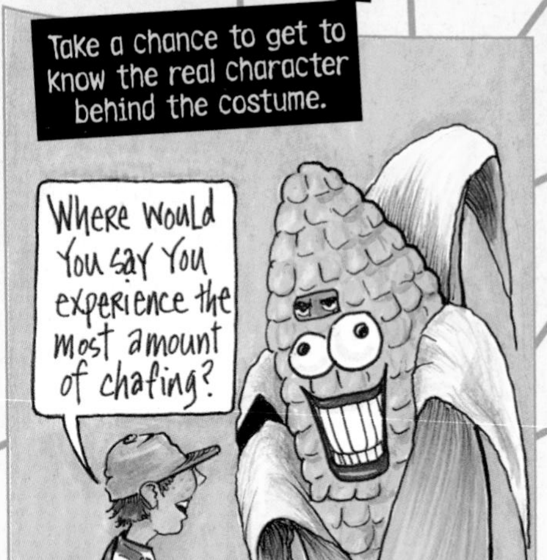
Where would You say You experience the most amount of chafing?

Getting Soaked

When nature calls, don't waste your time on bathroom lines — relief is as close as the nearest water ride.

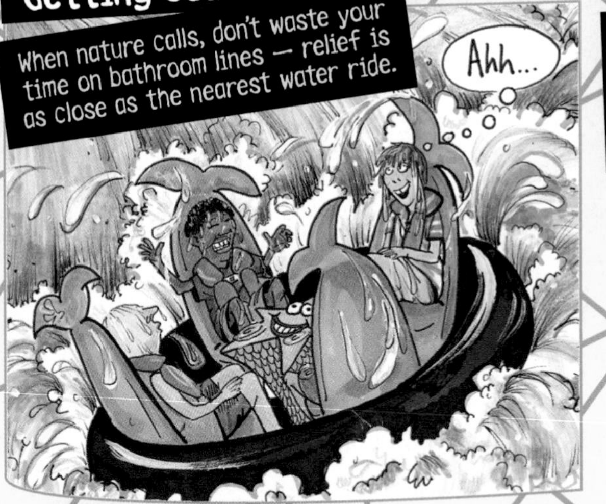
Ahh...

Getting Digested

Between wolfing down a funnel ca and rotor riding, calm your stoma and make your own attraction by obstructing the warning sig in front of certain rides.

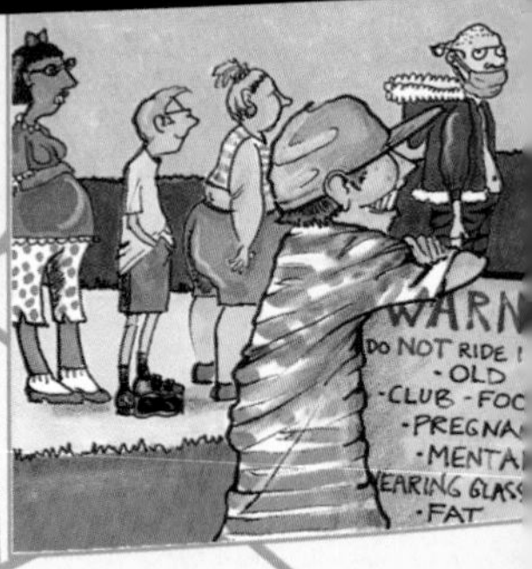
WARN
DO NOT RIDE !
-OLD
-CLUB-FOO
-PREGNA
-MENTA
WEARING GLASS
-FAT

Getting Derailed

If forced to ride the snore-inspiring monorail, make your own thrills with a game of spittle-suck.

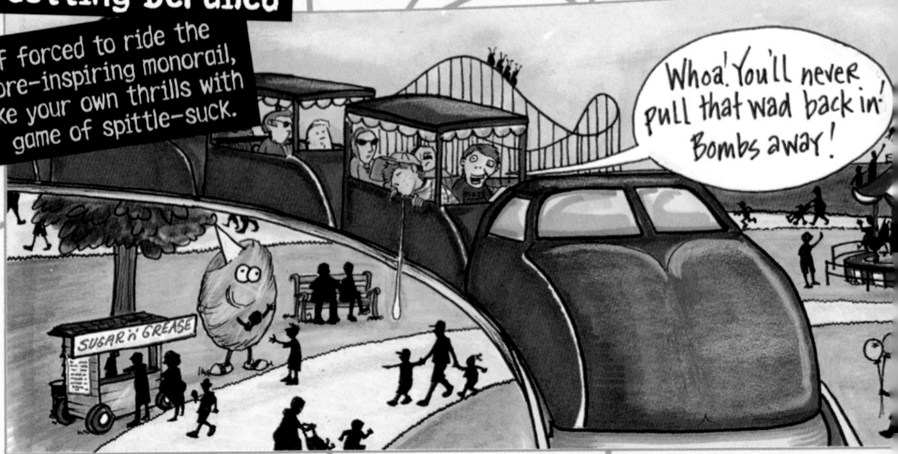
Whoa! You'll never pull that wad back in! Bombs away!
SUGAR 'n' GREASE

WRITER AND ARTIST: TERESA BURNS PARKHURST

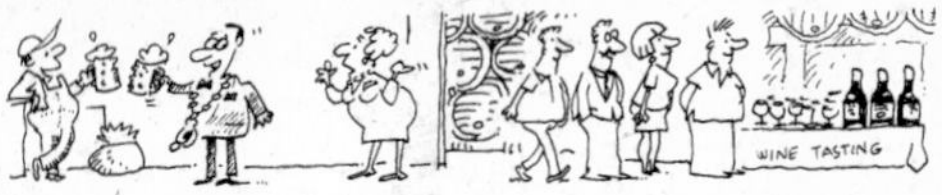
WINE TASTING

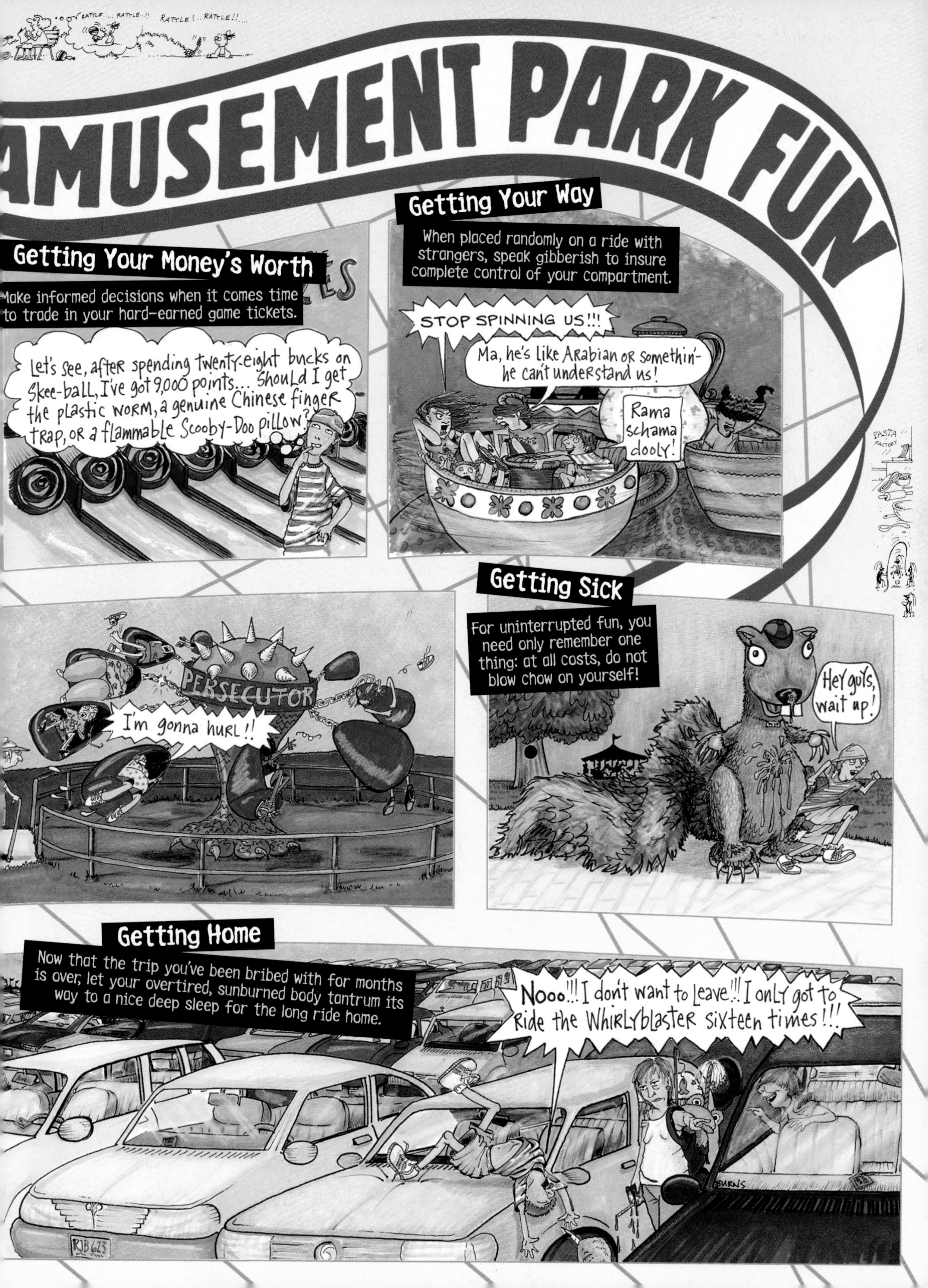

RATTLE..... RATTLE...!!! RATTLE!...RATTLE!!...
AMUSEMENT PARK FUN
Getting Your Money's Worth
Make informed decisions when it comes time to trade in your hard-earned game tickets.
Let's see, after spending twenty-eight bucks on Skee-ball, I've got 9,000 points... Should I get the plastic worm, a genuine Chinese finger trap, or a flammable Scooby-Doo pillow?
Getting Your Way
When placed randomly on a ride with strangers, speak gibberish to insure complete control of your compartment.
STOP SPINNING US!!!
Ma, he's like Arabian or somethin'- he can't understand us!
Rama schama dooly!
PASTA FACTORY
PERSECUTOR
I'm gonna hurl!!
Getting Sick
For uninterrupted fun, you need only remember one thing: at all costs, do not blow chow on yourself!
Hey guys, wait up!
Getting Home
Now that the trip you've been bribed with for months is over, let your overtired, sunburned body tantrum its way to a nice deep sleep for the long ride home.
Nooo!!! I don't want to leave!!! I only got to ride the Whirlyblaster sixteen times!!!
RJB 623
BURNS

ONE EVENING AT HOME

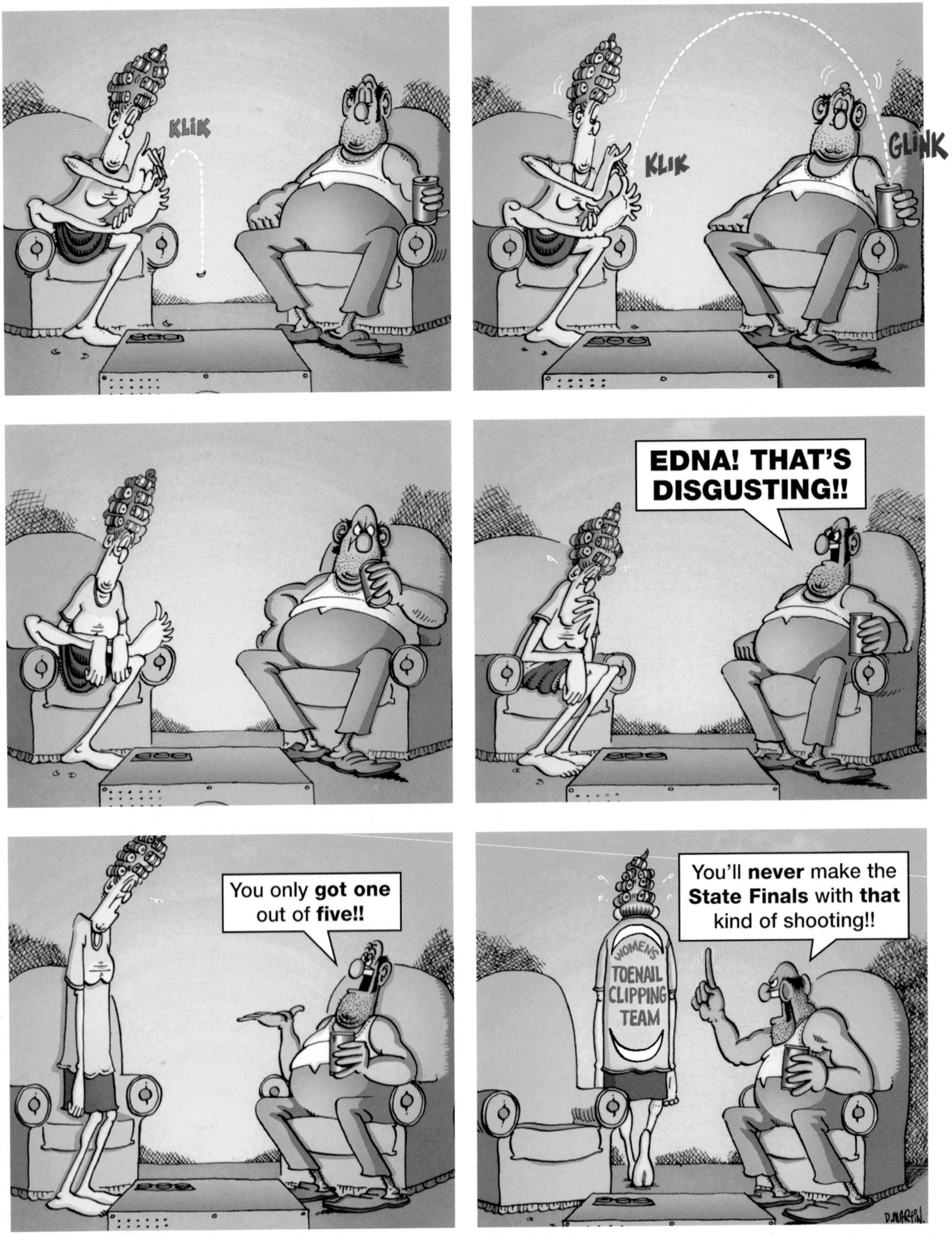
KLIK
KLIK
GLINK
EDNA! THAT'S DISGUSTING!!
You only got one out of five!!
WOMENS TOENAIL CLIPPING TEAM
You'll never make the State Finals with that kind of shooting!!
D. MARTIN.

WRITER AND ARTIST: DON MARTIN

Not long ago, we ran "The League of Rejected Superheroes" — but what good are crappy heroes without equally pathetic villains to fight? So, we enlisted some of comics' hottest stars (who had a pretty good run up until they took part in this career-ender) to illustrate these...

LESSER-KNOWN COMIC BOOK VILLAINS

WRITER: JEFF KRUSE

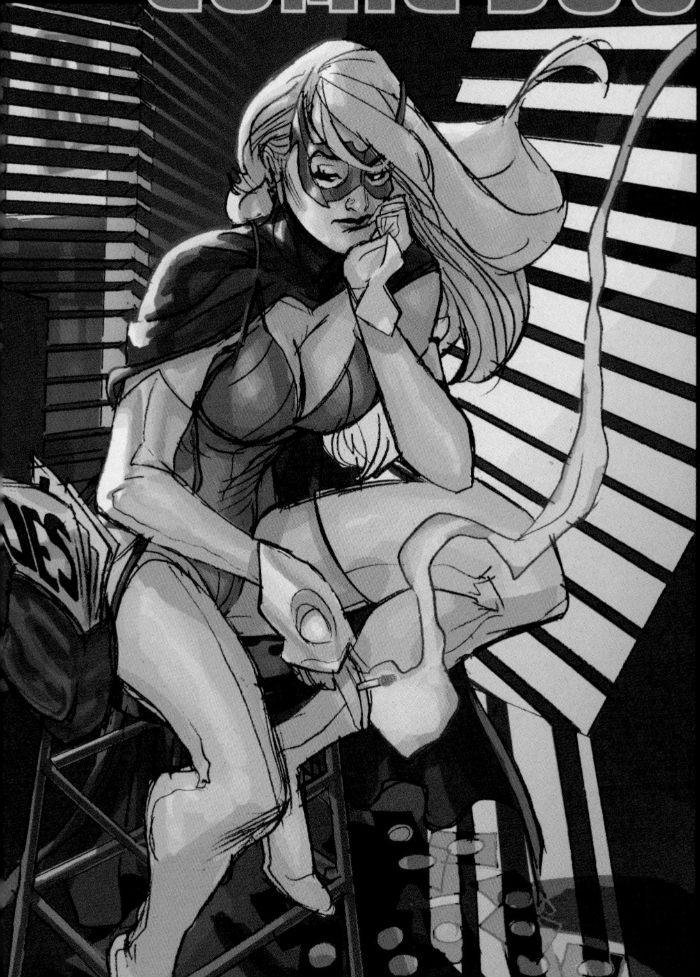

The Vague Viper

COMIC BOOK DEBUT: *Just Die, Already* #133, 1989.

ENEMIES: That Guy in the Green Boots; LadyPerson.

SUPER-POWER: After being exposed to radiation, she developed amazing skill at the card game Uno.

SPLIT PERSONALITY: Sometimes joins with the forces of good, which is in keeping with her role as leader of the Ambivalence League of America.

WEAPON: The Pamphlet of Lies.

M.O.: One of the rare non-violent bad gals, she ties up crime fighters with nuisance lawsuits.

ARTIST: TERRY DODSON

Professor Generico

COMIC BOOK DEBUT: *Teen Geezer* #14, 1996.

ORIGIN OF EVIL: Experimented with a bizzarre potion that made him think he was a member of the '87 San Diego Padres.

BACKGROUND: Acknowledged as one of the most brilliant scientists in his field, which, unfortunately, was intestinal bacteria. The creators could never find a way to make his evil non-disgusting.

CLAIM TO INFAMY: Gained a small measure of fame in 1997 when he became the one millionth "Scientist Gone Bad."

AMAZING POWER: Has the ability to re-grow his hair, should he lose any.

DIABOLICAL INVENTION: The PortaClock, an ingenious timepiece so small that it can be worn on one's wrist.

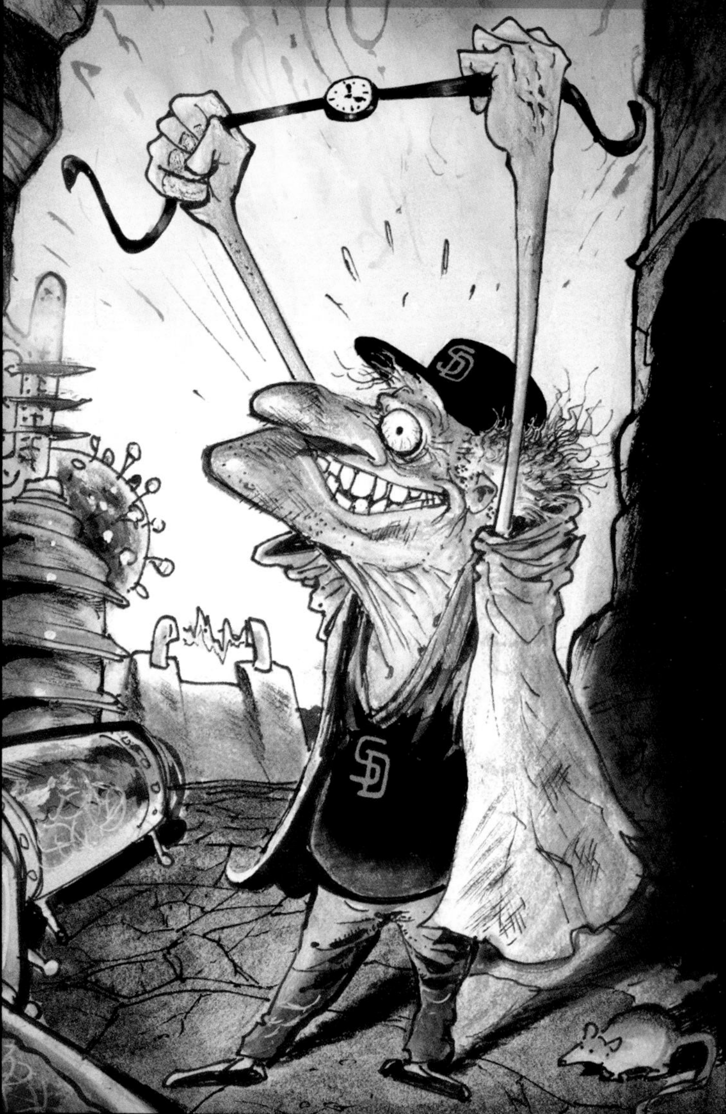

ARTIST: SAM KIETH

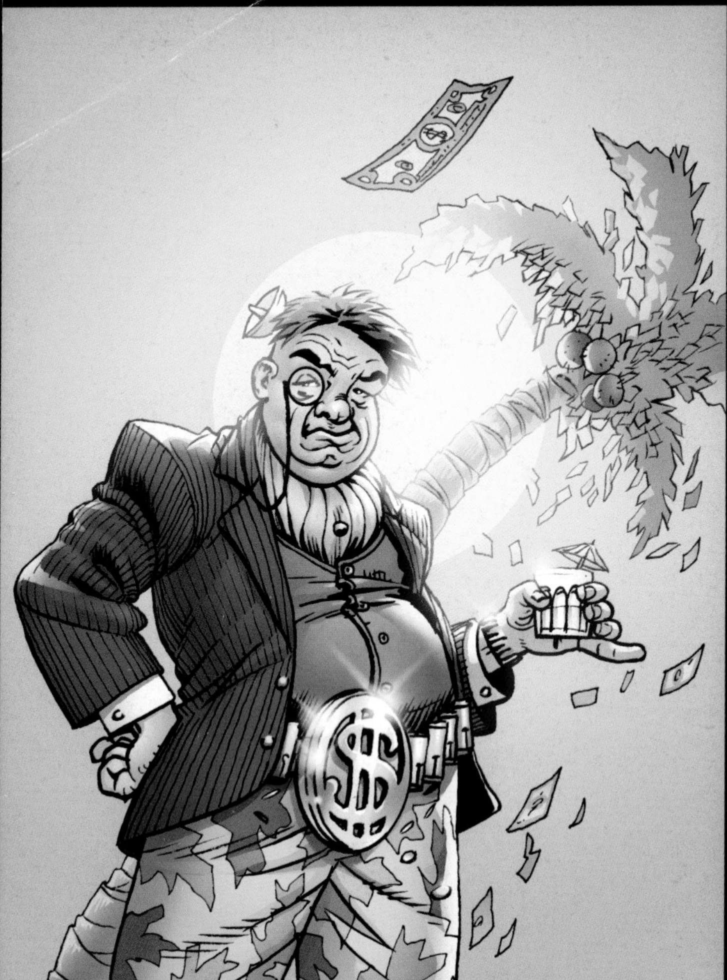

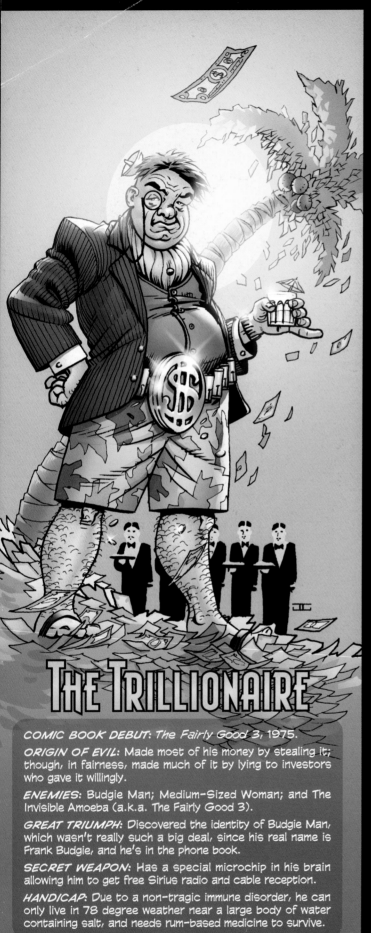

THE TRILLIONAIRE

COMIC BOOK DEBUT: *The Fairly Good 3*, 1975.

ORIGIN OF EVIL: Made most of his money by stealing it; though, in fairness, made much of it by lying to investors who gave it willingly.

ENEMIES: Budgie Man; Medium-Sized Woman; and The Invisible Amoeba (a.k.a. The Fairly Good 3).

GREAT TRIUMPH: Discovered the identity of Budgie Man, which wasn't really such a big deal, since his real name is Frank Budgie, and he's in the phone book.

SECRET WEAPON: Has a special microchip in his brain allowing him to get free Sirius radio and cable reception.

HANDICAP: Due to a non-tragic immune disorder, he can only live in 78 degree weather near a large body of water containing salt, and needs rum-based medicine to survive.

THE YAKMASTER

COMIC BOOK DEBUT: *Wonderful Stories of Wondrous Wonderment*, 1956.

BACKGROUND: This comic was originally written in a Himalayan dialect spoken by around 200 people, and the translation is very iffy.

ORIGIN OF EVIL: The Yakmaster was the Son of the Emperor in the mountain kingdom of Mushni Timbala (or a hat maker, it's not really clear) when his father banished him, presumably to further the plot.

WEAPON: Something that looks like a blender with sharpened bamboo sticks protruding from it.

REVERSAL OF CLICHÉ: Though there's a Buddhist monastery close by, he traveled to Mississippi to be trained by Southern Baptist ministers.

CATCHPHRASE: Hard to tell — he's a bit of a mumbler.

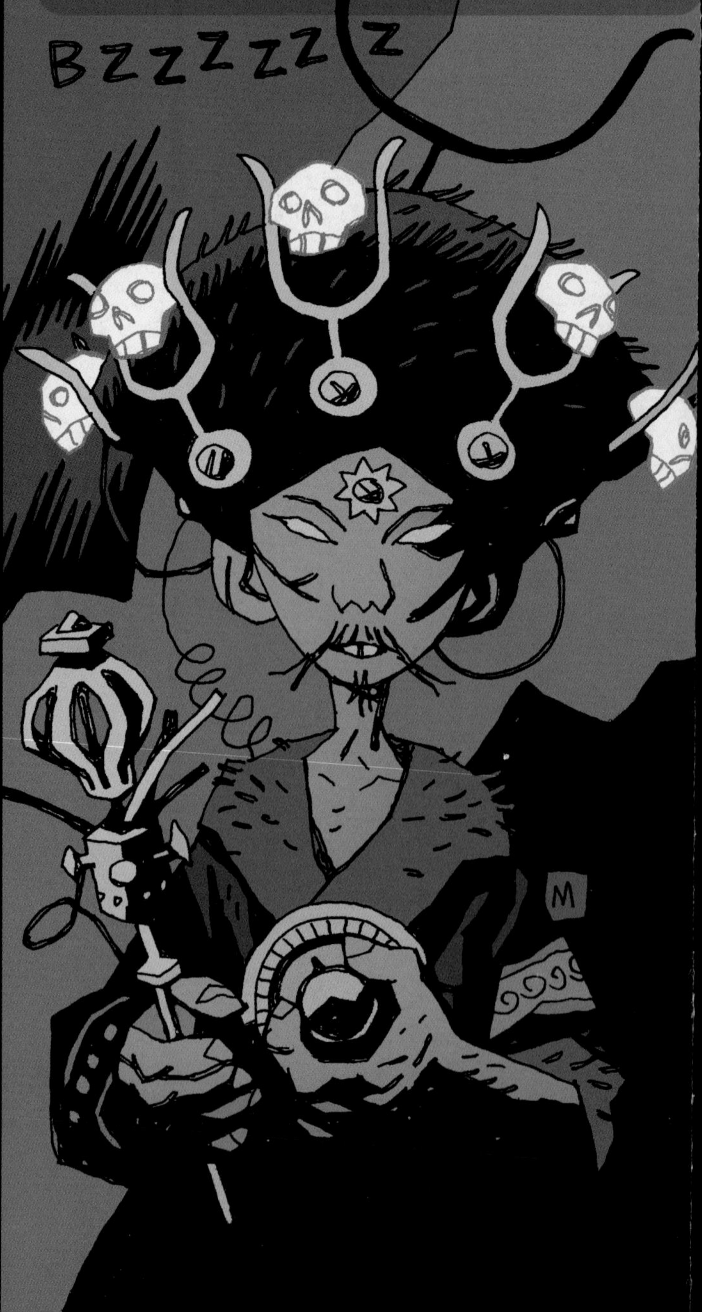
BZZZZZZ Z

 ARTIST: JOHN CASSADAY COLORIST: LAURA MARTIN

ARTIST: MIKE MIGNOLA COLORIST: DAVE STEWART

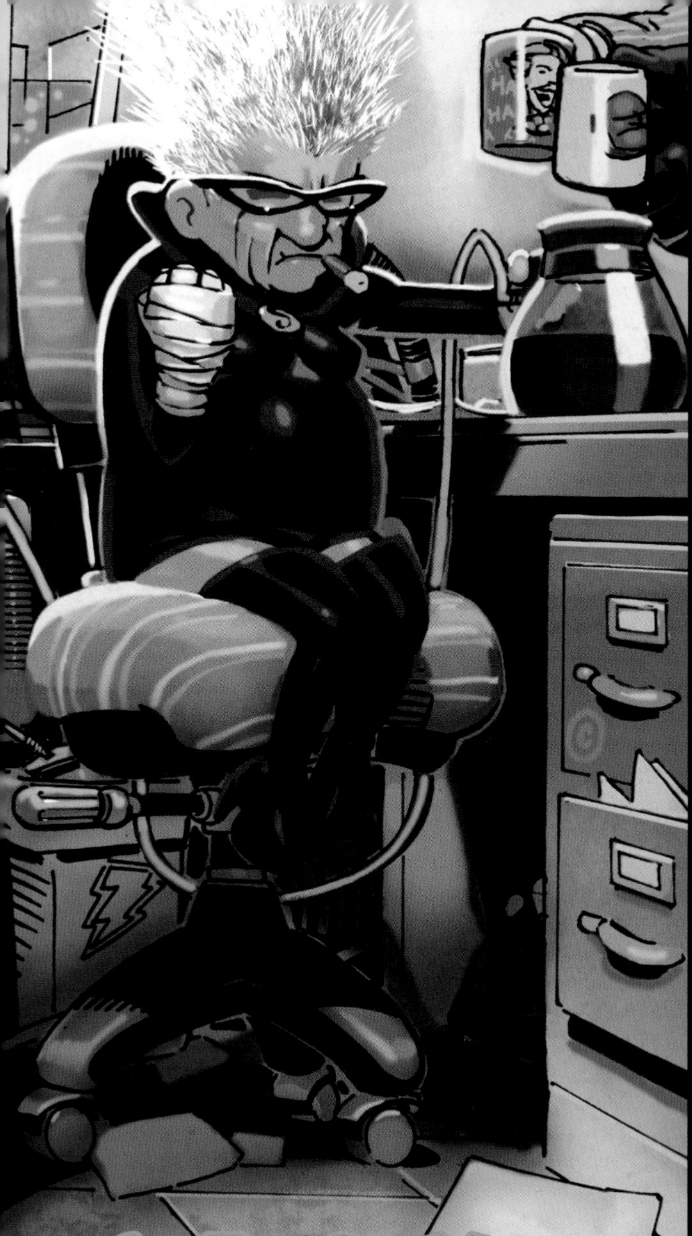
HA
HA

SARCASMA

COMIC BOOK DEBUT: *Triumph of Col. Goodguy, Like You Couldn't See That One Coming #73.*

ORIGIN OF EVIL: Became mutated as a result of a top secret government experiment involving Hostess Twinkies and a George Foreman Grill. Well, actually her fingers just got singed, but it was enough to make her vow revenge on all of humanity.

CATCHPHRASE: "Oooh, your brightly-colored Spandex outfit really scares me."

TURNING POINT: Became truly wicked after selling her soul, right before eBay disallowed those things.

FEAT: First appeared to Emperor G'Zav, leader of the Qaltrynn people of Planet Xlothon, and helped them come up with names that were less pretentious and easier to spell.

BIGGEST REGRET: Although women have made great strides in fighting on the side of darkness, the male villains still ask her do the filing and make coffee.

DR. UMBRAGE

COMIC BOOK DEBUT: *Goldfish HellTroopers*, 1989.

ORIGIN OF EVIL: Embarked on a life of crime when his high school guidance counselor suggested he was best suited for that field.

SCIENTIFIC BREAKTHROUGH: Can turn his internal organs invisible — but not his skin, so it's pretty useless.

DISCOVERY: Created a serum that causes excruciating pain, disfigurement and slow death. Although he could never find a way to use it for the betterment of mankind, the FDA fast-tracked it.

OTHER SCIENTIFIC BREAKTHROUGH: Discovered that he could create new life by mating with women. Not that this has ever happened.

REDEEMING QUALITY: Drives an alternative-fuel vehicle. Granted, it runs on the blood of his victims, but still, every little thing we can do for the environment helps.

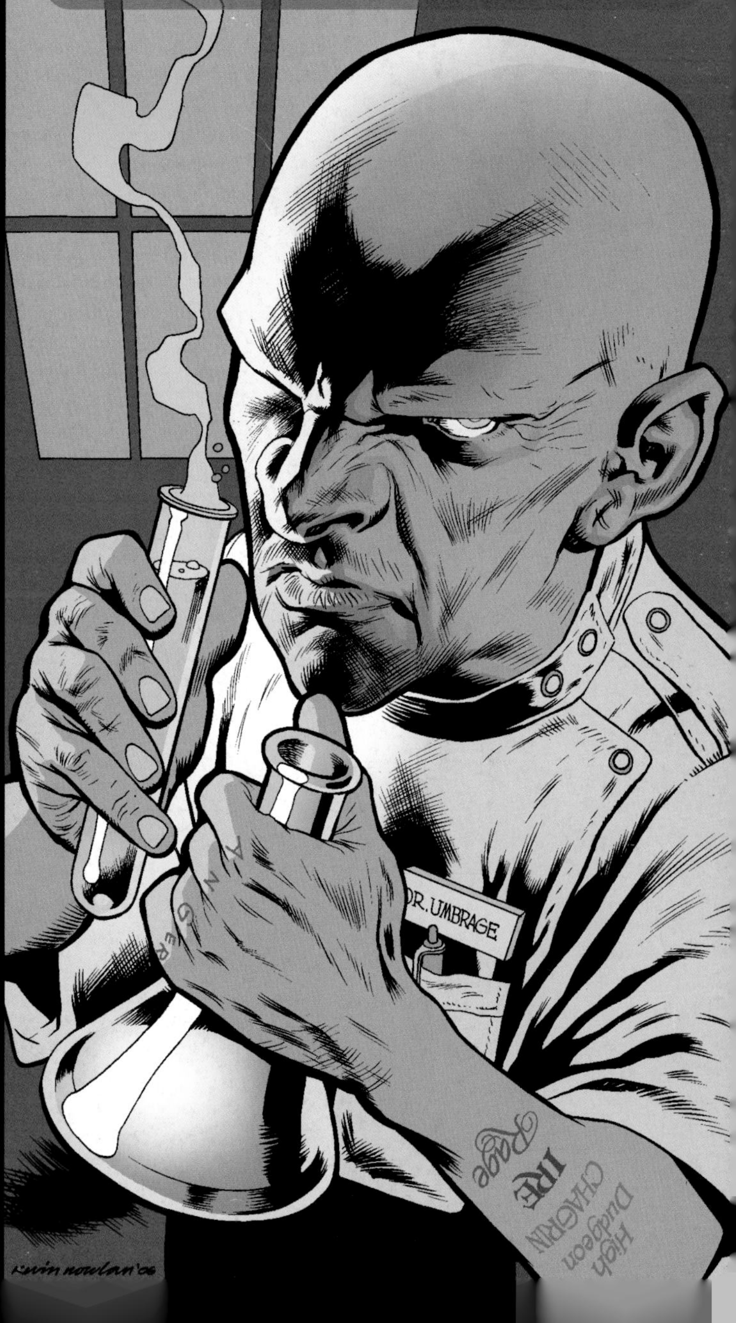
DR. UMBRAGE
Rage
IRE
CHAGRIN
High Dudgeon
kevin nowlan '06

A.N.N.O.Y

COMIC BOOK DEBUT: *Sgt. Hatemonger & Pals*, 1982.

MOST ANNOYING ASPECT: The acronym doesn't actually stand for anything.

HANDICAP: Speaks with both a stutter and a lisp, making him "The most misunderstood villain in the comic universe."

WEAPON: The Big Gun That Shoots Bullets.

GIMMICK: A clothing obsession similar to the other villain, Mad Hatter — only involving lobster bibs.

DEMISE: Hit in the groin by a meteorite. (Fans were given a unique opportunity to vote online what type of death he would receive: unspeakable, horrific, appalling, or ghastly. They chose horrific.)

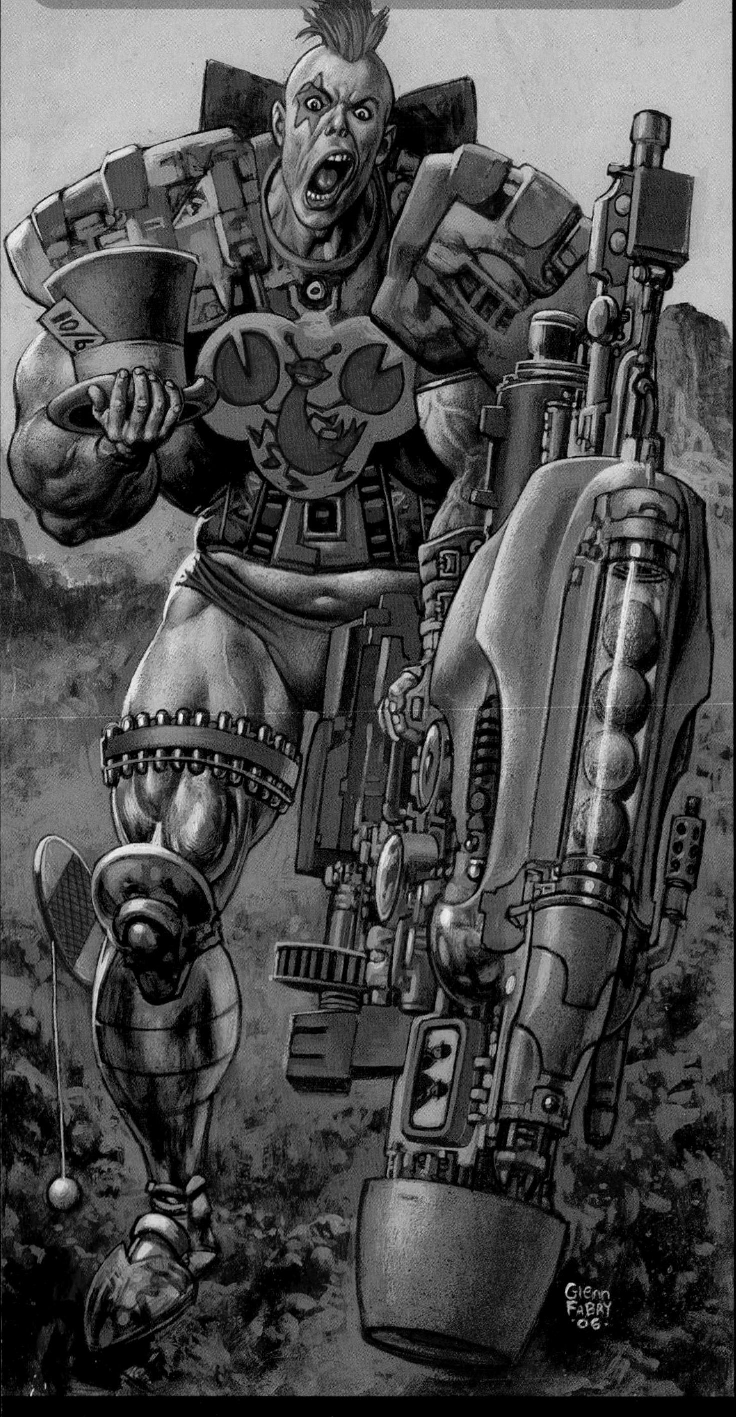
GLENN FABRY '06

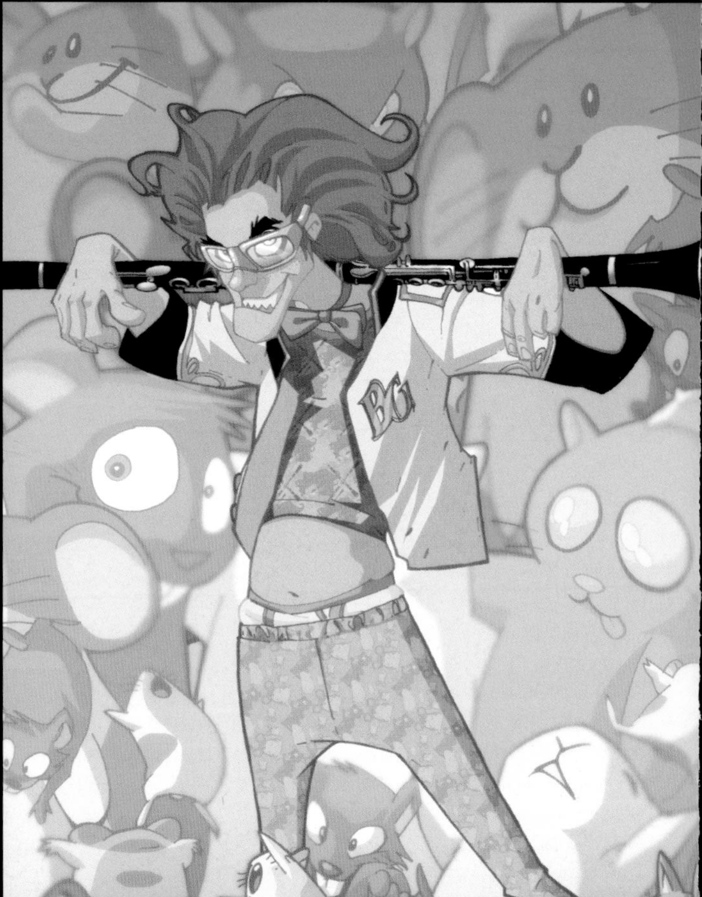

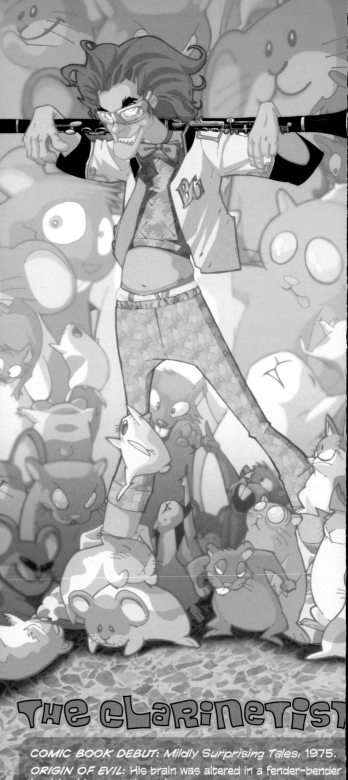

THE CLARINETIST

COMIC BOOK DEBUT: *Mildly Surprising Tales*, 1975.

ORIGIN OF EVIL: His brain was altered in a fender-bender involving his car and another car.

COSTUME: Green bowtie, racquetball goggles and Underoos with his own likeness.

DOWNFALL: Was driven insane by the HamsterDance song, which he could not get out of his head.

WEAPON: A special potion gives him the agility of a rhino and the strength of a hummingbird.

FUN FACT: The Clarinetist was created by Stan Lee, but, of course, not *the* Stan Lee.

ARTIST: GLENN FABRY

ARTIST: HUMBERTO RAMOS **COLORIST: LEONARDO OLEA**

JOKE & DAGGER DEPT.

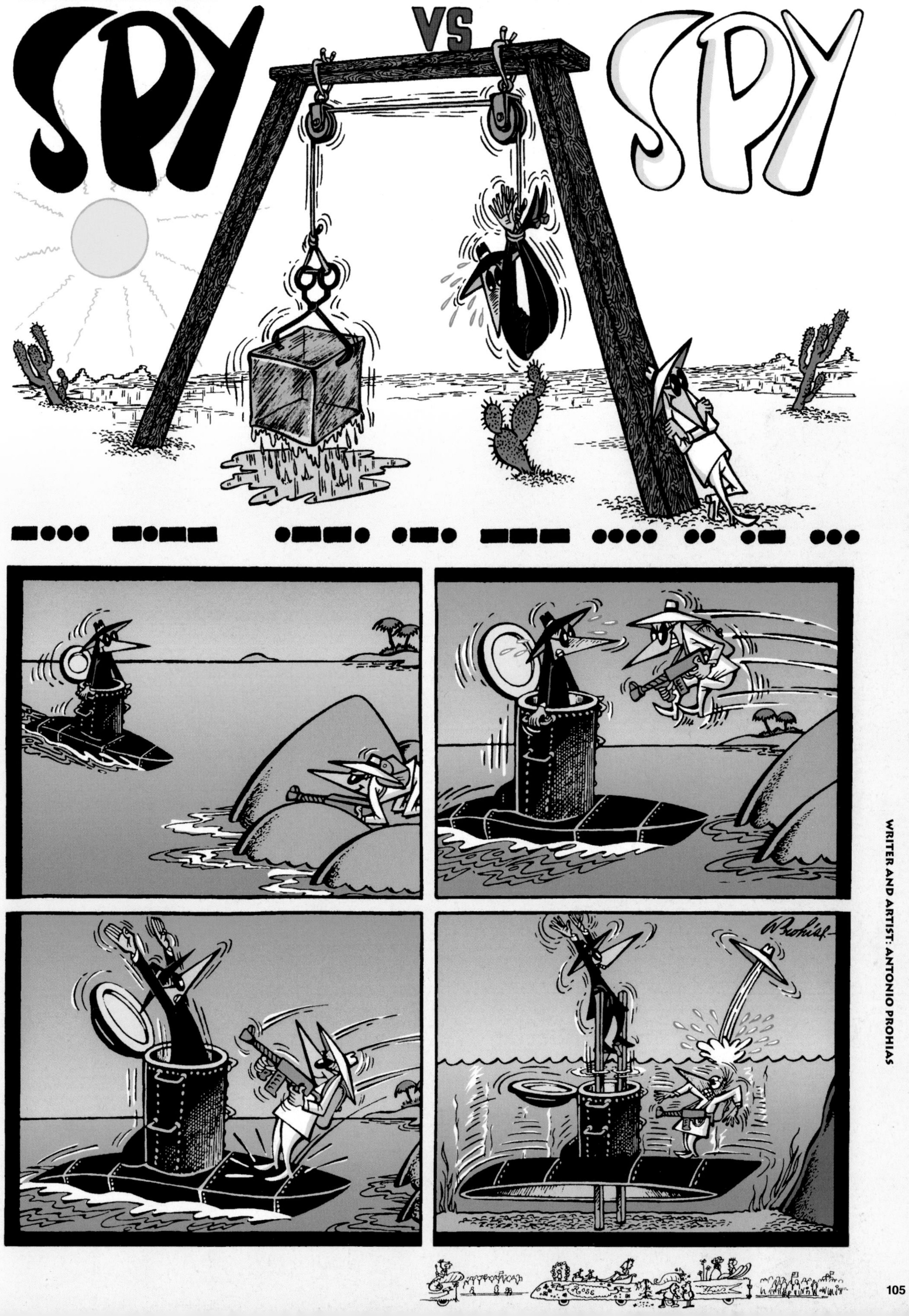
SPY VS SPY
Prohias

WRITER AND ARTIST: ANTONIO PROHIAS

Sergio Aragonés Presents A MAD LOOK AT

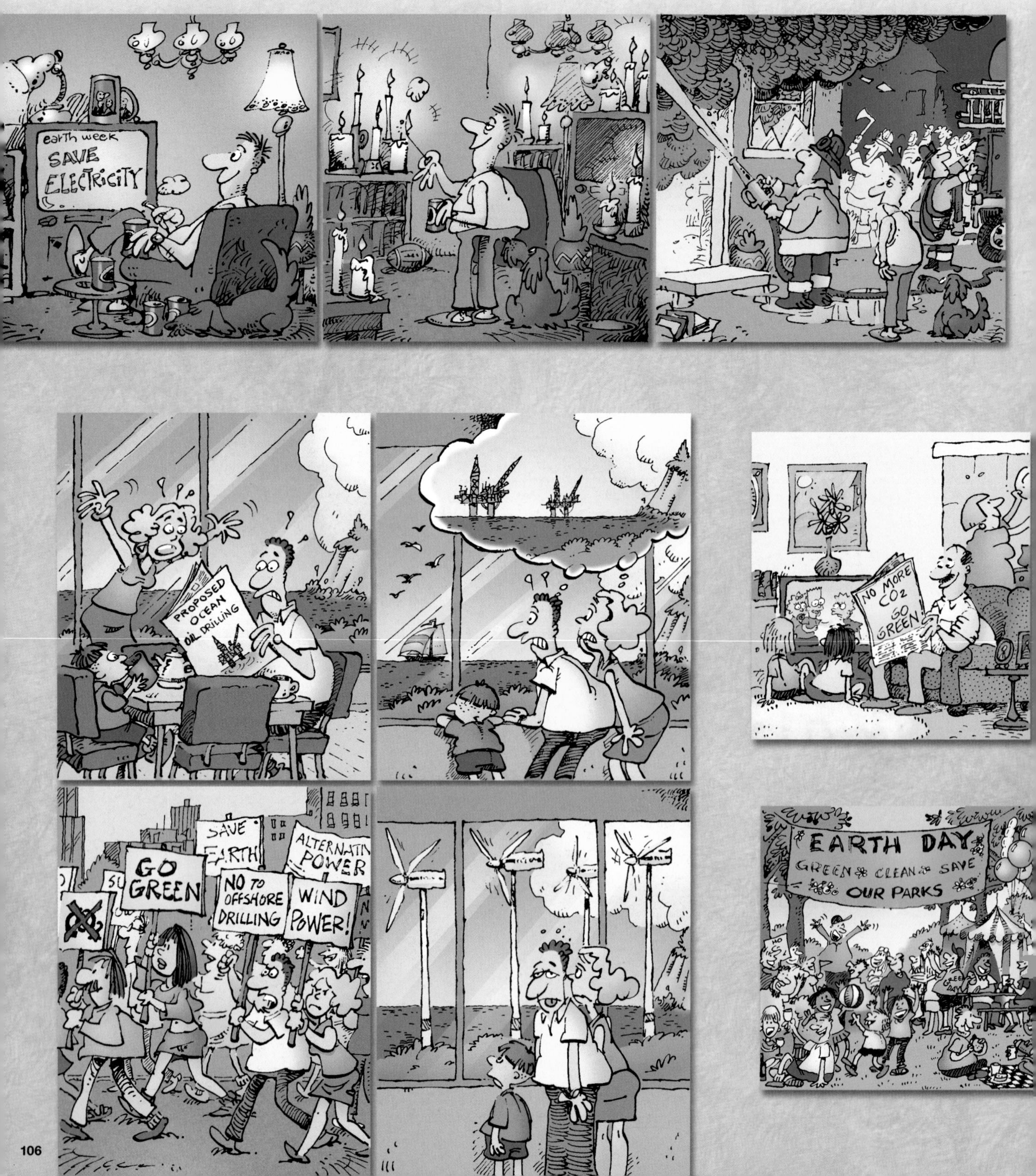
earth week
SAVE ELECTRICITY
PROPOSED OCEAN OIL DRILLING
NO MORE CO2 GO GREEN
SAVE EARTH
GO GREEN
NO TO OFFSHORE DRILLING
ALTERNATIV POWER
WIND POWER!
EARTH DAY
GREEN CLEAN SAVE
OUR PARKS

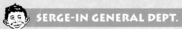

GOING GREEN

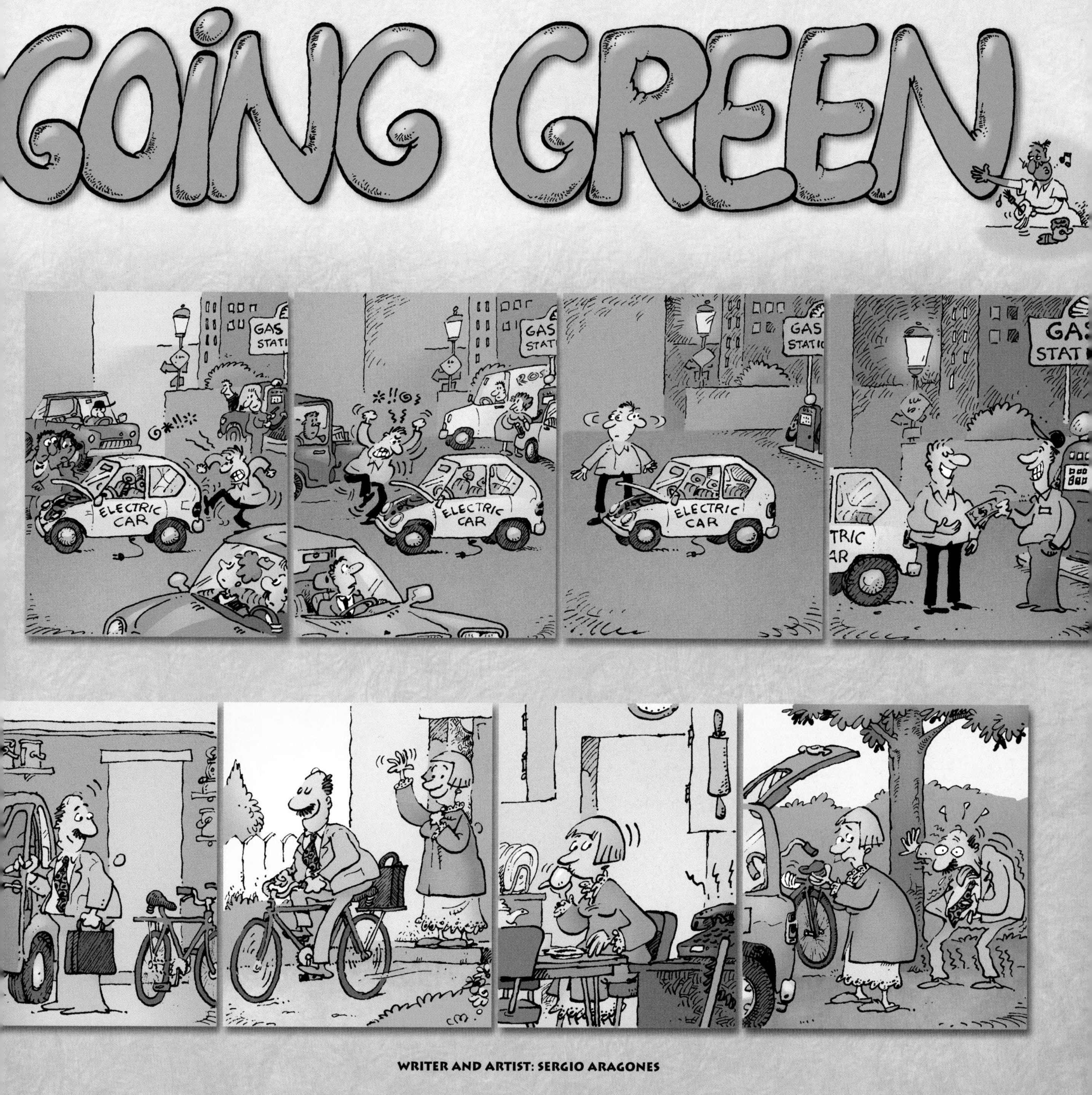

GAS STATION
ELECTRIC CAR
GAS STATION
ELECTRIC CAR
GAS STATION
ELECTRIC CAR
GAS STAT

WRITER AND ARTIST: SERGIO ARAGONES

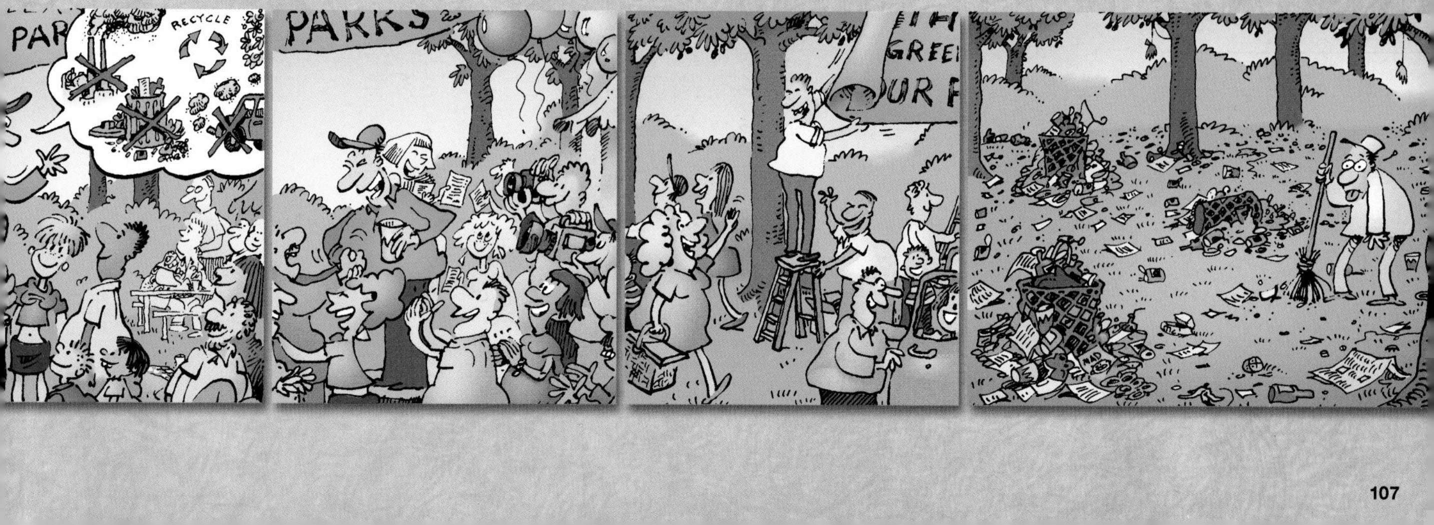

PAR
RECYCLE
PARKS
GREE
OUR

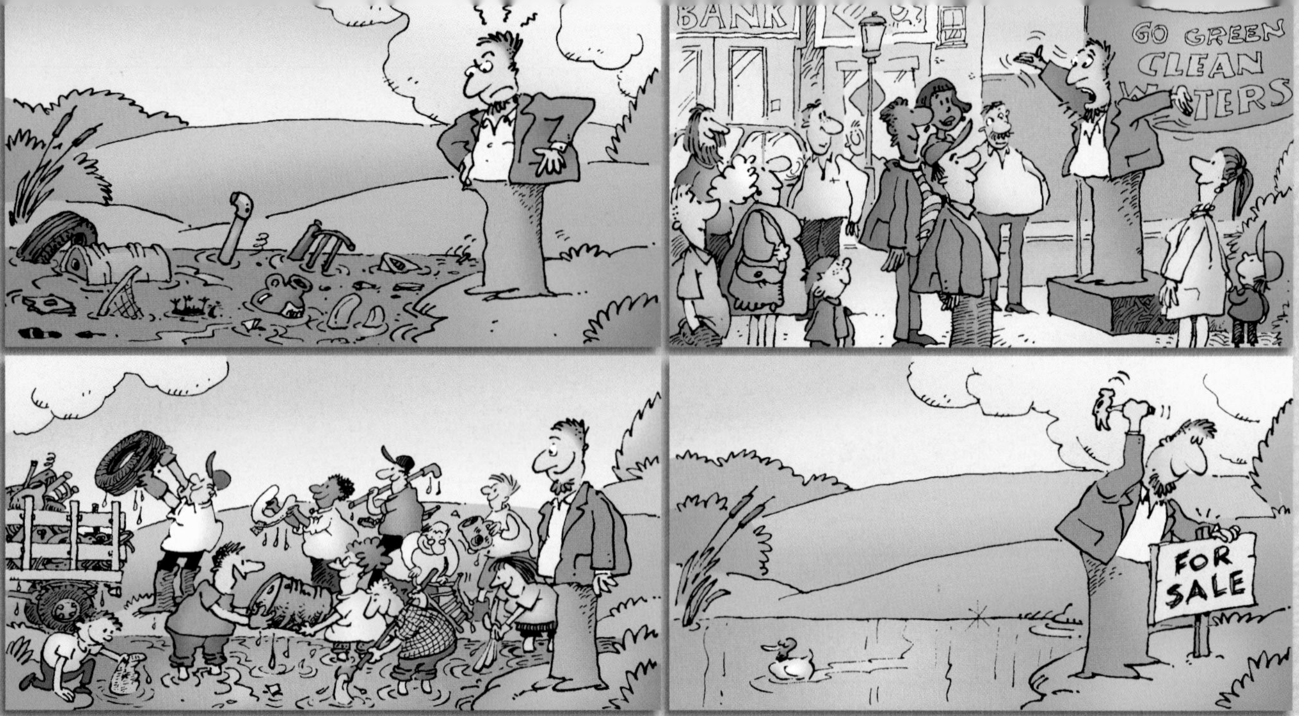
BANK
GO GREEN
CLEAN
WATERS
FOR SALE

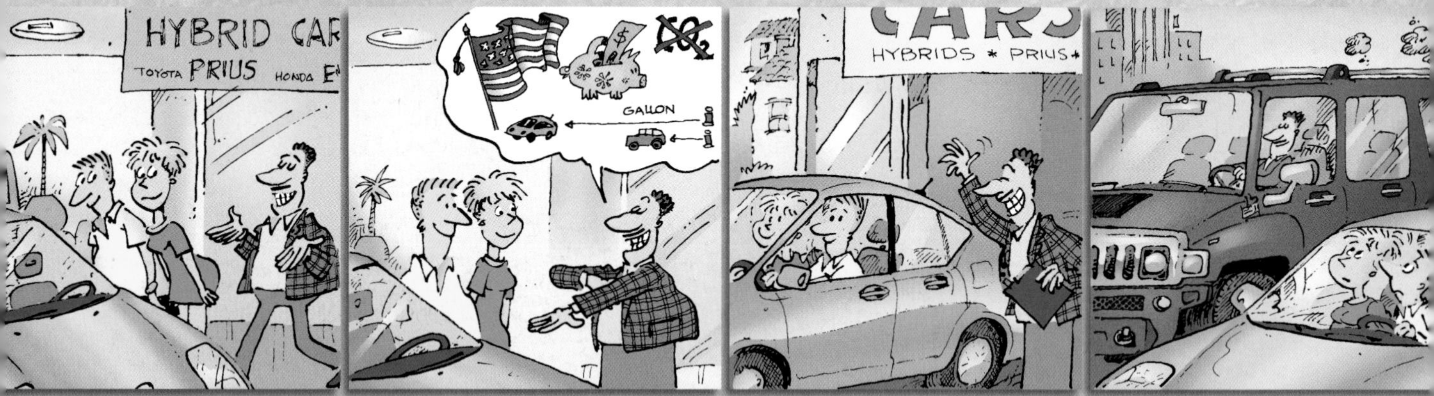
HYBRID CAR
TOYOTA PRIUS
GALLON
HYBRIDS * PRIUS *

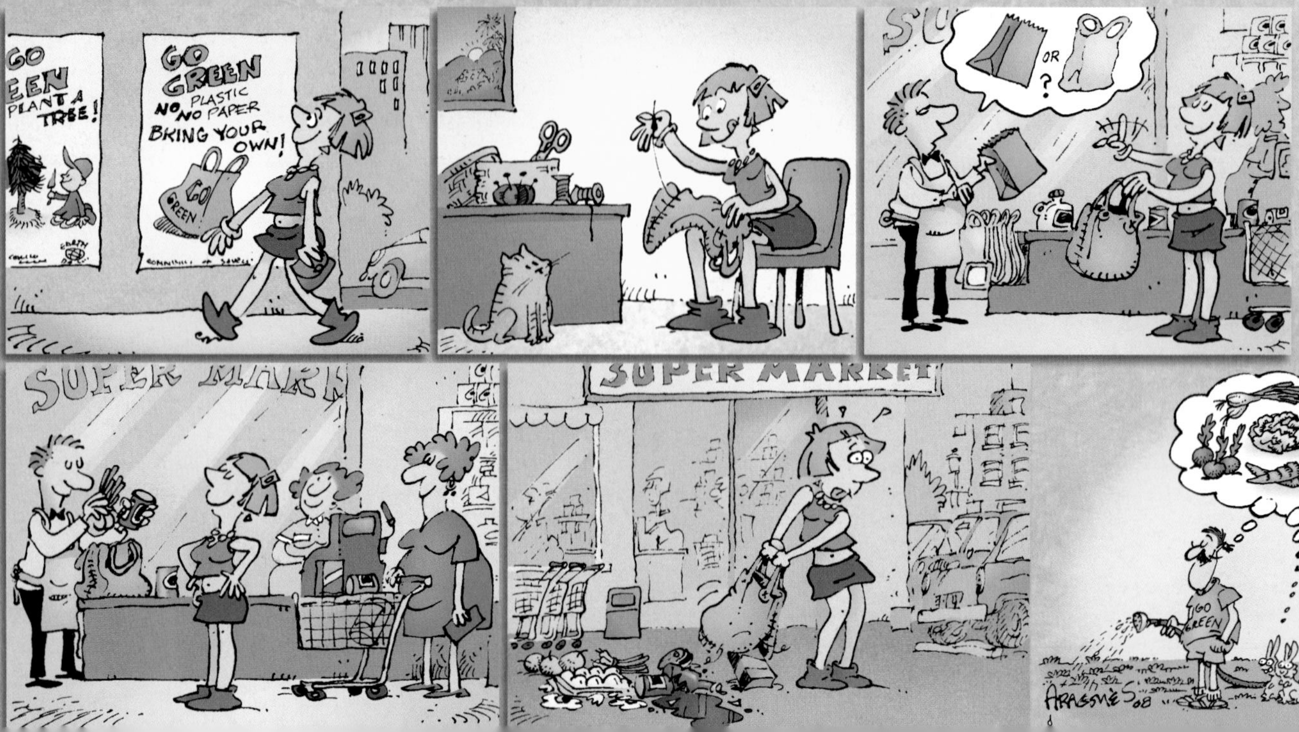
PLANT A TREE!
GO GREEN
NO PLASTIC
NO PAPER
BRING YOUR OWN!
OR
?
SUPER MARKET
GO GREEN

FOOLASTIC BOOK CLUB

Fan-Favorite Sequels!

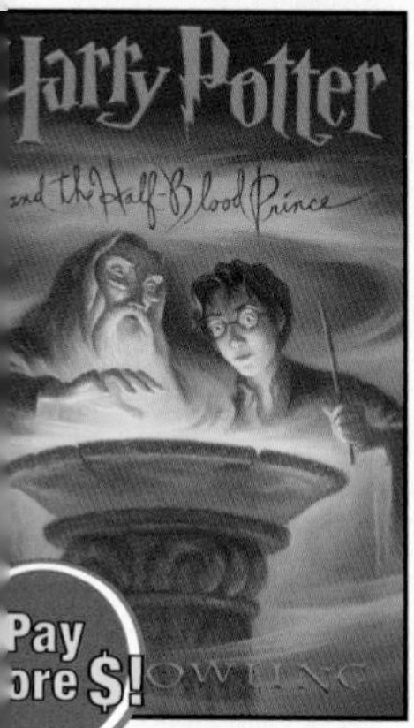

Harry Potter
and the Half-Blood Prince

Pay More $!

Harry Potter and the Half-Blood Prince
J.K. Rowling 652 pages
Own the latest Harry Potter adventure – even though all your friends already read and discussed it long ago. Perfect for students whose parents were too lame to let them stay up to buy it right at midnight when it first came out!
~~$19.95~~ **$21.50**

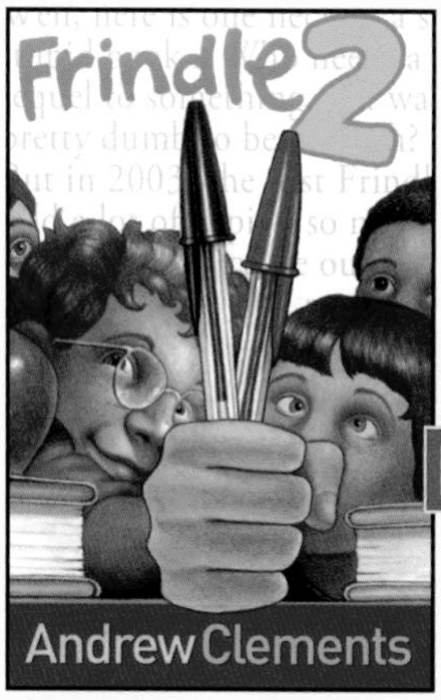

Frindle 2
Andrew Clements

NEW!

Frindle 2: On Second Thought...
Andrew Clements 25 pages
In fifth grade, clever troublemaker Nick Allen asked why a pen needed to be called a pen – why couldn't it be called a...Frindle? Before he knew it, his crazy experiment had become a national phenomenon and everyone was calling pens "Frindles." In this satisfactory sequel, Nick decides that maybe "Pen" was a better name after all and that whole "Frindle" stuff was just a stupid waste of time. As the book ends, a pen is no longer a Frindle – it's a pen!
$7.95

Falling Up the Light Sidewalk Where the Attic Ends
Shel Silverstein 184 pages
This brand new book features never-before-seen poems from the late Shel Silverstein. Of course, they've never been seen before because they're all awful and were cut from his really good books. Collected from his old garbage can!
$19.98 ~~$18.98~~

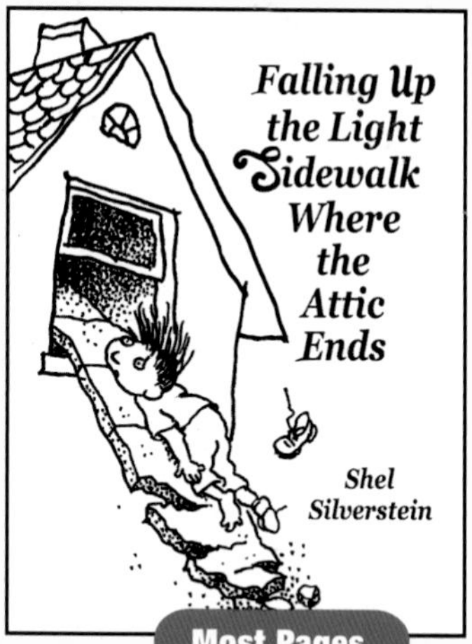

Falling Up the Light Sidewalk Where the Attic Ends
Shel Silverstein

Most Pages Are Numbered!

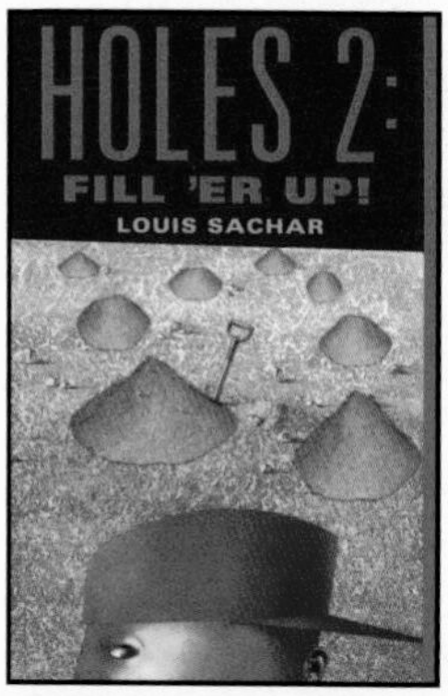

HOLES 2:
FILL 'ER UP!
LOUIS SACHAR

Holes 2: Fill 'Er Up!
Louis Sachar 262 pages
Jonathan Nahtanoj's luck has run out! He's been sentenced to Camp Green Lake for a crime he didn't commit. The warden has a new punishment to help the young inmates "develop character" — namely, filling in all those stupid holes she had them dig in the first book, so that sod can be laid down. You'll learn important lessons about friendship, integrity and landscaping.
$11.35

All Sales Final!

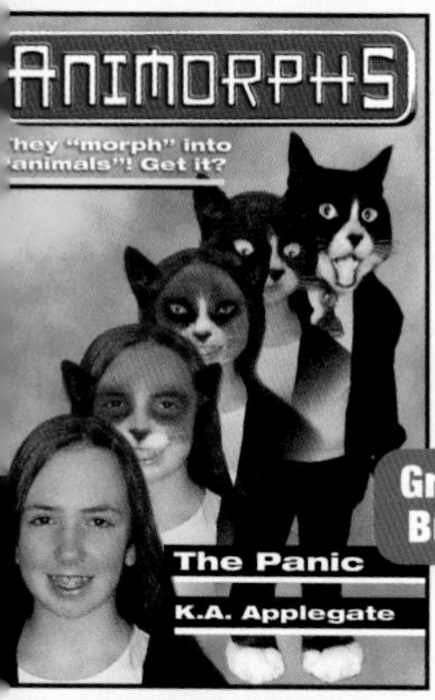

ANIMORPHS
They "morph" into animals"! Get it?
The Panic
K.A. Applegate

Great for Burning!

nimorphs: The Panic"
. Applegate 202 pages
en the Yeerk aliens threaten to launch a ssive attack that threatens everyone on e planet, how will the Animorphs stop em? Probably by morphing into animals, ht? Isn't that kind of what they always do?
.95

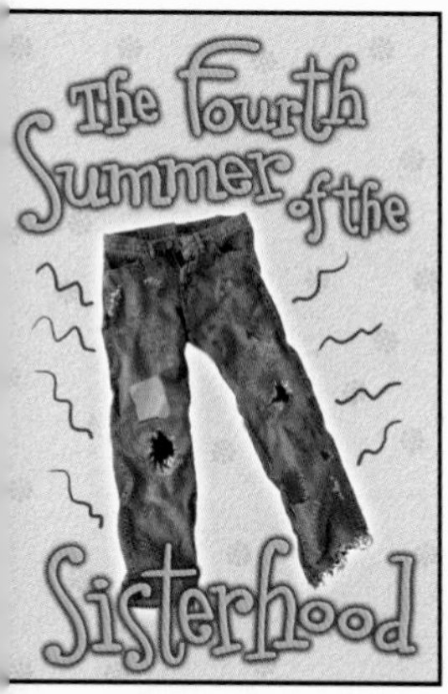

The Fourth Summer of the Sisterhood

e Fourth Summer of the Sisterhood
n Brashares 402 pages
ia, Bridget, Carmen and Tibby are back – d so are their traveling pants! Join them as ey embark on adventures of love, life and e Laundromat – to finally wash those dirty, oss pants they've been sharing for the last ee years. It's about time!
~~95~~ **$8.95**

If You Love Harry Potter, Then You'll Kind of Like These Knock-offs!

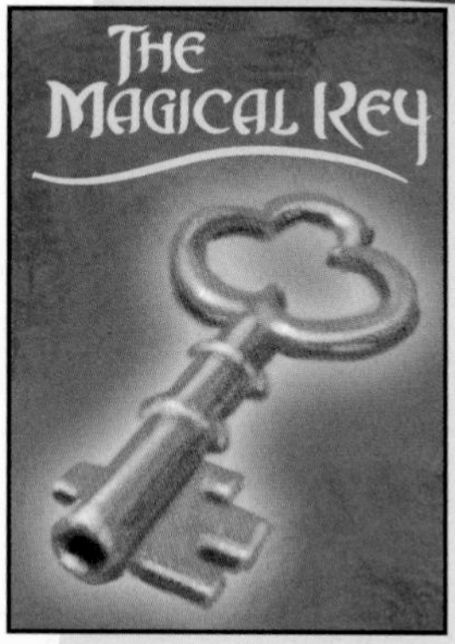

The Magical Key

The Magical Key
Hector Spackle 285 pages
Marvin's dad has a magical key that could lead to amazing powers – or just unlock that linen closet! Even after finishing the book, it won't be clear. First book in a series of 20!
$7.95

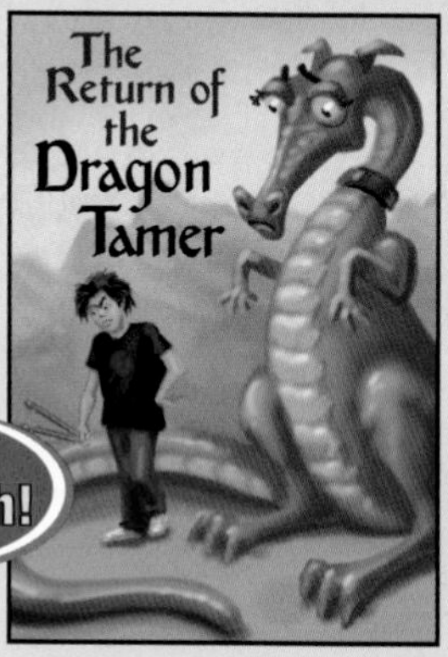

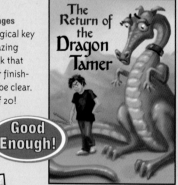

The Return of the Dragon Tamer

Good Enough!

The Return of the Dragon Tamer
Franklin Slacks 308 pages
On his 10th birthday, Kevin learns that he comes from a long line of magical dragon tamers! But Kevin wants to be a drummer in a band when he grows up, so he's not that into it.
$8.49

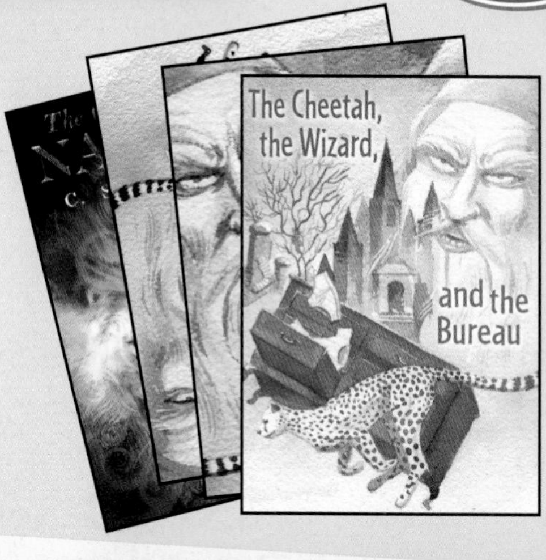

The Cheetah, the Wizard, and the Bureau

The Chronicles of Narnia Fantasy Grab Bag
Want *The Lion, the Witch, and the Wardrobe*? Well, if you do, you also have to take 3 other vaguely-related books that you'd never buy any other way! Comes with *The Cheetah, the Wizard, and the Bureau, Magicfire: The Curse of Troll Grove* and *Zelborn Revisted — Book the Third: The Saga of Norzibeth* — all magically forgettable!
$42.50

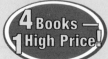

4 Books — 1 High Price!

WRITER: DAVE CROATTO ARTISTS: SCOTT BRICHER AND GARY HALLGREN

FOOLASTIC
BOOK CLUB

HISTORY COMES ALIVE BY BEING SLIGHTLY LESS BORING THAN SCHOOL!

No Good!

NEW!

THE COMPLETE HISTORY OF THE
WORLD

The Complete History of the World

Marshall Phlegm 48 pages

From the Big Bang to cavemen to the 1967 World Series to today, learn what happened during all 13.7 billion years! 48 exciting pages — plus stickers!

$2.95

The Great American Journey

Meg Chunder 304 pages

Felicity and Abigail are leaving their home in Richmond, Virginia to explore the wild frontiers of America! Will these courageous cousins survive the long, lonely trip to California and the many obstacles they'll face along the way? Things are looking pretty good, since it's 2005 and they're flying business class on a 747!

$10.95 ~~$9.95~~

THE
GREAT AMERICAN
JOURNEY

No Longer Printed with Toxic Ink!

Save Nothing!

Miranda Hudge:
Freedom Fighte

Miranda Hudge: Freedom Fighter

Tiffany Flump 215 pages

Read this amazing true story about a girl just like you! W except that she spent her childhood freeing slaves, fight censorship and working with the Queen — while you pre much go straight home and eat Doritos in front of the TV

$11.95

Sci-Fi, Fantasy, Thrillers and Who-Cares-Who-Dun-Its!

FUTURE SHOCK
WALLY BACKWASH

Cheap Materials!

Future Shock!

Wally Backwash 225 pages

In the future, everyone is born with 302 eyelashes — except for Jacob! Living with only 300 eyelashes, how far will he go to keep his secret — and would anyone even care?

$8.50

GORDON KORMAN
ON THE RUN
ROAD RAGERS
FOOLASTIC

On the Run: Road Ragers

Gordon Korman 160 pages

Aiden and May Falconer's parents are facing life in prison for a crime they didn't commit. With their parents trapped in jail with no way out, Aiden and May secretly travel the country with just one mission in mind — to have the coolest, most fun-filled roadtrip ever! It's nonstop fun from New York to San Francisco with no parents, no bedtimes, no curfews and no rules!

$4.99

Expensive!

"A Summer to... Remember?"
FOOLASTIC
J.B. SPOOKINGTON

"A Summer to...Remember?"

J.B. Spookington 185 pages

Lily has amnesia and can't remember if she the reason her hamster died 10 years ago — even worse, she's just moved to a new town and suspects that her neighbors may be vampires! Can Lily endure the Civil Rights tensions of 1964 — and her first real crush! - during a summer she won't soon forget?

$7.95

the Castle's Secret

New-ish!

The Castle's Secret

R. I. P. Deadingham 207 pages

A mysterious couple is keeping Riley prisoner! Can his best friend Charlie uncover the secret of the Castle of Mirrors to save him? Yes, he can. Sorry if that ruined the ending... but you'll still buy it, right?

~~$6.59~~ **$7.50**

A Series of Uneventful Misfortunes
THE SIMILAR SEQUEL

Includes Pages and Cover!

Lemony Snicket's A Series of Uneventful Misfortunes — The Similar Sequel

Lemony Snicket 325 pages

If you love the first 12 books, you'll love this one, since it's the exact same story over and over aga

$15.89

No Refunds!

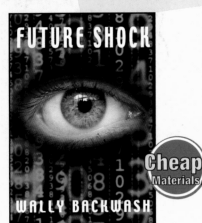

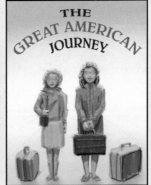

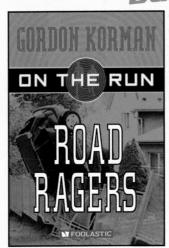

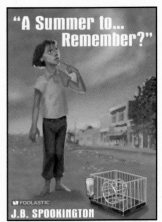

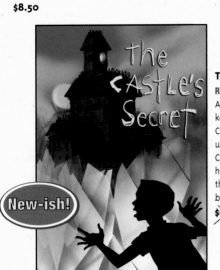

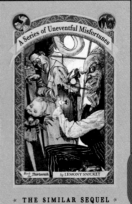

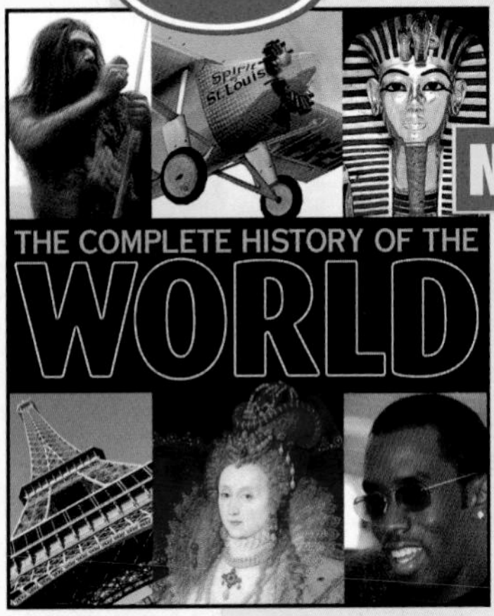

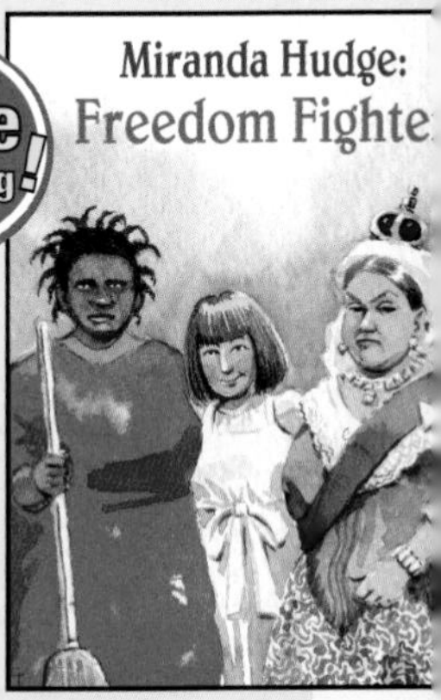

FOOLASTIC BOOK CLUB

NOT QUITE READING!

Zoey 101
School Daze
FOOLASTIC

Zoey 101: School Daze

112 pages

Read this hilarious new adventure, based on the hit TV show that your parents yelled at you for watching too much – which is what started them nagging you to read more to begin with!

$2.95

What Do You Expect for $2.95?

LIVE
EA SPORTS
MADDEN NFL 07
EXCLUSIVE NFL LICENSE

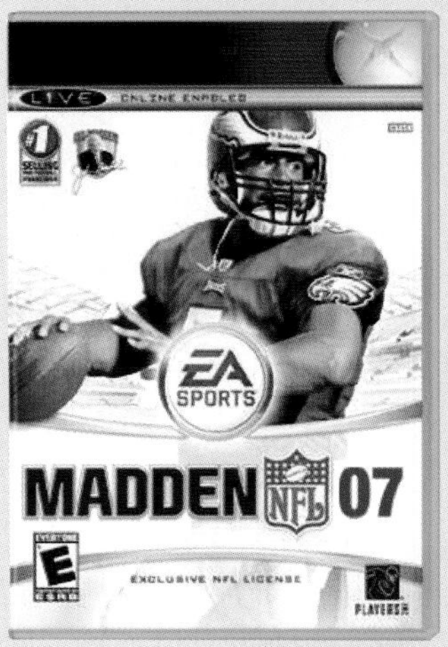

Madden 07

PainStation2 and Ecch-Box

It's got nothing to do with books, school or learning, but maybe if your parents aren't paying attention, you can check it on the order form and dupe them into paying for it! You get your game, we get the money — everybody's happy!

~~$49.95~~ **$60.50**

VERY Expensive!

Sudoku

Check out the ancient Japanese number game that's sweeping the country! 43 puzzles requiring intense concentration and problem-solving skills! It's like having extra math homework that you do just for fun!

$5.95 ~~$4.50~~

Guaranteed Highest Price!

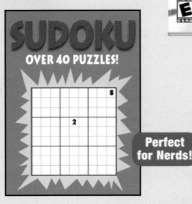

SUDOKU
OVER 40 PUZZLES!
8
2

Perfect for Nerds!

What a Load of Craft! Learn calligraphy, knitting, pottery and more!

Wendy O'Bendy 112 pages

Now you can MAKE birthday and holiday gifts for all your friends – and you can take all the money you would have spent on them and just spend it on yourself! Like on more books! Right...?

$14.95

what a load of craft!
Learn calligraphy, knitting, pottery and more!

Hangin' With Hilary Duff
When the Going Gets Duff, the Duff Gets Going!
FOOLASTIC

Hilary Duff: When the Going Gets Duff, the Duff Gets Going

Jerome McTatertot 18 pages

She's one of the hottest stars alive! But what's she really like? What was her life like before she got famous? What makes Hilary tick? These questions and many more won't be answered by this 18-page booklet of trivia you already knew and lame old photos from back when she was still on *Lizzie McGuire*! But it's glossy!

$3.25

Rejected for a Caldecott Medal!

A Series of Uneventful Misfortunes
MAD LIBS
A super silly way to fill in the ________!

A Series of Uneventful Misfortunes MAD Libs!

48 pages

If you love the adventures of the Baudelaire Orphans, now you can write you own silly adventures. Pick the name of a new guardian for the orphans, a new alias for Count Olaf and a new town name and you're done. Come to think of it, it's not like Lemony Snicket does much more than that in each book anyway...

$1.95

Personal Organizer and Spellchecker

Requires 7 D Batteries

Now you can organize your assignments, mark down important test dates, even check the grammar and spelling on your homework. The perfect tool to help you in your studies! At least that's what you'll tell your parents – they don't need to know that you only want it because you can also play "Hangman" and 12 other cool games on it!

$12.95

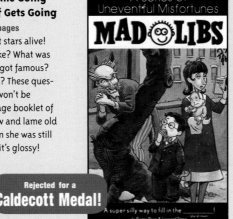

DURACELL

NEW!

Lame!

101 Jokes, Riddles and Puns That Will Leave You Baffled

Boyd Will B. Boyd 38 pages

"How many unicorns does it take to screw in a lightbulb? Eight... nine if it's a Wednesday!" "What do a flashlight and a substitute teacher have in common? They both love a *leap* year!" Plus 99 other weird jokes that make no sense! From the Creators of *101 Poorly-Translated Foreign Jokes*

$5.50 ~~$4.25~~

101 JOKES, RIDDLES AND PUNS THAT WILL LEAVE YOU BAFFLED!
VRRR
FOOLASTIC

FOOLASTIC
BOOK CLUB

Books that Come With Necklaces
(Don't Worry, You Can Just Throw Out the Book)

Ballet

Ballet
Valerie Van Clam 49 pages
Perfect for ballet lovers! This book comes with a collectible ballerina necklace you can wear while you read! Just don't wear it while you're dancing, though – it'll probably swing up in your face and chip your tooth.
$12.95

Books That Come With Necklaces

Books That Come With Necklaces
Valerie Van Clam 49 pages
Perfect if you love our line of books that come with necklaces! This book is all about books that come with necklaces, and it comes with a collectible necklace of a book about necklaces that you can wear while reading other books that come with necklaces. Confusing, huh? Don't worry, this book will explain it all!
$12.95

Puppies
Valerie Van Clam 49 pages
Perfect for puppy lovers! This book comes with a collectible puppy necklace you can wear while you're begging your mom to please, PLEASE let you get a dog, even though your stupid brother is allergic, the big crybaby.
$12.95

PUPPIES

KIDS' KORNER
THE BOOK YOUR MOM MAKES YOU ORDER FOR YOUR LITTLE BROTHER AN[D] EVERYONE MAKES FUN OF YOU FOR!

Franklin's
BIG TRIP

Franklin's Big T[rip]
Paulette Bourgeois
12 pages
When Franklin trip[s] and lands flat on h[is] back, he's stuck! Unable to get up himself, and with n[o] one to help him, he learns valuable lessons about posit[ive] thinking and the can-do spirit as he slowly loses con[-]sciousness and the hot summer sun scorches his helple[ss] body. The exciting final adventure!
$2.95

Just Read the Description, Jerk!

Save Nothing

Inspiring Inspirational Tales Sure to Inspire!

Thumbs Up!

Thumbs Up!
Peter "Pete" Peterson 215 pages
Jake Framington is determined to be the best thumbwrestler in his class! But there's only one problem – he was born without thumbs! Does he have what it takes to gain the acceptance of his classmates, win the regional championships AND save his family's farm in the process?
~~$4.95~~ **$5.95**

TOO LITTLE
TOO LATE
FOOLASTIC

Too Little Too Late
Turk Pudding
3 pages
The amazing tr[ue] story of a boy w[ho] risked it all to s[ave] his family – bu[t] still came up sh[ort]
$0.75

ORDER FORM

	QTY	PRICE	AMT
Captain Underpants and the Day He Finally Put on Some Khakis		$3.95	
Clifford the Big Red Dog and the Big Brown Carpet Stain		$4.24	
Curious George and the L'Oréal Testing Facility		$6.50	
Everybody Poops...But, Man, What's Your Father Eating?		$9.25	
General Fartypants and the Big-Butted Underwear Nerds of Toilet Town		$3.50	
If You Leave a Mouse a Cookie on a Mousetrap		$2.95	
The Berenstein Bears Hibernate for the Entire Story		$4.50	
The Cat in the Hat Gets Fixed		$6.50	
The Guinness Book of World Records — Just Pictures of Circus Freaks Edition!		$4.25	
The Magic School Bus Hits Arthur and Drags Him 40 Feet		$3.50	
The Very Hungry Caterpillar and the Even Hungrier Sparrow		$1.95	
SpongeBob's Deep Sea Jokebook — 400 Jokes Where the Punchline is Always "Barnacle"		$2.50	
Learn to Draw SpongeBob and Still Look Like You're Taking Notes in Class		$3.75	
Batman Begins: The Novelization of the Motion Picture That Wasn't That Great to Start With		$6.50	
Frindle 3: Return of the Frindle		$2.95	
The Prinze's Diaries by Freddie Prinze Jr.		$4.75	
Flatulent Stanley (Now in Scratch 'N' Sniff!)		$3.50	
The Hardy Boys and the Case of the Kids Who Keep Making Fun of Their Last Name		$4.25	
Nancy Drew: The Really Tough Case That She Didn't Even Bother With		$3.75	
The Extreme Gamer's Ultimate Strategy Guide: Tic Tac Toe		$4.95	
Garfield: Still Fat, Lazy and Unfunny — His 217th Book		$5.50	
The Guinness Book of World Records You'll Really Hurt Yourself Trying to Break		$4.75	

A MAD FAKEOUT FLIER

YOU CAN'T SPELL "EDUCATIONAL BOOKS ARE FUN" WITHOUT "EDUCATIONA[L] BOOKS"!

GET MATHIN' WITH
TEEN TITANS

Get Mathin' With the Teen Titans!
89 pages
With Robin, Cyborg, Raven and the rest of the team on hand, multiplication and division will become as exciting as your favorite superheroes! Actually, most kids find that instead of making math more exciting, it just makes their favorite heroes much more boring. See for yourself!
$11.95

Newbery Loser!

JumpStart
Learn Phonics with the Looney Tunes!

Jumpstart! Learn Phonics with the Looney Tunes!
78 pages
Suthferin' sucatash, it's dithpica[ble] how easy it is to learn reading a[nd] writing! The included CD uses th[e] voices of those wascally varmin[t] Looney Tunes to help you to rec[og]nize and learn new words! Stutt[er,] stammer, lisp and sputter along [with] Elmer, Porky, Daffy, Sylvester an[d] Tweety – and don't even get us started on the Tazmanian Devil's son! (From the Makers of Jumps[tart] Learn Phonics with Fat Albert & [the] Junkyard Gang and Jumpstart! L[earn] Phonics with WWE SmackDown!)
~~$12.49~~ **$13.49**

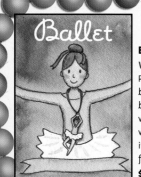

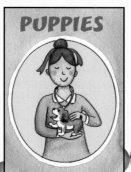

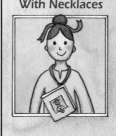

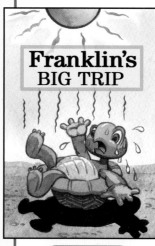

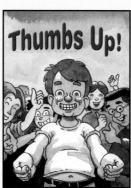

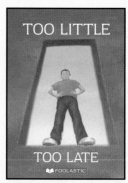

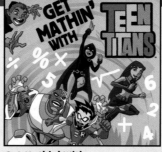

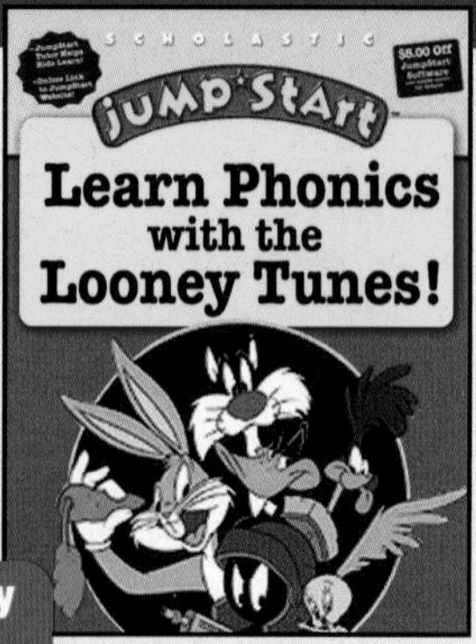

WHEN ADVERTISING TAKES OVER THE PLEDGE OF ALLEGIANCE

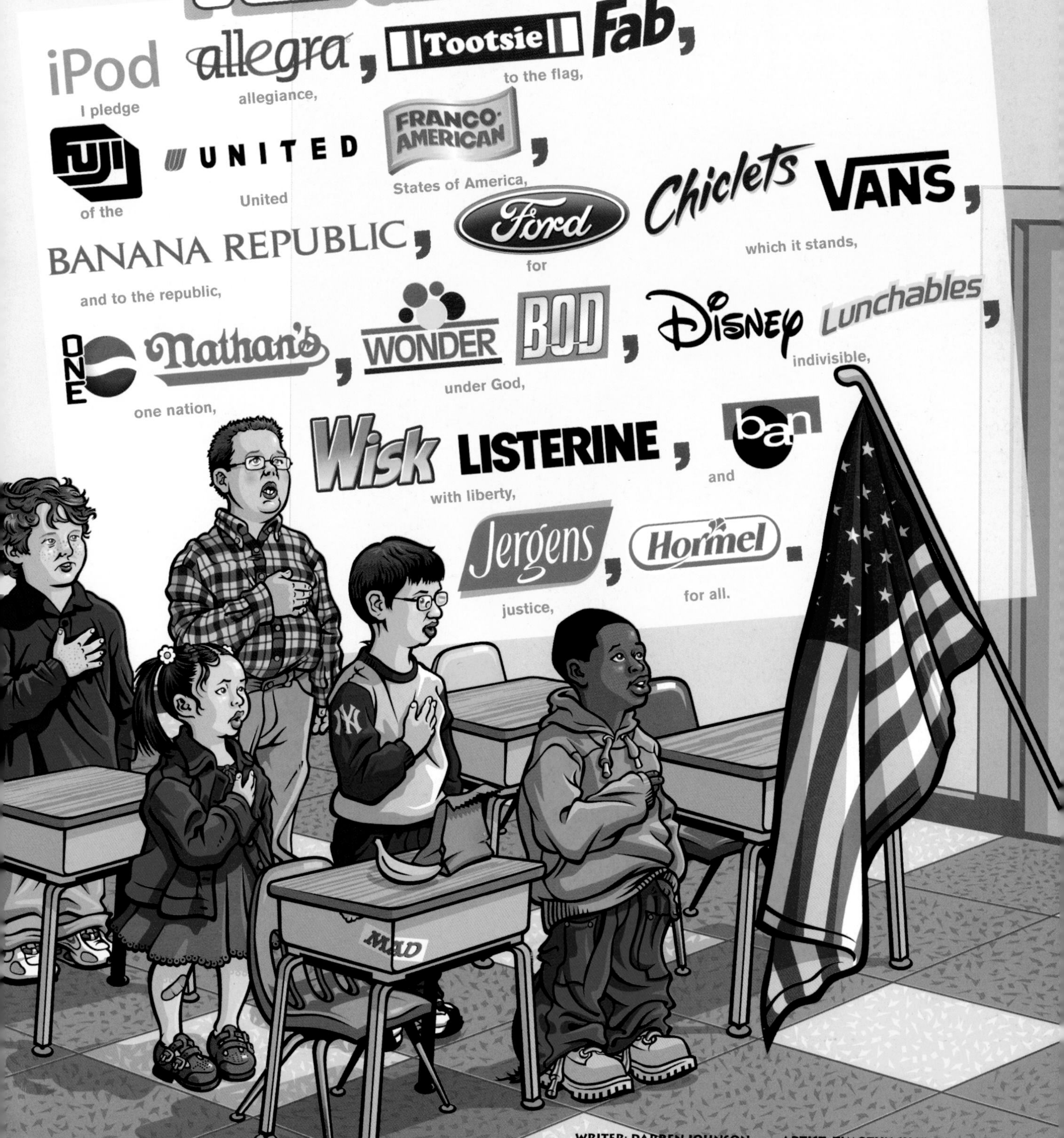
iPod allegra, Tootsie Fab,
I pledge allegiance, to the flag,
FUJI UNITED FRANCO-AMERICAN,
of the United States of America,
BANANA REPUBLIC, Ford Chiclets VANS,
and to the republic, for which it stands,
ONE Nathan's, WONDER BOD, Disney Lunchables,
one nation, under God, indivisible,
Wisk LISTERINE, ban
with liberty, and
Jergens, Hormel.
justice, for all.
MAD

WRITER: DARREN JOHNSON ARTIST: TIMOTHY SHAMEY

COMING DETRACTIONS DEPT.

Ah, a night at the movies! The modern multiplex experience features stadium seating, Dolby multi-channel sound, superwide screens and ultra-sharp projection technology. But before you get to that, you're forced to spend 20 minutes looking at boring factoids and moronic "quizzes" on grainy, washed-out slides that aren't up to the quality of your Aunt Thelma's vacation pics taken at Lake George in 1958! If only they were more like these...

PRE-MOVIE

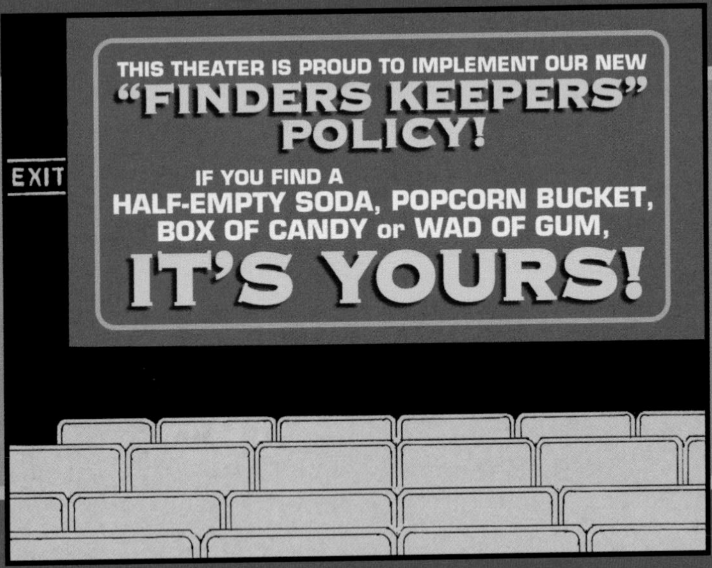

EXIT
THIS THEATER IS PROUD TO IMPLEMENT OUR NEW
"FINDERS KEEPERS" POLICY!
IF YOU FIND A
HALF-EMPTY SODA, POPCORN BUCKET, BOX OF CANDY or WAD OF GUM,
IT'S YOURS!

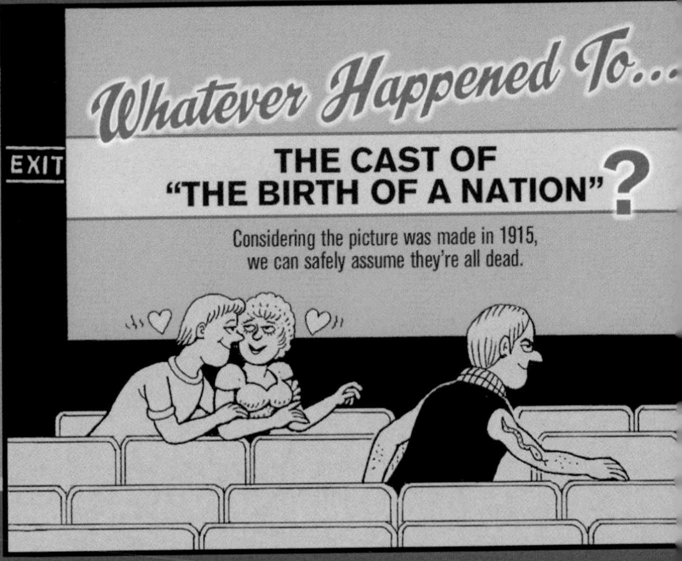

EXIT
Whatever Happened To...
THE CAST OF "THE BIRTH OF A NATION"?
Considering the picture was made in 1915, we can safely assume they're all dead.

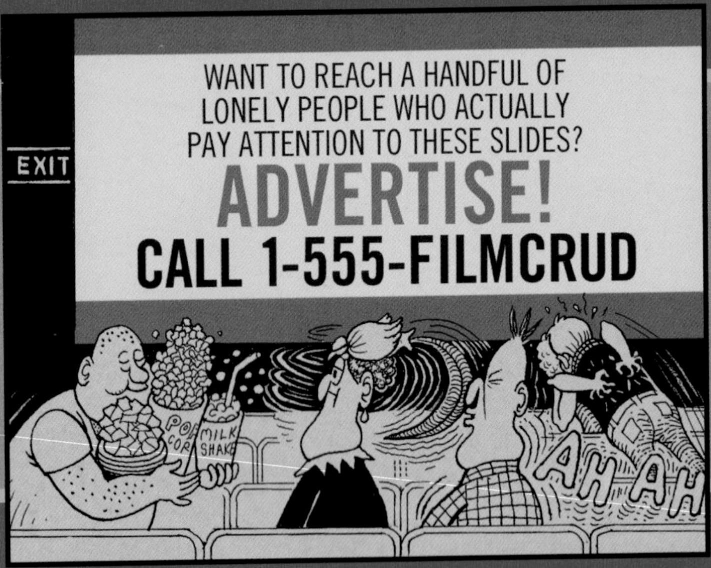

EXIT
WANT TO REACH A HANDFUL OF LONELY PEOPLE WHO ACTUALLY PAY ATTENTION TO THESE SLIDES?
ADVERTISE!
CALL 1-555-FILMCRUD
POP CORN
MILK SHAKE
AHAH

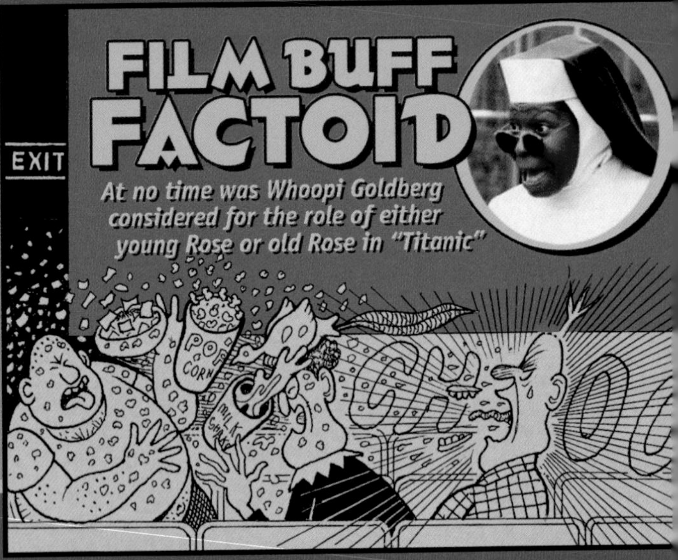

EXIT
FILM BUFF FACTOID
At no time was Whoopi Goldberg considered for the role of either young Rose or old Rose in "Titanic"
POP CORN
MILK SHAKE

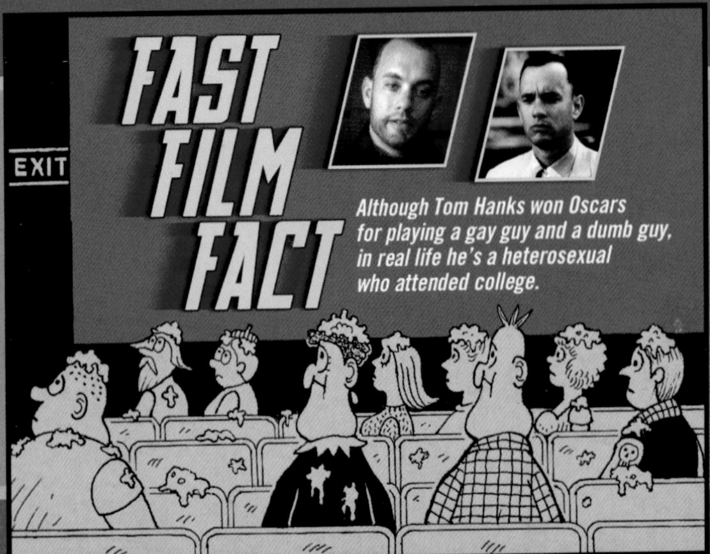

EXIT
FAST FILM FACT
Although Tom Hanks won Oscars for playing a gay guy and a dumb guy, in real life he's a heterosexual who attended college.

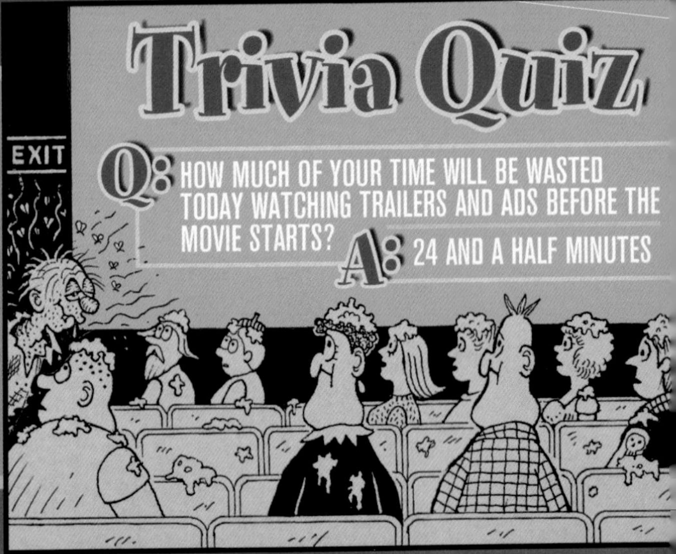

EXIT
Trivia Quiz
Q: HOW MUCH OF YOUR TIME WILL BE WASTED TODAY WATCHING TRAILERS AND ADS BEFORE THE MOVIE STARTS?
A: 24 AND A HALF MINUTES

ARTIST: AL JAFFEE

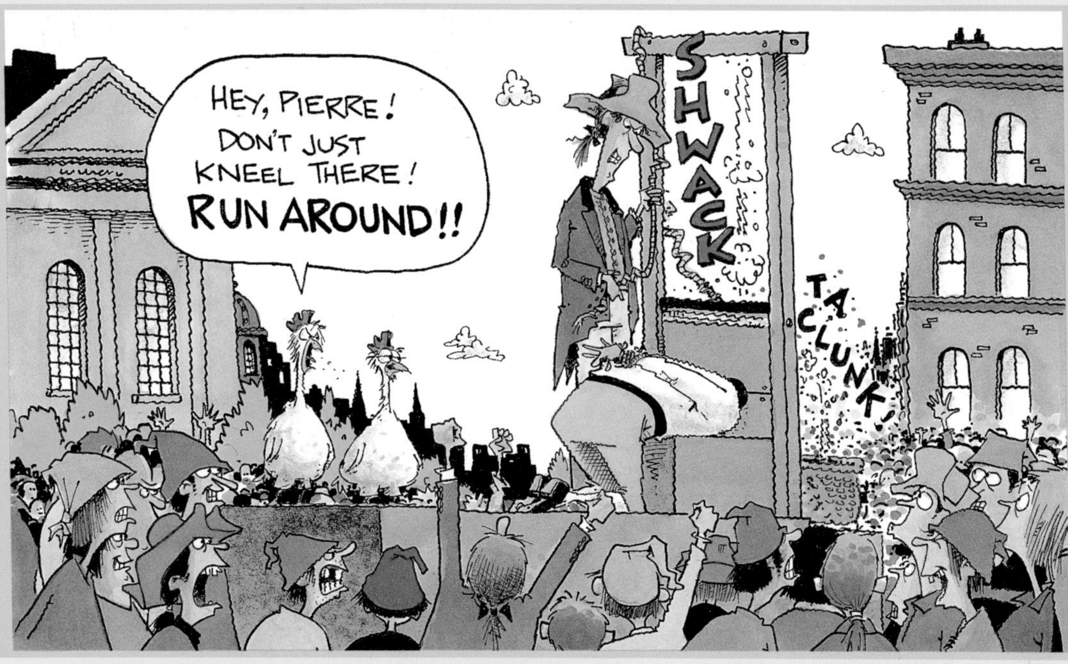
HEY, PIERRE! DON'T JUST KNEEL THERE! RUN AROUND!!
SHWACK
TA CLUNK!

Just for laughs, they'd spend a little time taking in the French Revolution
—when *people's* heads were being chopped off

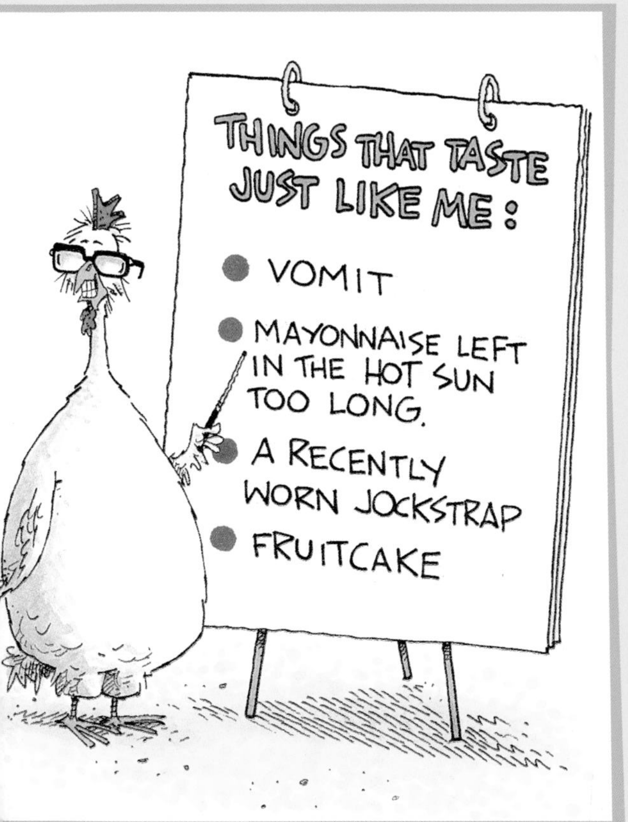
THINGS THAT TASTE JUST LIKE ME:
VOMIT
MAYONNAISE LEFT IN THE HOT SUN TOO LONG.
A RECENTLY WORN JOCKSTRAP
FRUITCAKE

They'd be calling all the shots in the
"things that taste just like chicken" department.

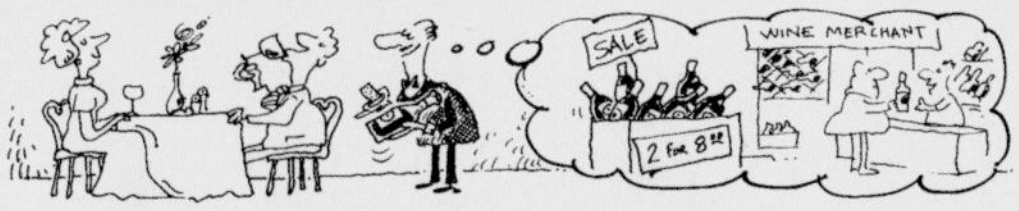

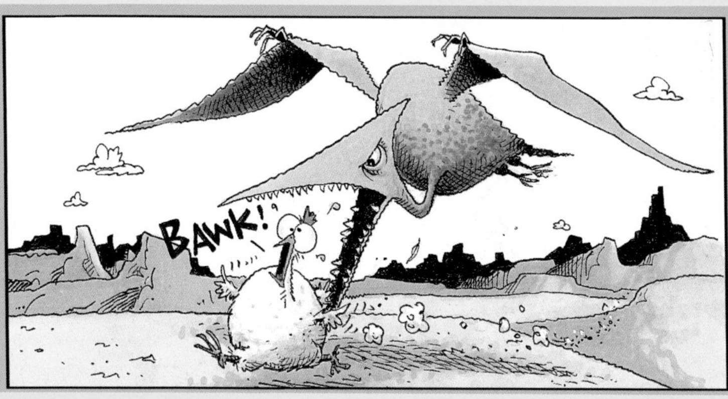
BAWK!

Some would learn the hard way, the dangers of
looking up their prehistoric ancestors

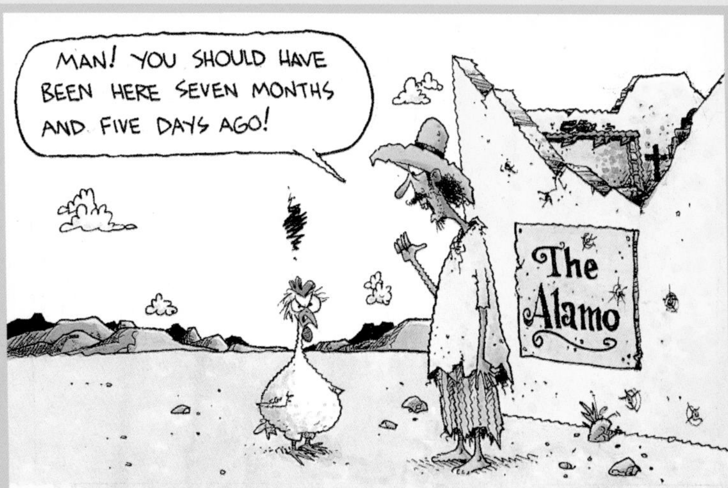
MAN! YOU SHOULD HAVE BEEN HERE SEVEN MONTHS AND FIVE DAYS AGO!
The Alamo

They would rarely set their arrival date correctly,
because at the end of the day, they're still frickin' chickens

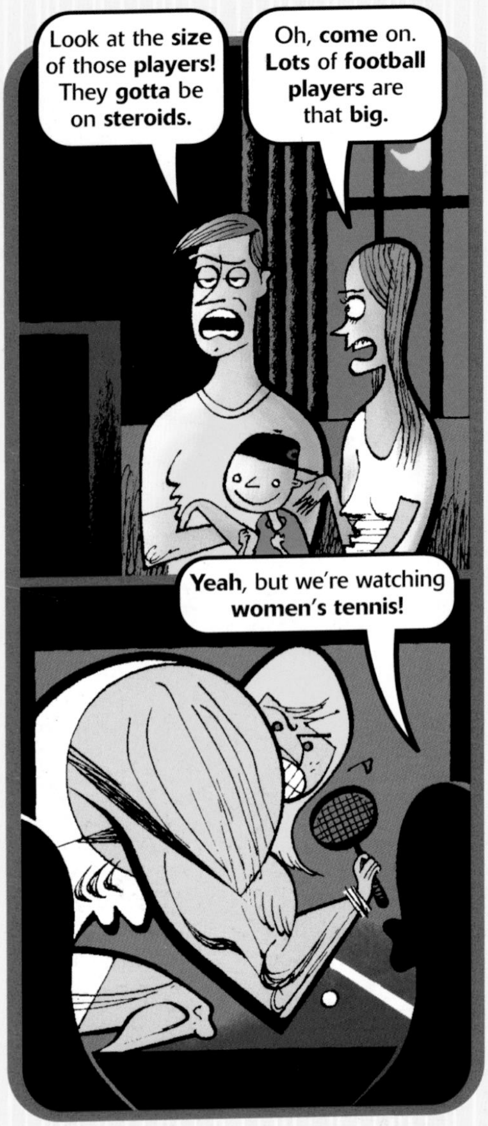
Look at the **size** of those **players!** They **gotta** be on **steroids.**
Oh, **come** on. **Lots** of **football players** are that **big.**
Yeah, but we're watching **women's tennis!**

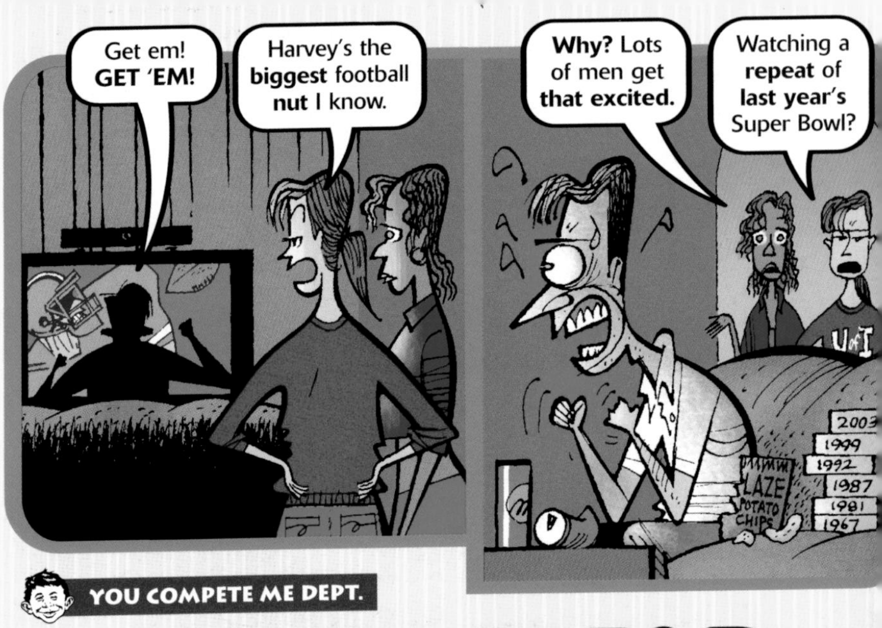
Get em! **GET 'EM!**
Harvey's the **biggest** football **nut** I know.
Why? Lots of men get **that excited.**
Watching a **repeat** of **last year's** Super Bowl?
2003
1999
1992
1987
1981
1967
LAZE POTATO CHIPS

YOU COMPETE ME DEPT.

The MAD WORLD of..

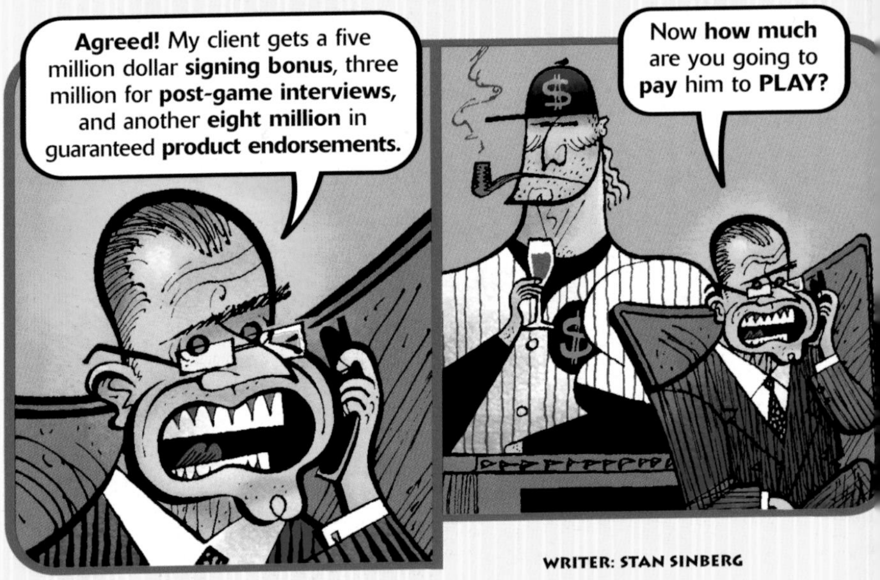
Agreed! My client gets a five million dollar **signing bonus**, three million for **post-game interviews**, and another **eight million** in guaranteed **product endorsements.**
Now **how much** are you going to **pay** him to **PLAY?**

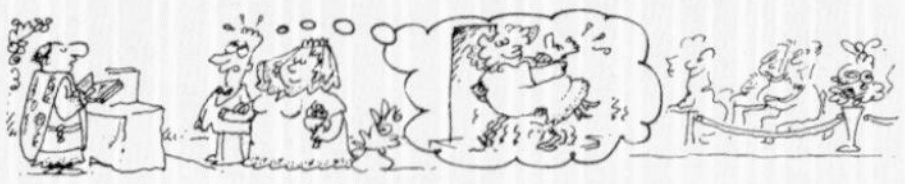

WRITER: STAN SINBERG

ARTIST: MARC HEMPEL

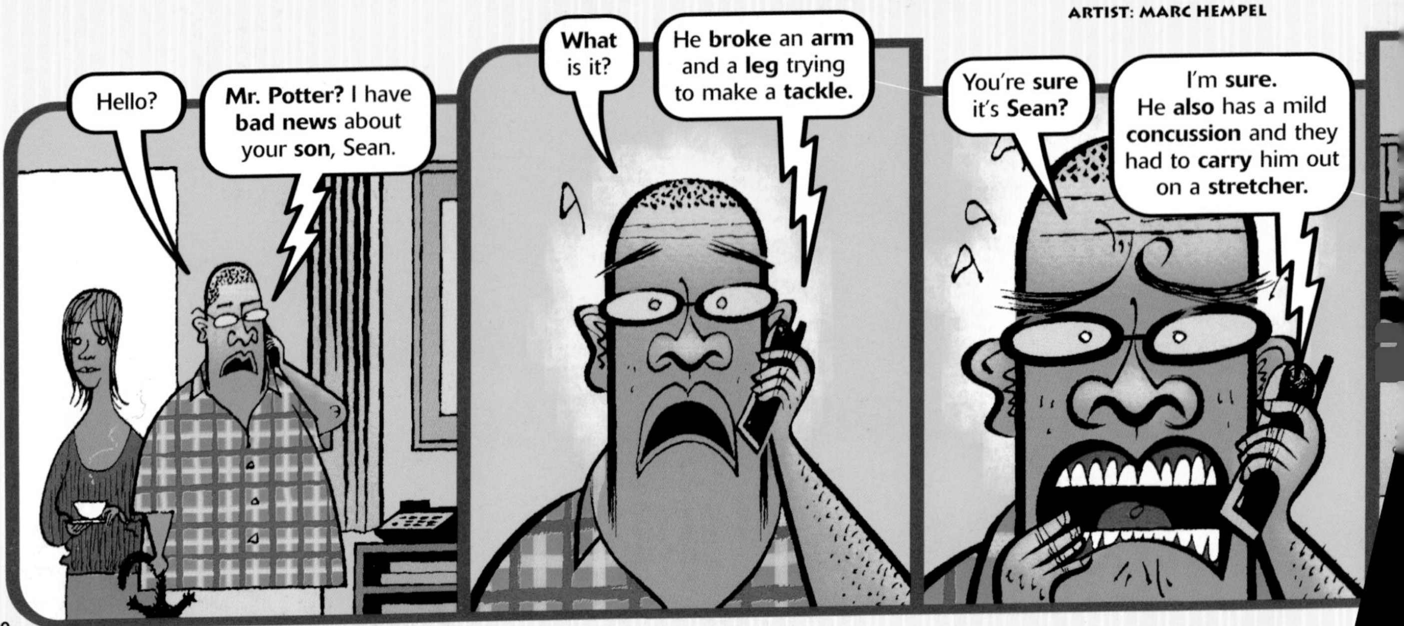
Hello?
Mr. Potter? I have **bad news** about your **son**, Sean.
What is it?
He **broke** an **arm** and a **leg** trying to make a **tackle.**
You're **sure** it's **Sean?**
I'm **sure.** He **also** has a mild **concussion** and they had to **carry** him out on a **stretcher.**

Say... Remind Them...

WRITER: JACOB LAMBERT
ARTIST: PETER BAGGE

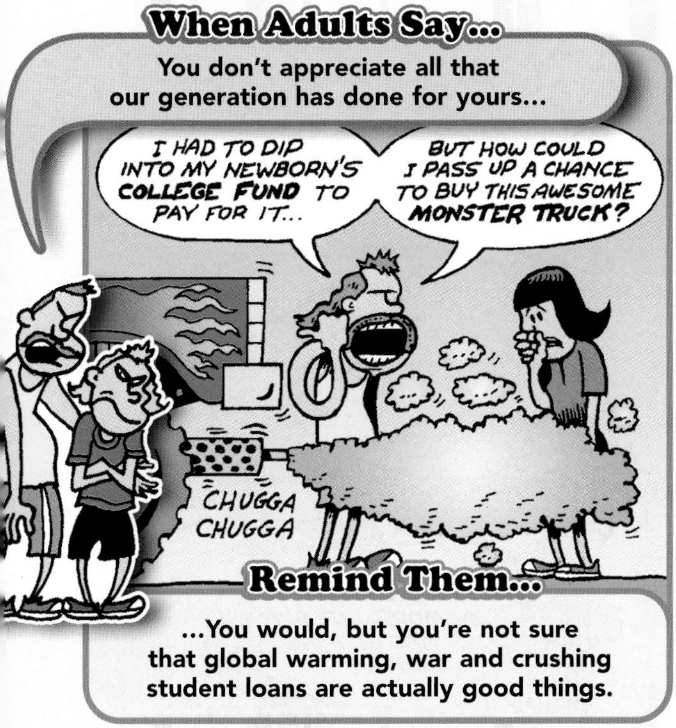
When Adults Say...
You don't appreciate all that our generation has done for yours...
I HAD TO DIP INTO MY NEWBORN'S COLLEGE FUND TO PAY FOR IT...
BUT HOW COULD I PASS UP A CHANCE TO BUY THIS AWESOME MONSTER TRUCK?
CHUGGA CHUGGA
Remind Them...
...You would, but you're not sure that global warming, war and crushing student loans are actually good things.

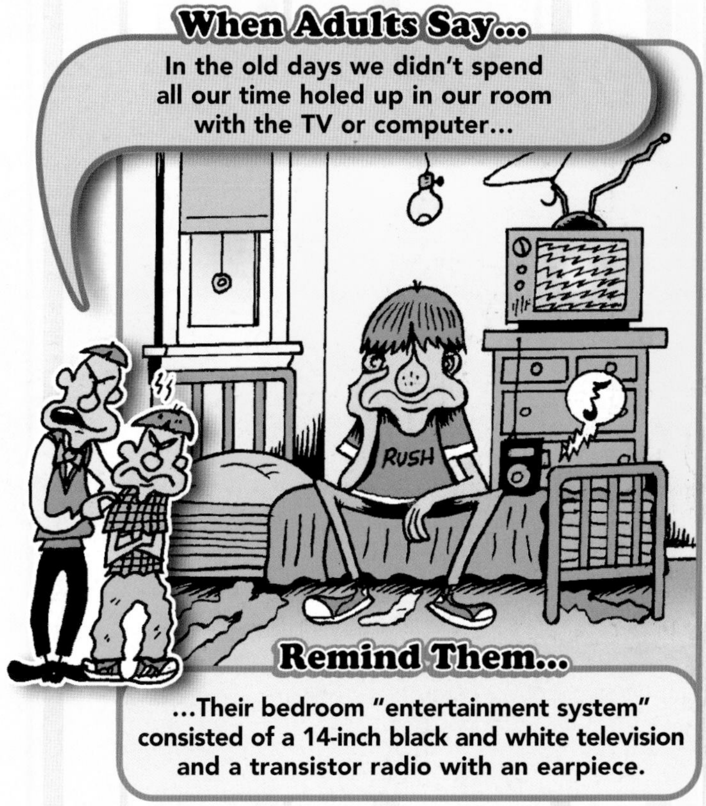
When Adults Say...
In the old days we didn't spend all our time holed up in our room with the TV or computer...
RUSH
Remind Them...
...Their bedroom "entertainment system" consisted of a 14-inch black and white television and a transistor radio with an earpiece.

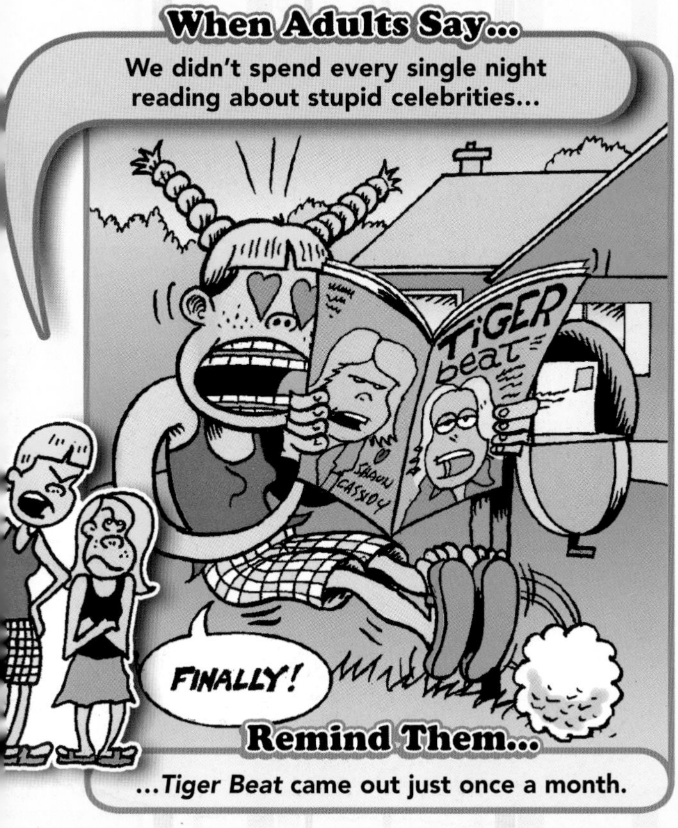
When Adults Say...
We didn't spend every single night reading about stupid celebrities...
TIGER beat
SHAUN CASSIDY
FINALLY!
Remind Them...
...Tiger Beat came out just once a month.

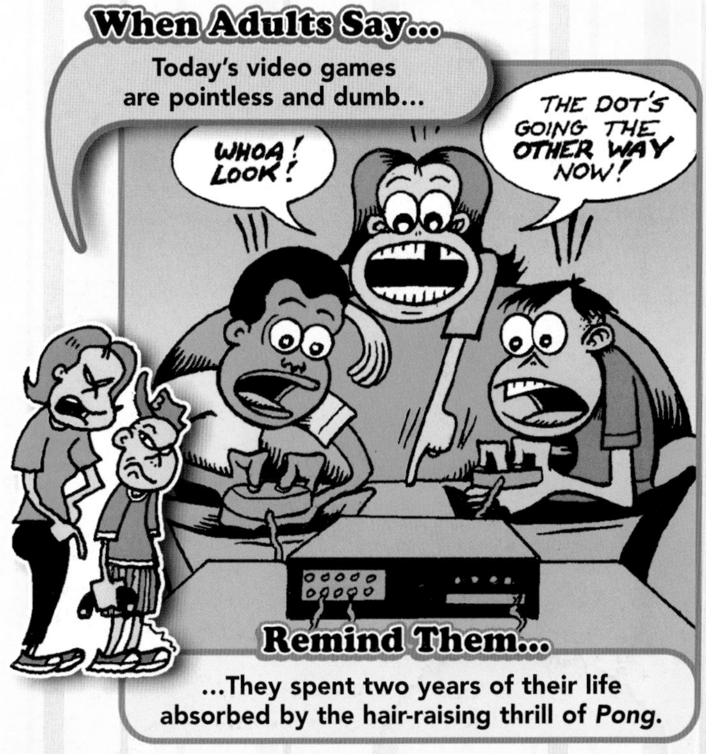
When Adults Say...
Today's video games are pointless and dumb...
WHOA! LOOK!
THE DOT'S GOING THE OTHER WAY NOW!
Remind Them...
...They spent two years of their life absorbed by the hair-raising thrill of Pong.

DON'T PHRASE ME, BRO DEPT.

It's been said that if you live long enough, eventually you'll "hear it all." Don't believe it! Most people resist change and cling to their ignorance. In fact, here are some...

COMMENTS YOU'LL NEVER HEAR NO MATTER HOW LONG YOU LIVE

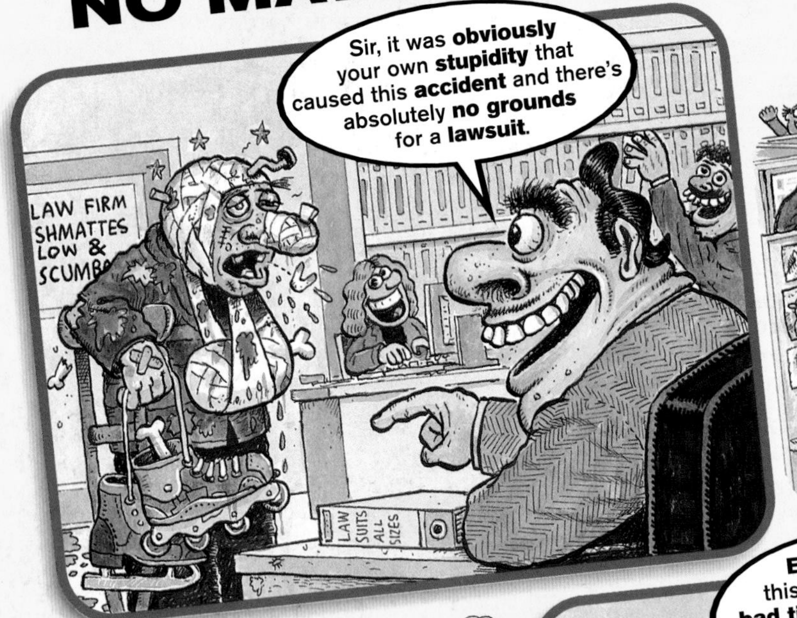

Sir, it was **obviously** your own **stupidity** that caused this **accident** and there's absolutely **no grounds** for a **lawsuit**.
LAW FIRM SHMATTES LOW & SCUMB
LAW SUITS ALL SIZES

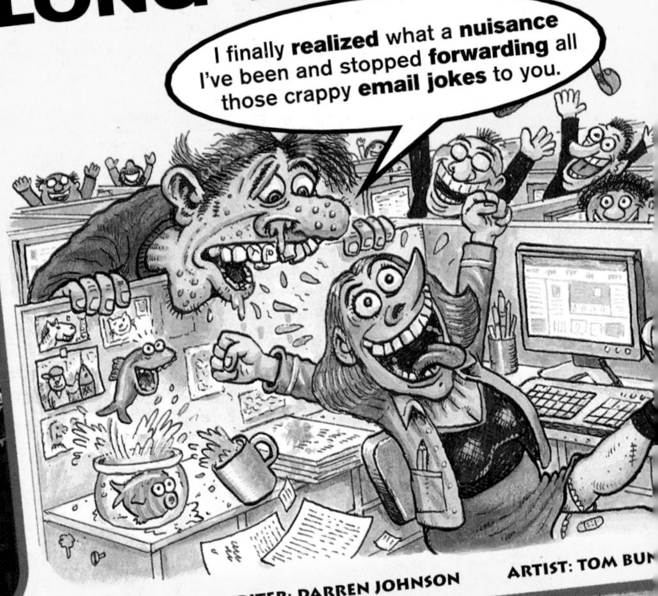

I finally **realized** what a **nuisance** I've been and stopped **forwarding** all those crappy **email jokes** to you.

WRITER: DARREN JOHNSON ARTIST: TOM BUN

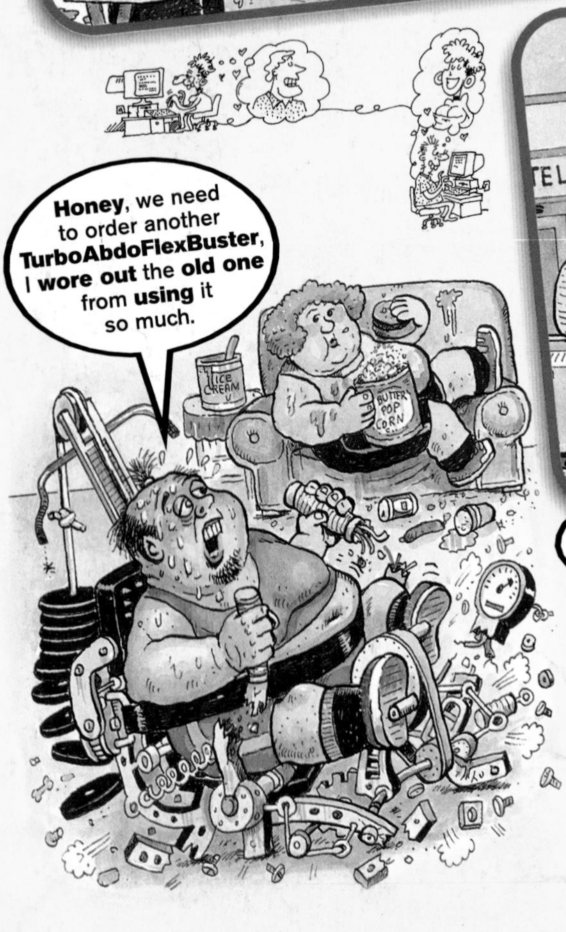

Honey, we need to order another **TurboAbdoFlexBuster**, I **wore out** the **old one** from **using** it so much.
ICE CREAM
BUTTER POP CORN

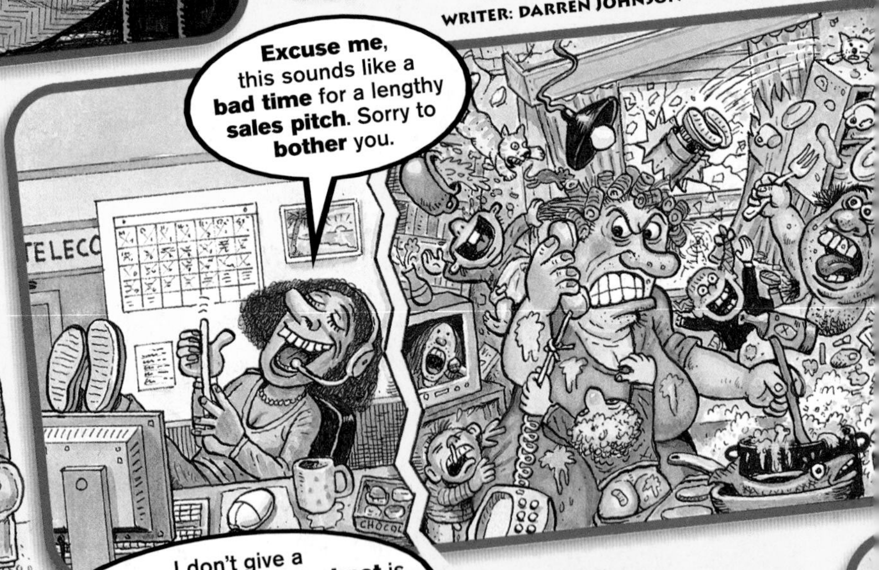

Excuse me, this sounds like a **bad time** for a lengthy **sales pitch**. Sorry to **bother** you.
TELECO
CHOCOL

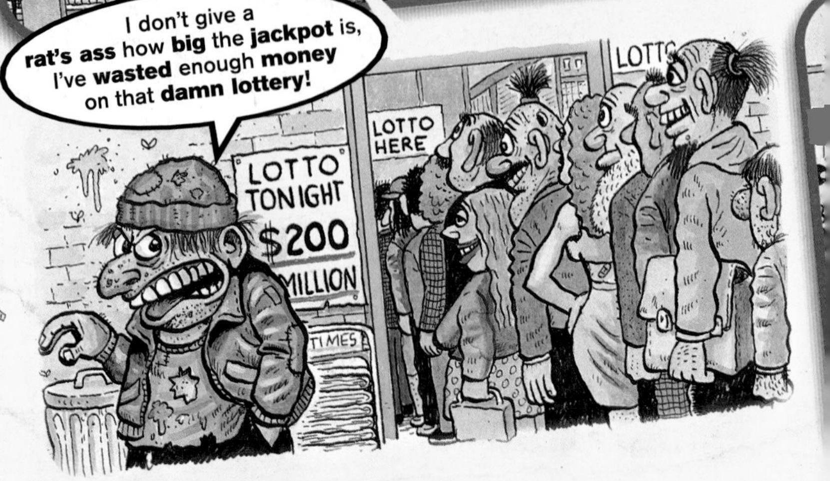

I don't give a **rat's ass** how **big** the **jackpot** is, I've **wasted** enough **money** on that **damn lottery**!
LOTTO HERE
LOTTO TONIGHT $200 MILLION
TIMES

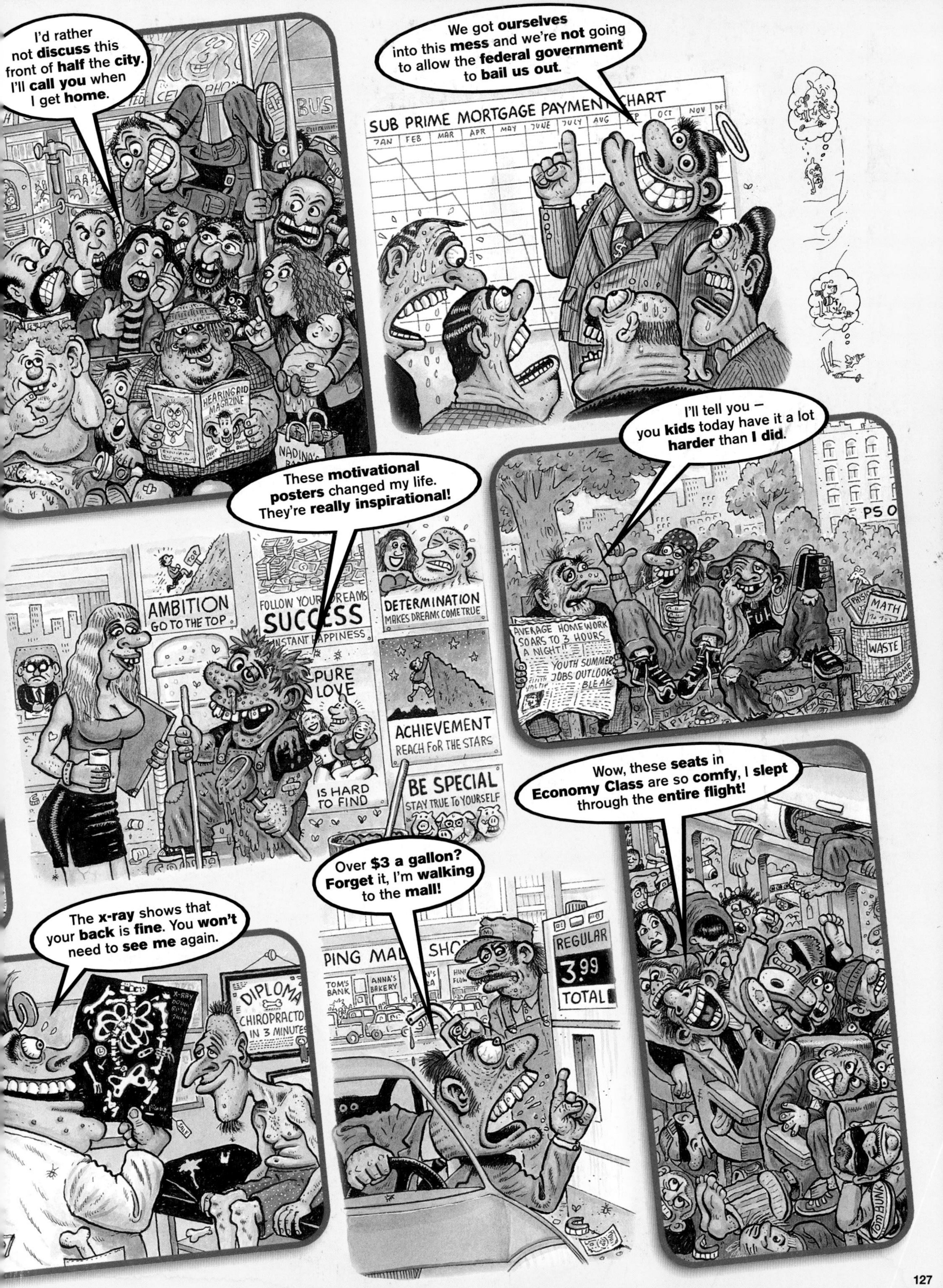
I'd rather not discuss this front of half the city. I'll call you when I get home.
HEARING AID MAGAZINE
We got ourselves into this mess and we're not going to allow the federal government to bail us out.
SUB PRIME MORTGAGE PAYMENT CHART
These motivational posters changed my life. They're really inspirational!
AMBITION GO TO THE TOP
FOLLOW YOUR DREAMS SUCCESS INSTANT HAPPINESS
DETERMINATION MAKES DREAMS COME TRUE
PURE LOVE IS HARD TO FIND
ACHIEVEMENT REACH FOR THE STARS
BE SPECIAL STAY TRUE TO YOURSELF
I'll tell you — you kids today have it a lot harder than I did.
AVERAGE HOMEWORK SOARS TO 3 HOURS A NIGHT!
YOUTH SUMMER JOBS OUTLOOK BLEAK
MATH
WASTE
The x-ray shows that your back is fine. You won't need to see me again.
DIPLOMA CHIROPRACTOR IN 3 MINUTES
Over $3 a gallon? Forget it, I'm walking to the mall!
REGULAR
3.99
TOTAL
Wow, these seats in Economy Class are so comfy, I slept through the entire flight!

SERGE-IN GENERAL DEPT.

A MAD LOOK AT ANGRY BIRDS

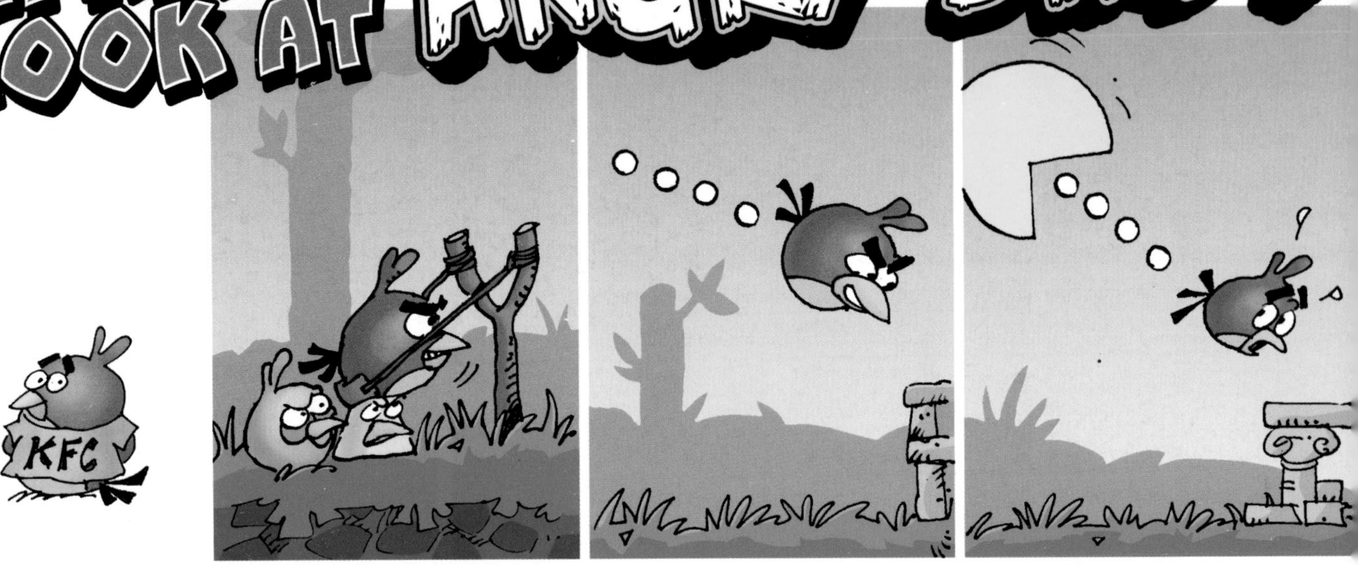
KFC

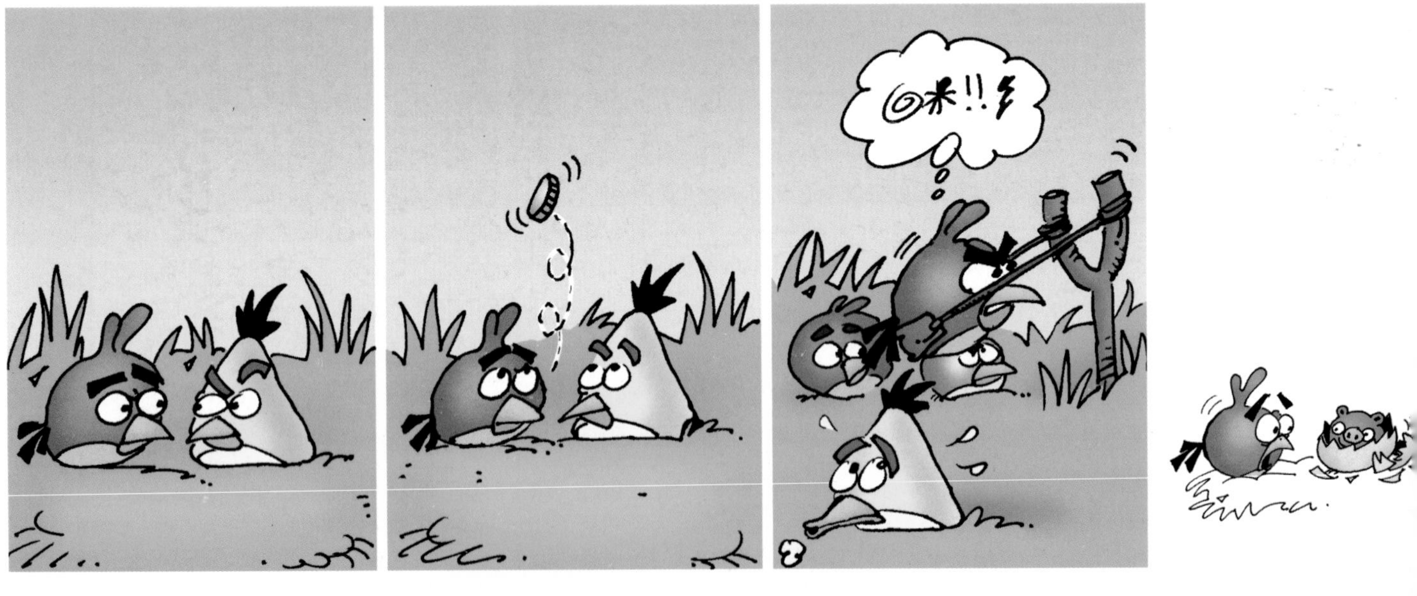

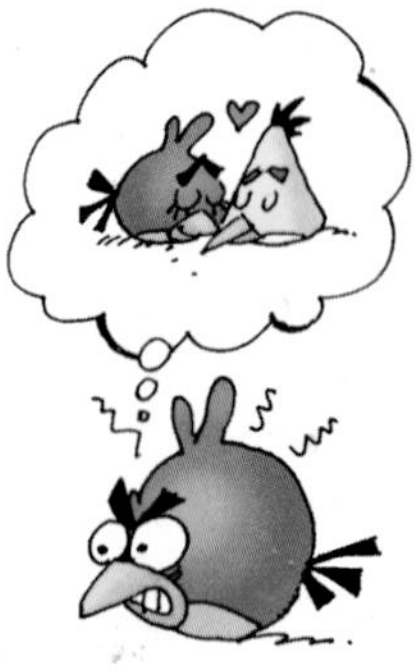

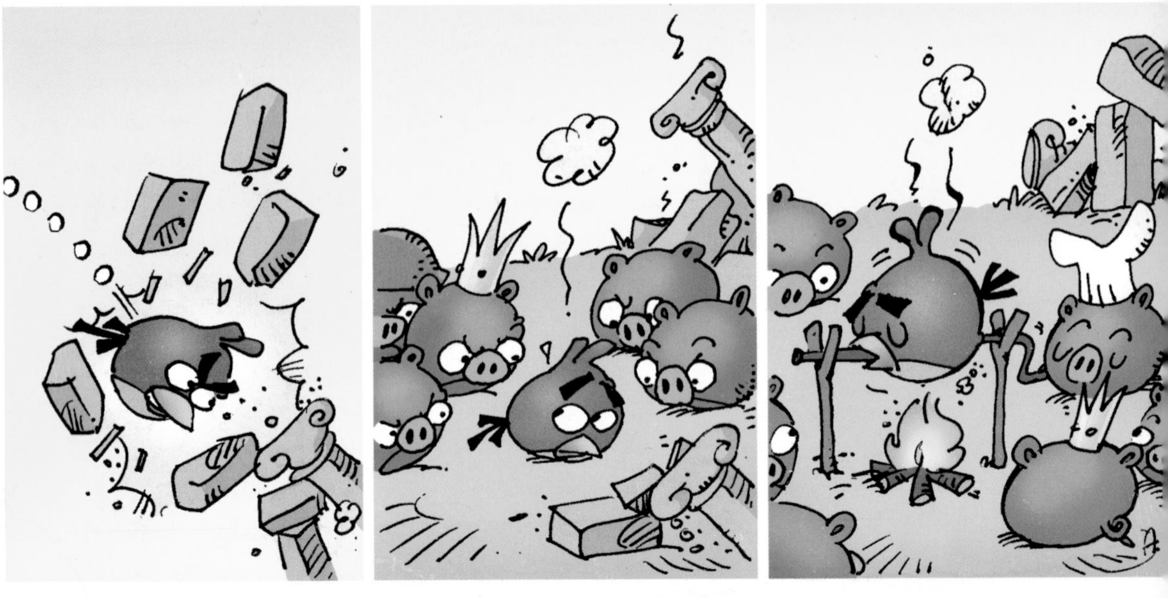

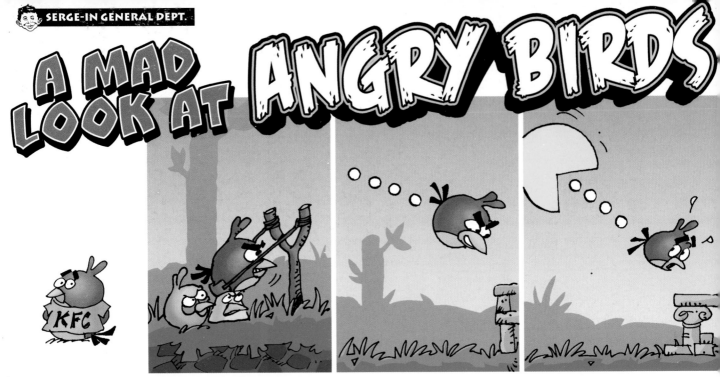

WRITER AND ARTIST: SERGIO ARAGONÉS

A a

apple

Trace and print **A** and **a**.

A A

a a

The anteater admires ants gathering acorns.
Circle the ants. Count the acorns.

SEE, HEAR, READ™

Bb

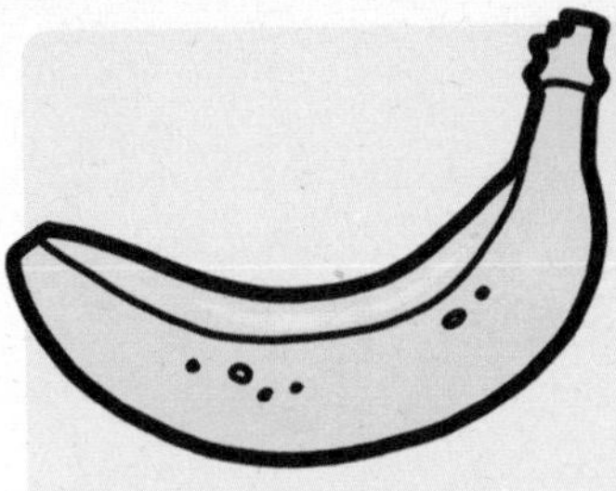

banana

Trace and print **B** and **b**.

B B

b b

A blue bear takes a bubble bath.

Color all the **B** spaces **brown**. Color all the **b** spaces **blue**.

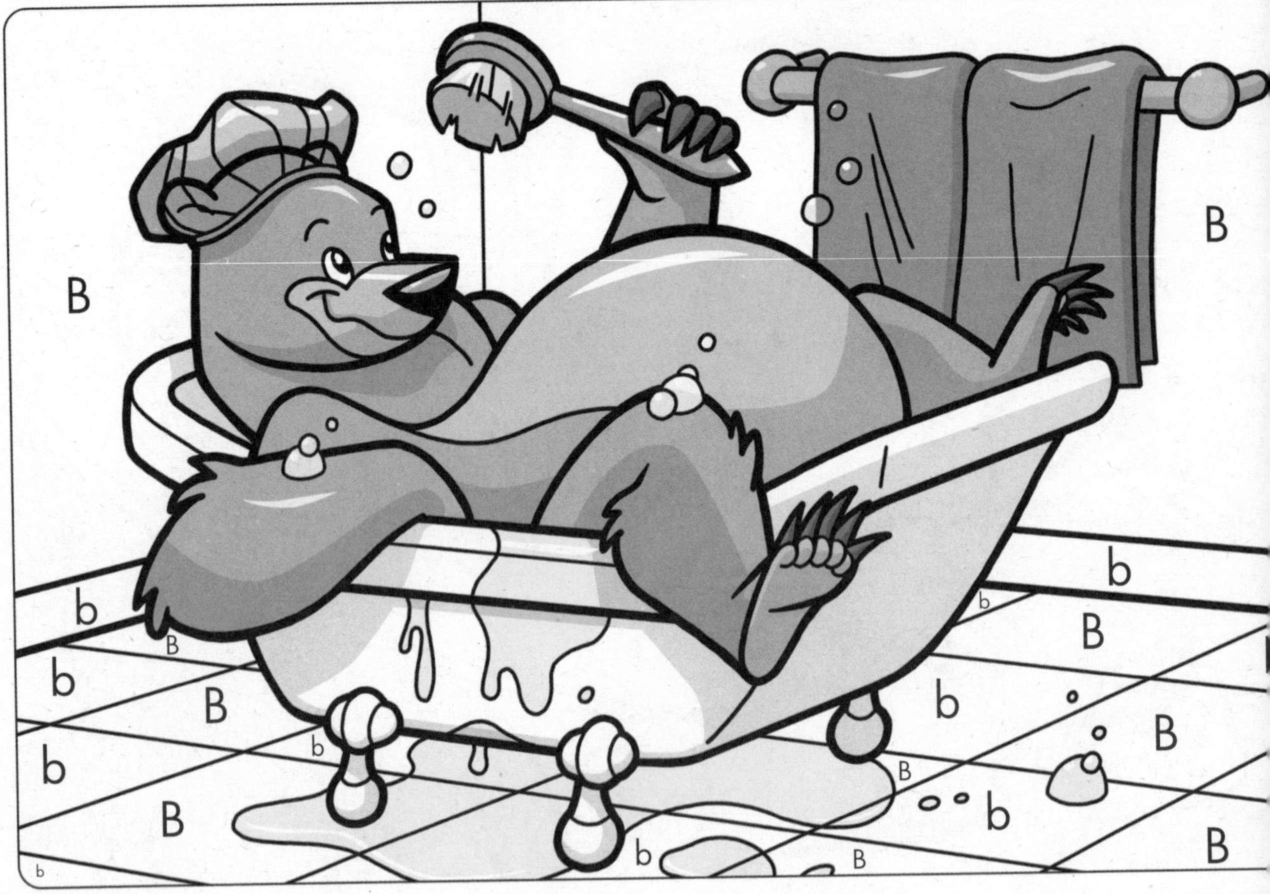
B
B
b
b
b
B
B
b
B
b
B
b
b
B
b
B
b
B
B
b

SEE, HEAR, READ™

Cc

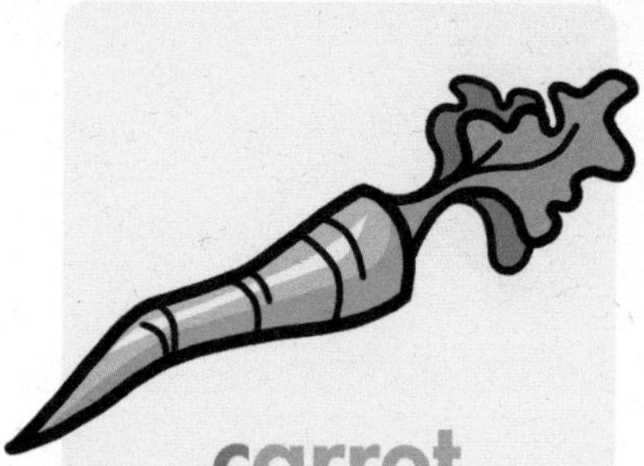
carrot

Trace and print **C** and **c**.

A calico cat naps on a cozy couch.

Connect the dots and color.

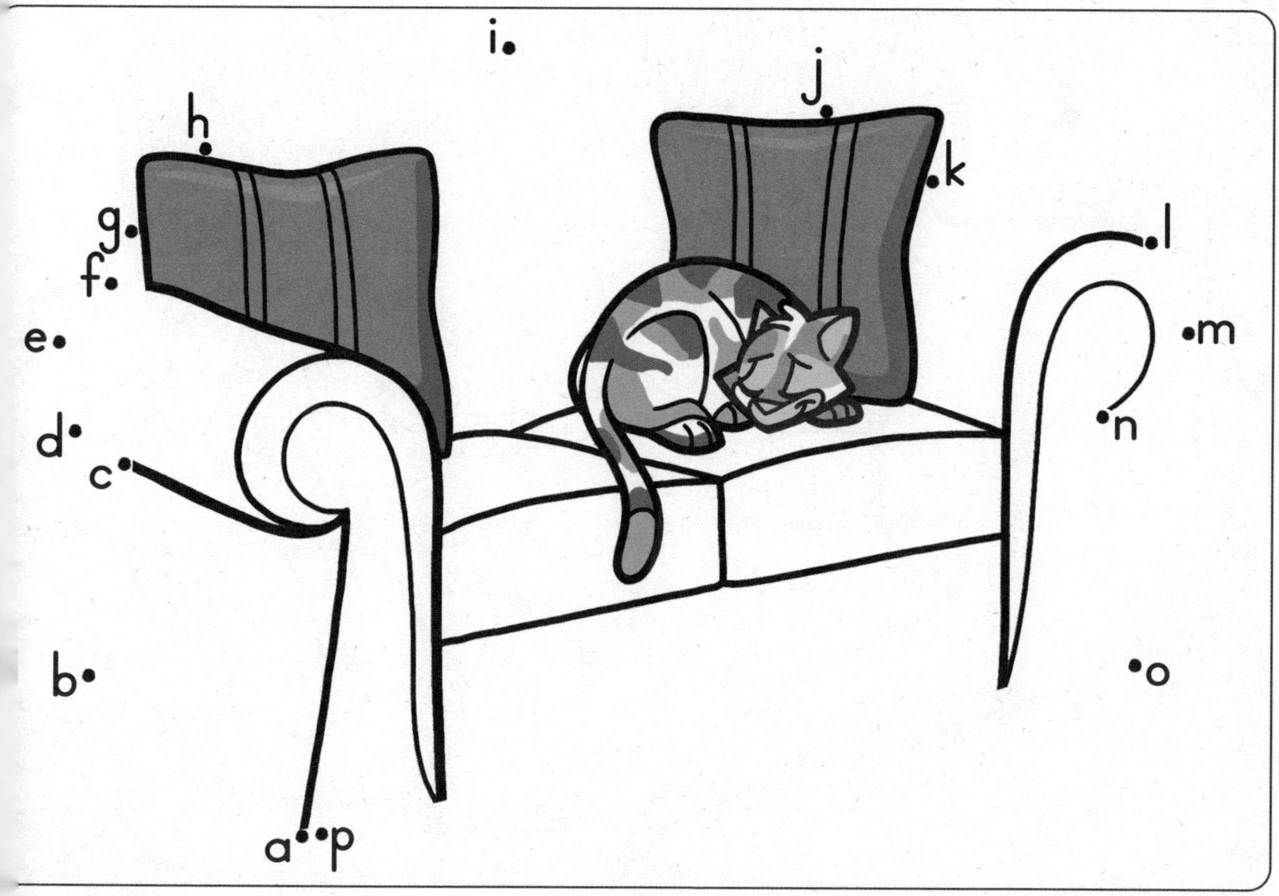
i
j
h
k
g
l
f
m
e
d
n
c
b
o
a
p

SEE, HEAR, READ™

Dd

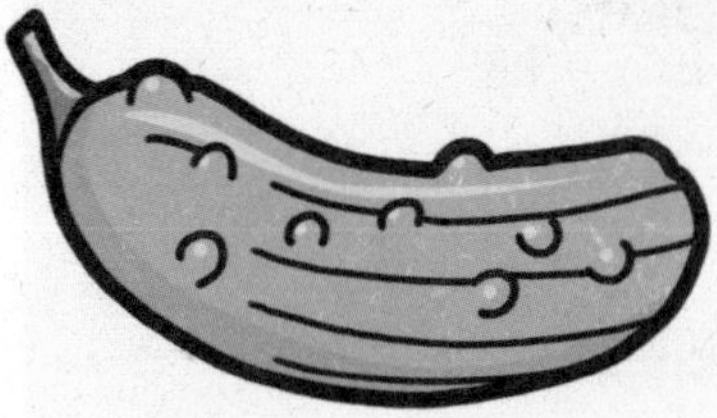

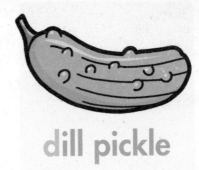

dill pickle

Trace and print **D** and **d**.

D D

d d

Dinosaurs play and dine in the dark den.

Circle the dinosaur that is different.

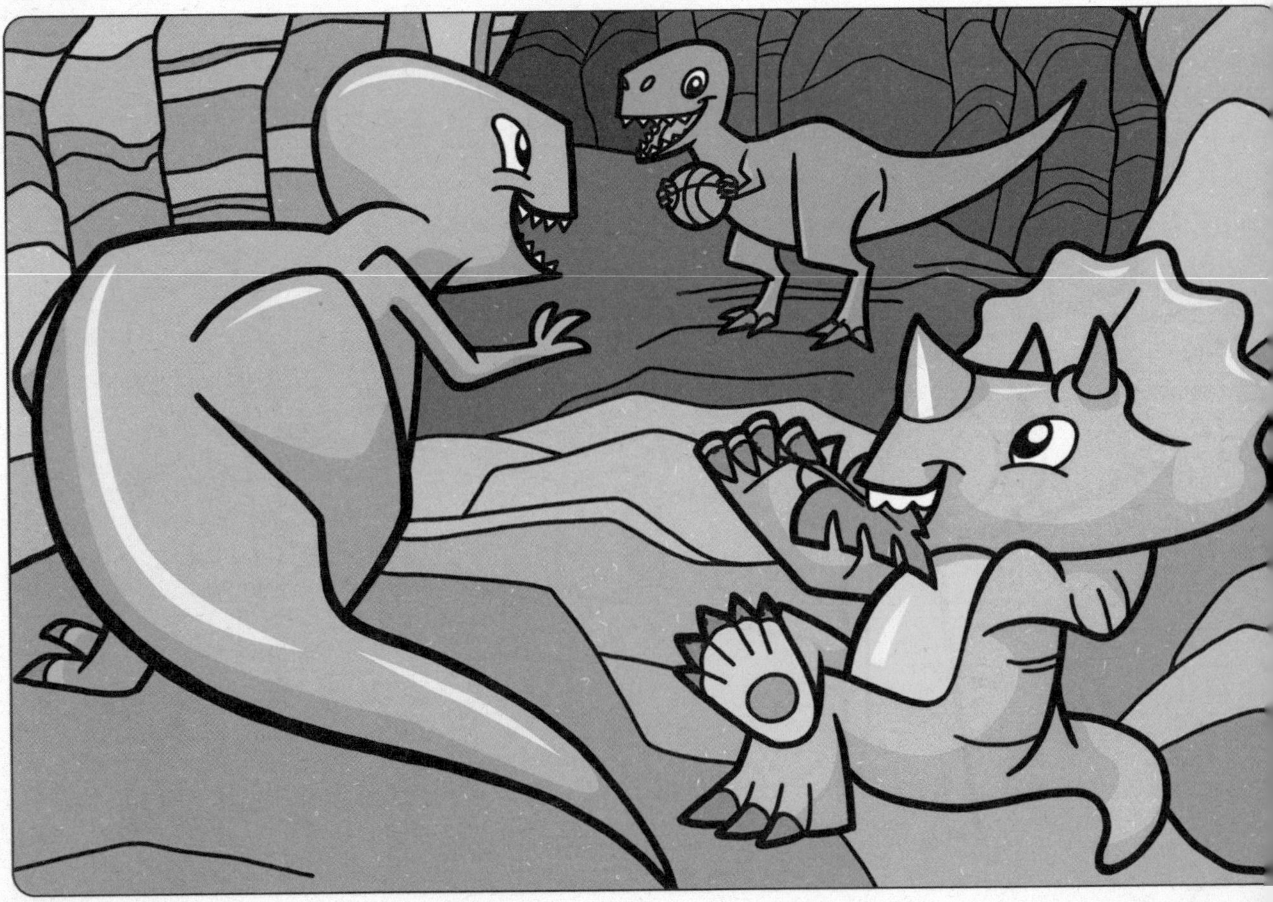

Ee

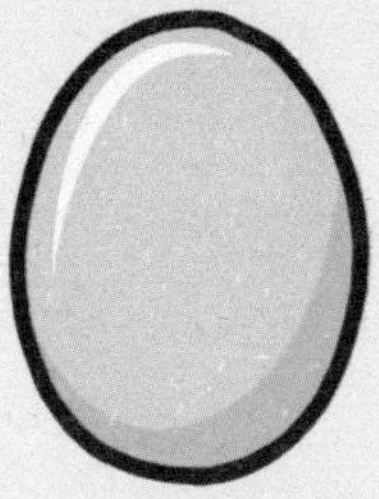

egg

race and print **E** and **e**.

E E

e e

An eager elephant drinks at the water's edge.
Connect the dots and color.

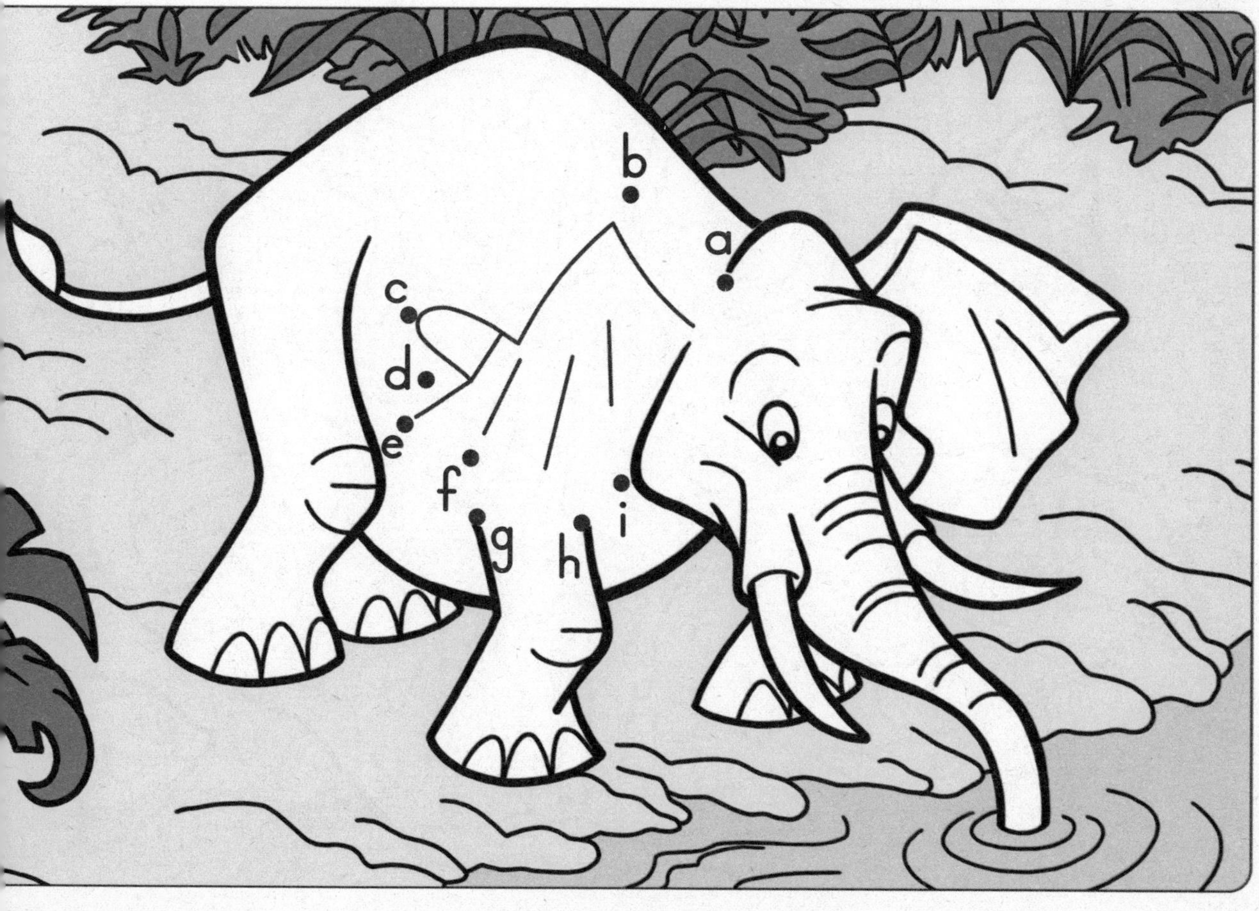
b
a
c
d
e
f
g
h
i

Ff

fig

Trace and print **F** and **f**.

F F

f f

A funny fish finds a friend.

Help the fish through the maze.

Start

Finish

Gg

grapes

race and print **G** and **g**.

G G G

g g

Gray goats graze on green grass.
Color the goats **gray**.

Hh

honey

Trace and print **H** and **h**.

Trace and print H and h image

The happy horse wears a hat.
Connect the dots and color.

Draw lines to match the letter pairs.

A B C D

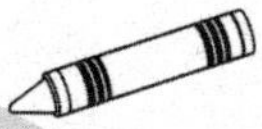

d c a b

E F G H

h g e f

I i

ice cream

Trace and print **I** and **i**.

Iggy the iguana visits India.
Find and circle 5 hidden iguanas.

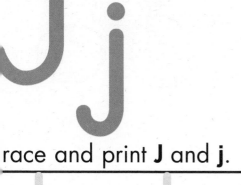

jelly

race and print **J** and **j**.

J J J

J J

j j

j j

Sleepy jaguars rest in the jungle.
Add black spots to the jaguars.

K k

kiwifruit

Trace and print **K** and **k**.

K   K

k   k

Katie the kangaroo likes to fly kites.
Draw a kite.

Ll

lemon

race and print **L** and **I**.

L

I

Liam the lion looks for Lucy the lioness.
Help the lion through the maze.

Start

Finish

13

Mm

mango

Trace and print **M** and **m**.

M M

m m

Monty the moose munches in the meadow.
Draw antlers for the moose.

Nn

noodles

race and print **N** and **n**.

N N

n n

Nancy the nightingale nears her nest.
Color and count the eggs.

Oo

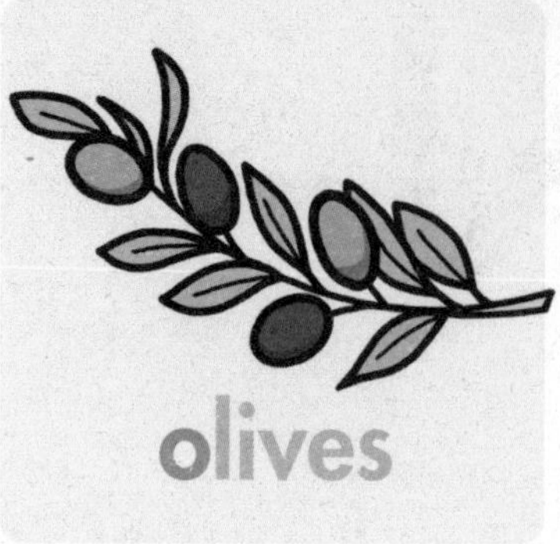
olives

Trace and print **O** and **o**.

O O

o o

Ollie the octopus enjoys eating oranges.

Color each octopus leg a different color and his head **orange**

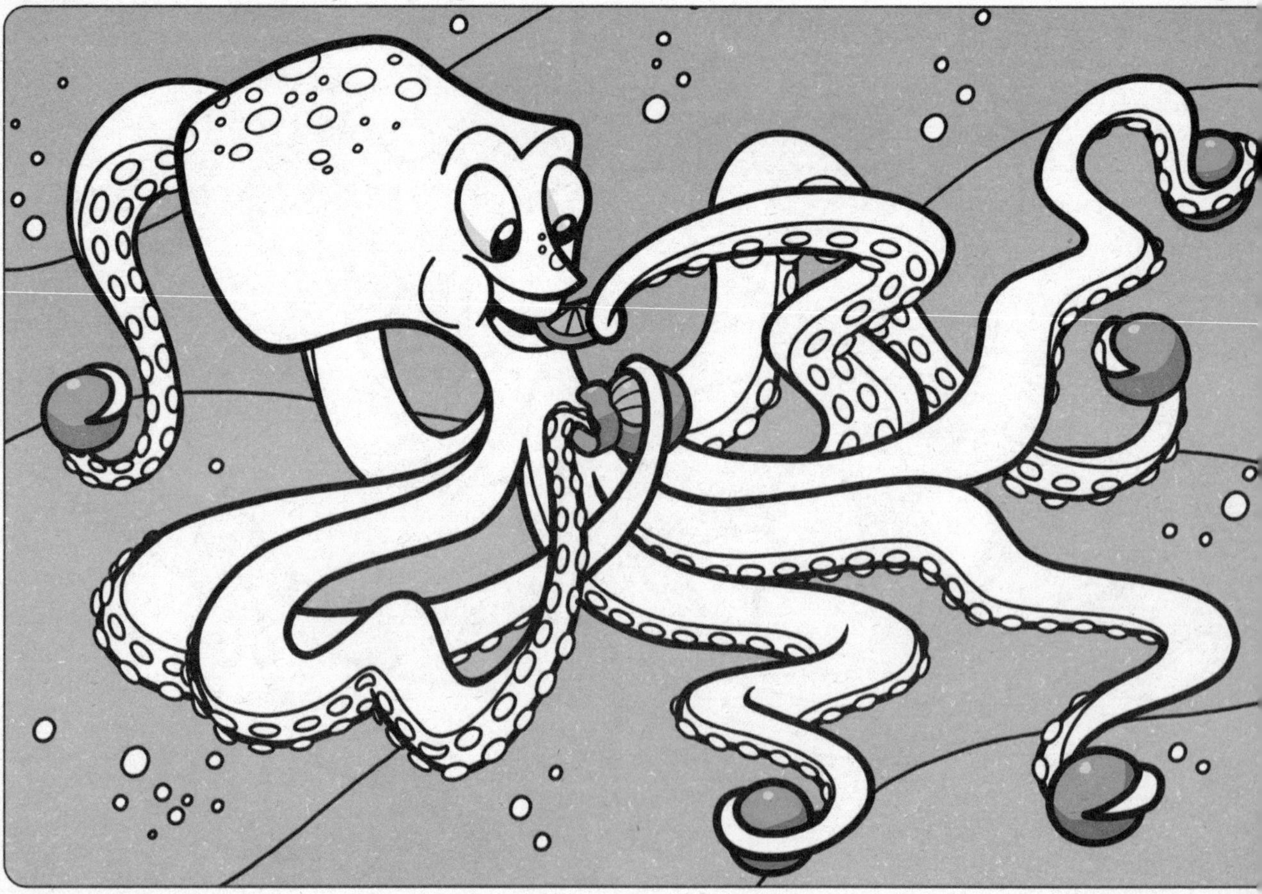

Pp

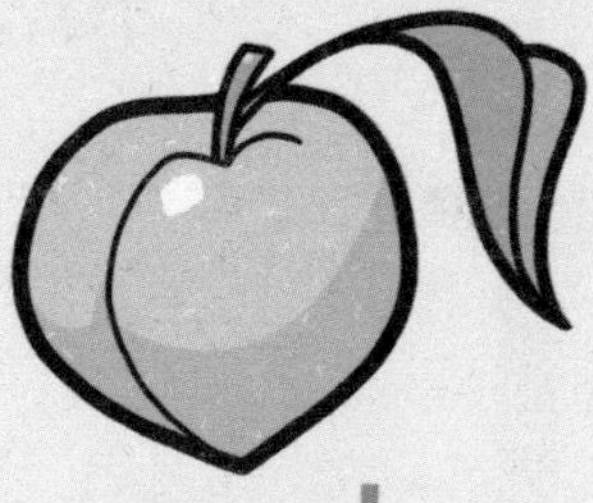

peach

Trace and print **P** and **p**.

P P

p p

Three penguins and a puffin perform a play.

Find and circle the puffin.

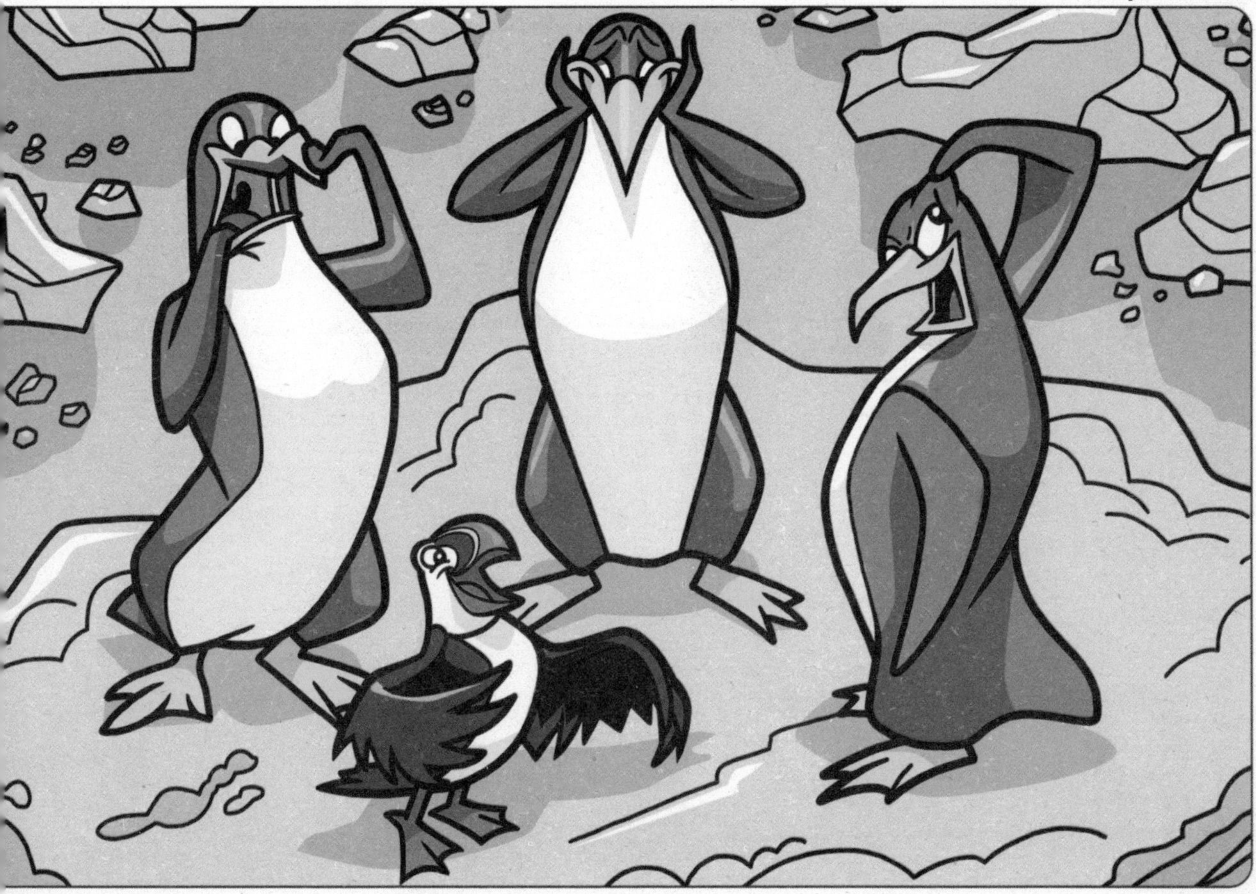

Draw lines to match the letter pairs.

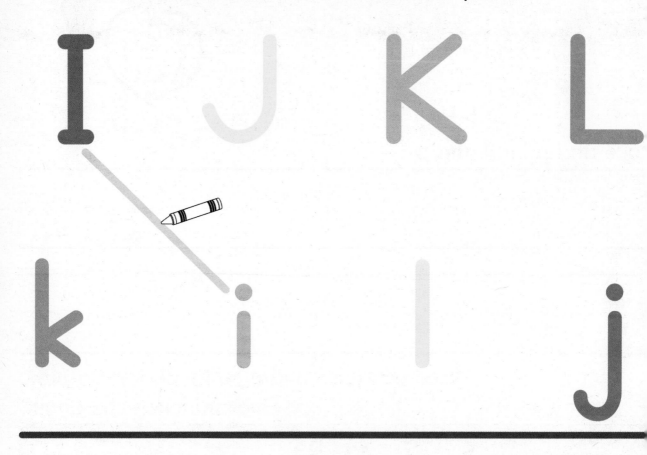

I   J   K   L

k   i   l   j

M   N   O   P

p   o   m   n

Qq

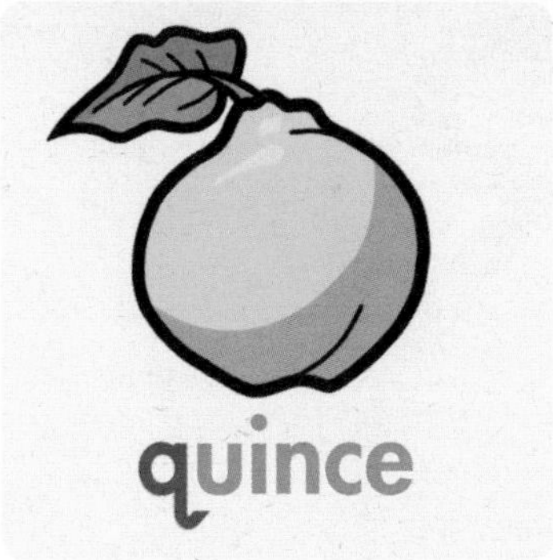
quince

race and print **Q** and **q**.

Q Q

q q

The queen bee quickly asks a question.

Follow the path to help the queen find her worker bees.

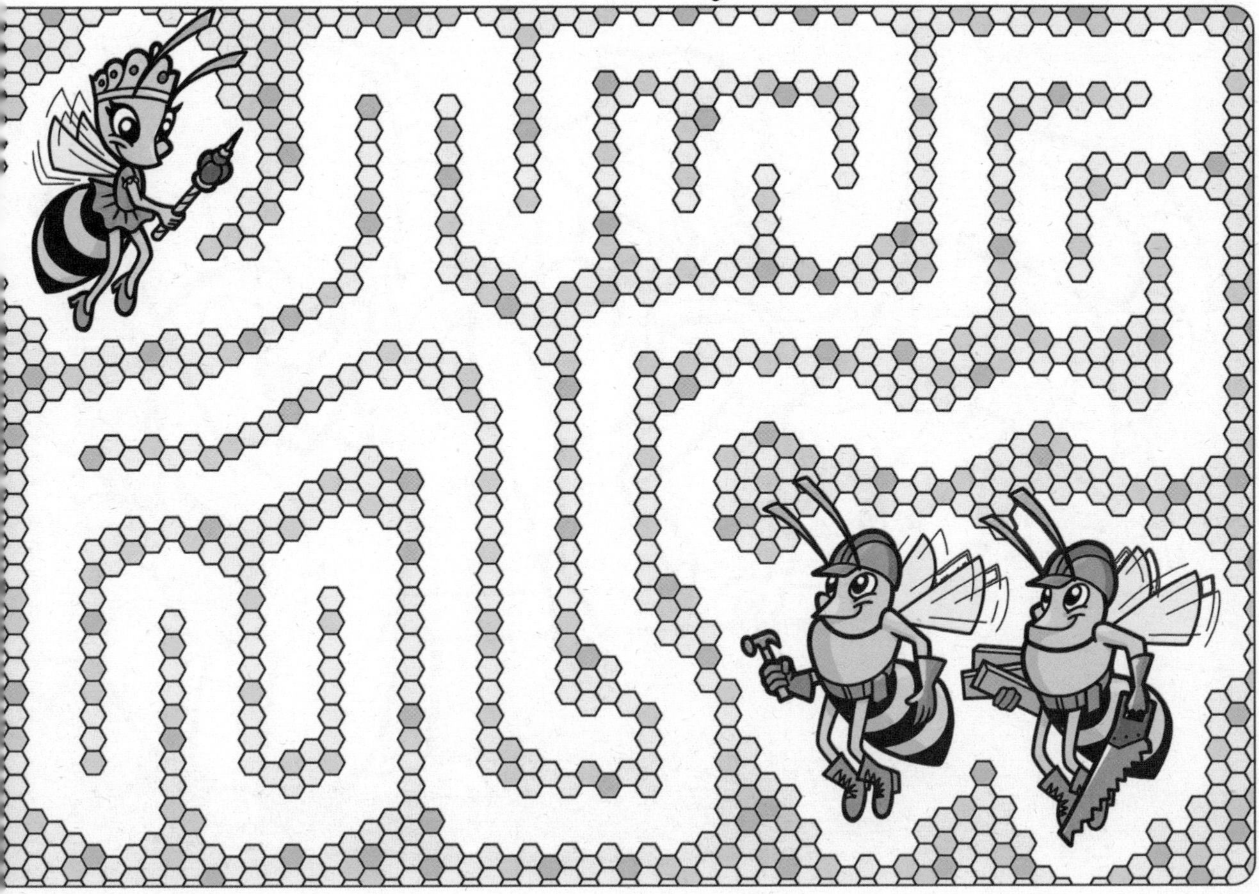

SEE, HEAR, READ

Rr

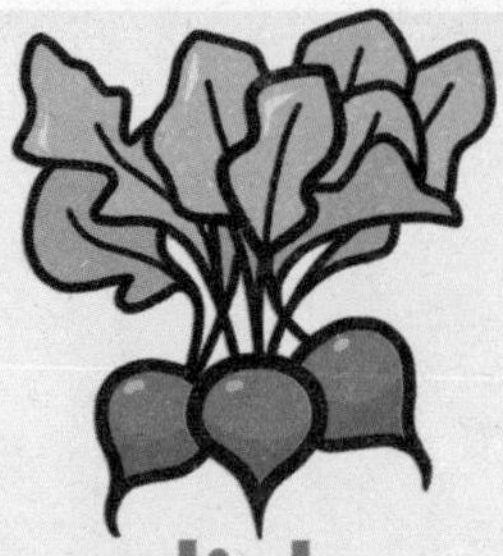
radishes

Trace and print **R** and **r**.

R R

r r

Rascally raccoons romp on a red rug.

Color all the **R** spaces **black**. Color all the **r** spaces **brown**.

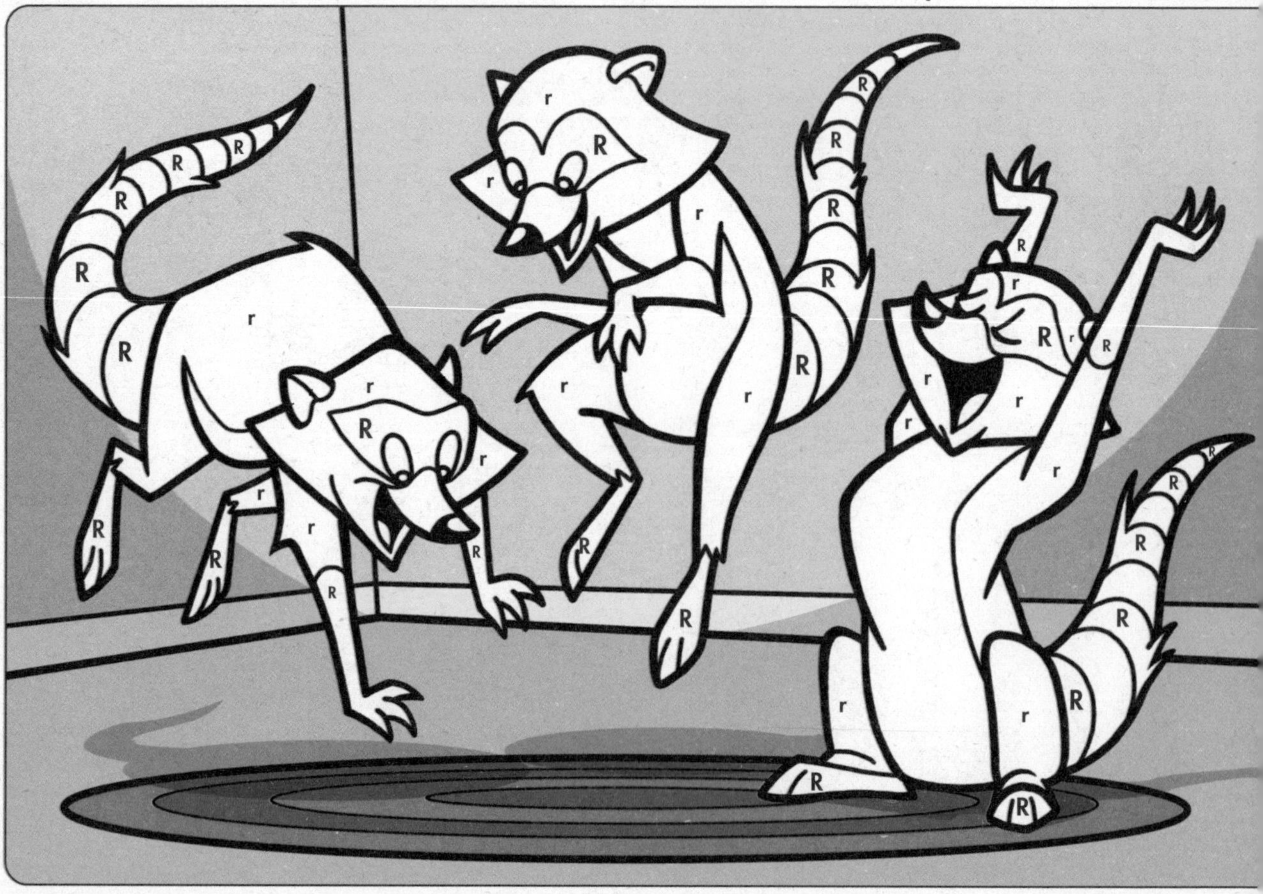

Ss

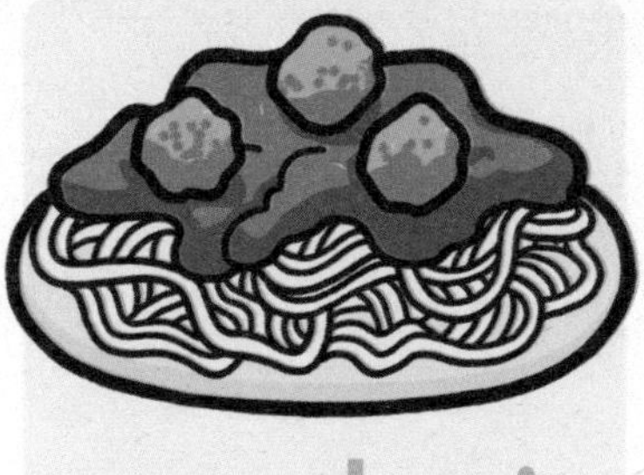
spaghetti

ace and print **S** and **s**.

S S

s s

A soaked skunk swims in a stream.

Connect the dots and color in the stripe.

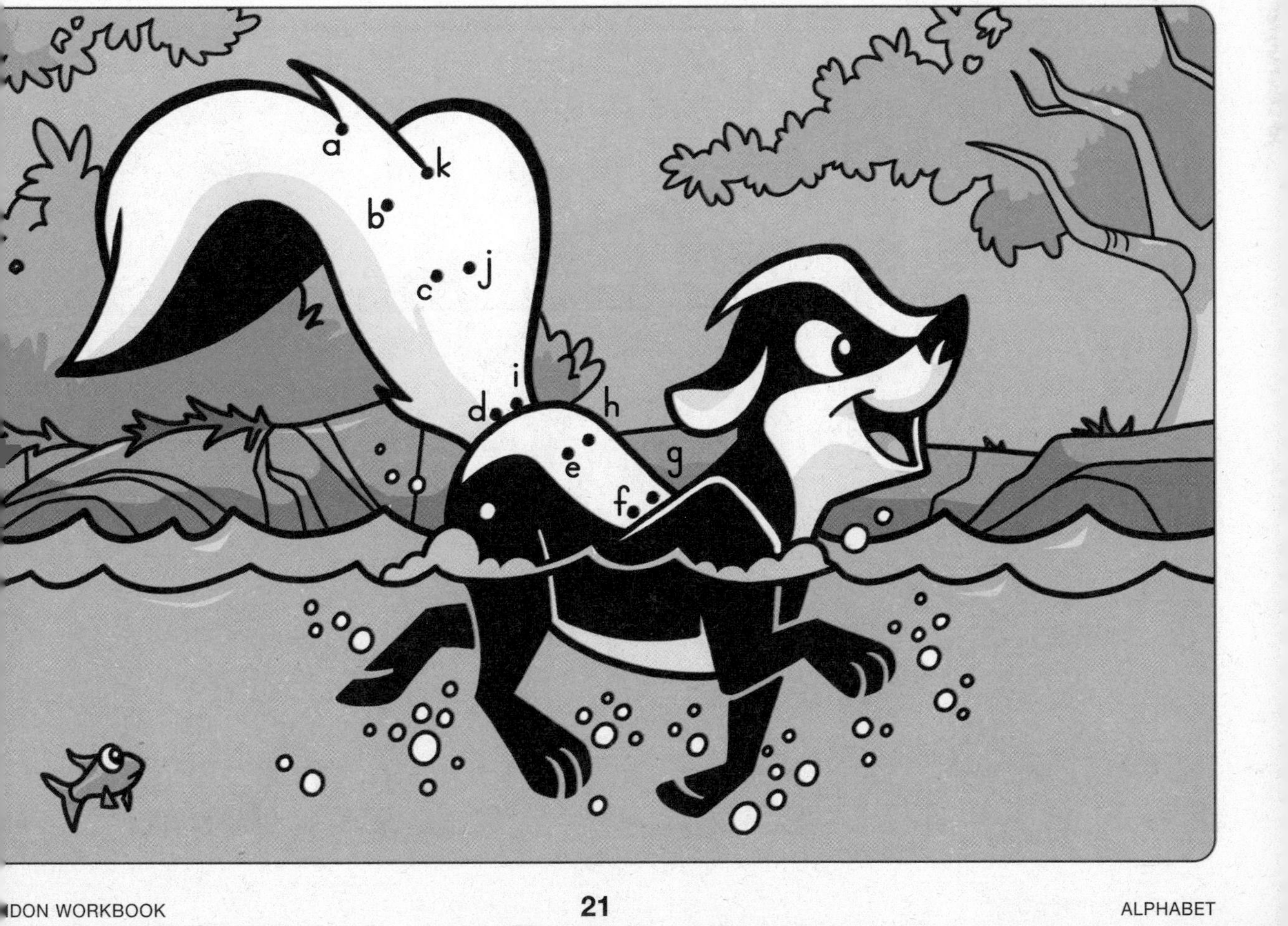
a
k
b
j
c
i
d
h
e
g
f

T t

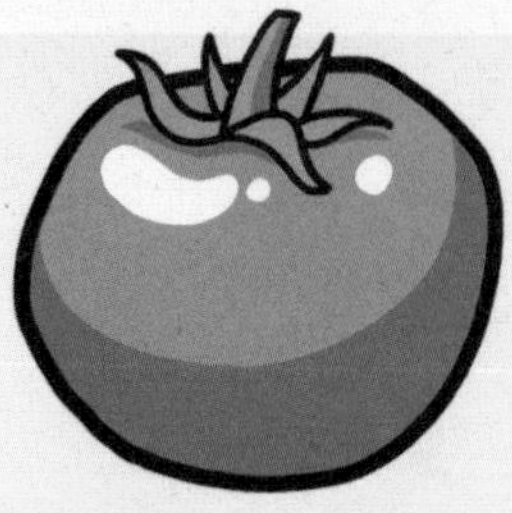

tomato

Trace and print **T** and **t**.

T T

t t

Tim the tiger talks to the turtle.

Color the turtle **teal**.

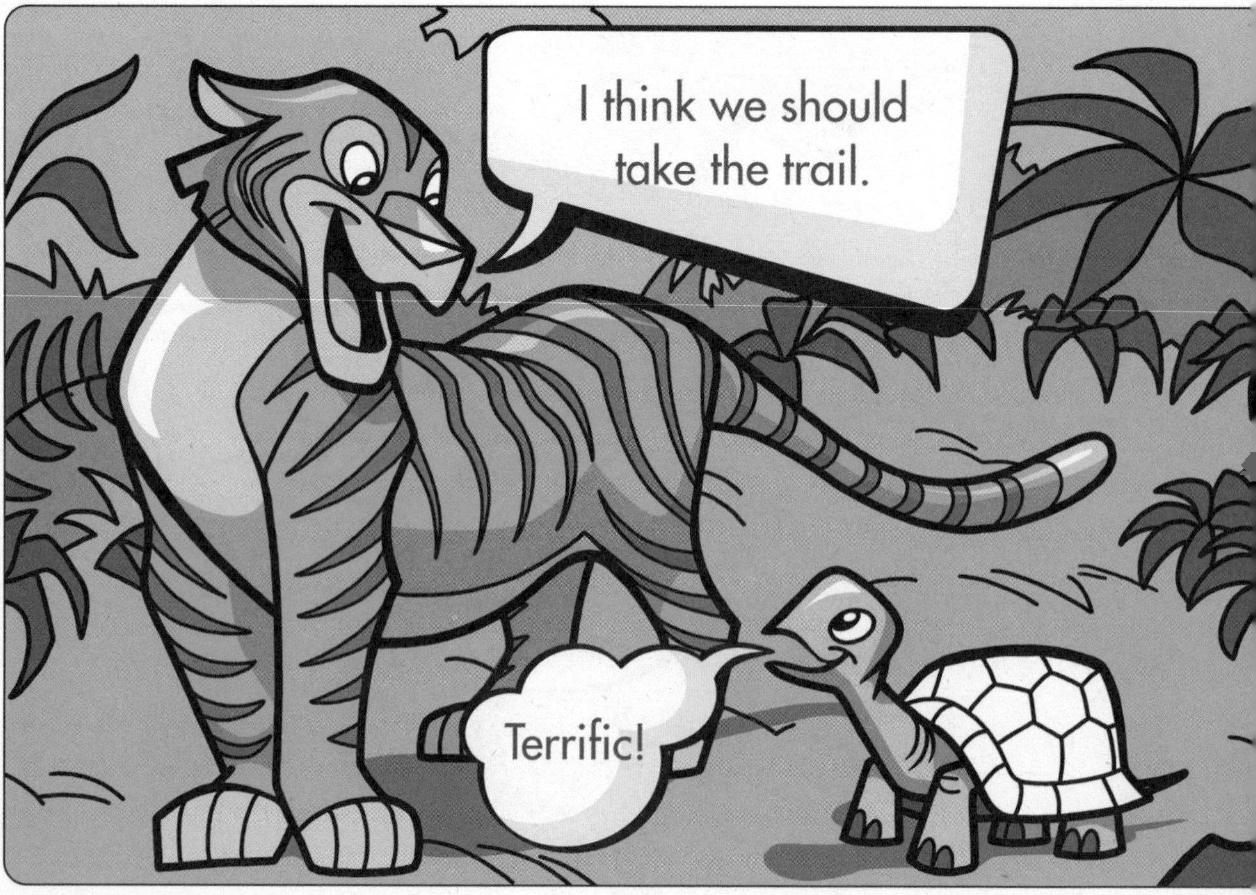
I think we should take the trail.
Terrific!

Uu

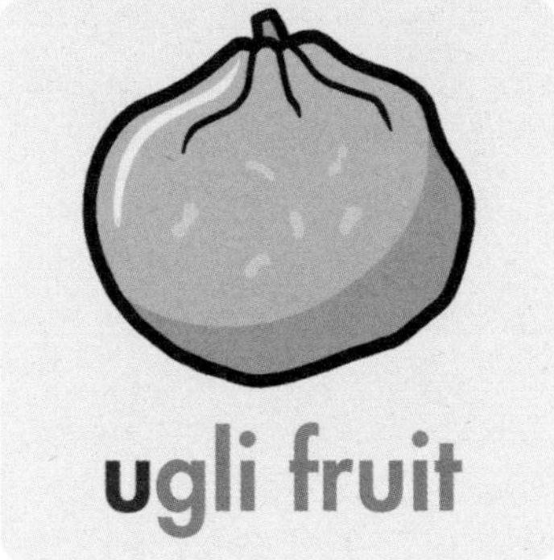
ugli fruit

ace and print **U** and **u**.

U U

u u

A beautiful unicorn rests under an umbrella.

Connect the dots.

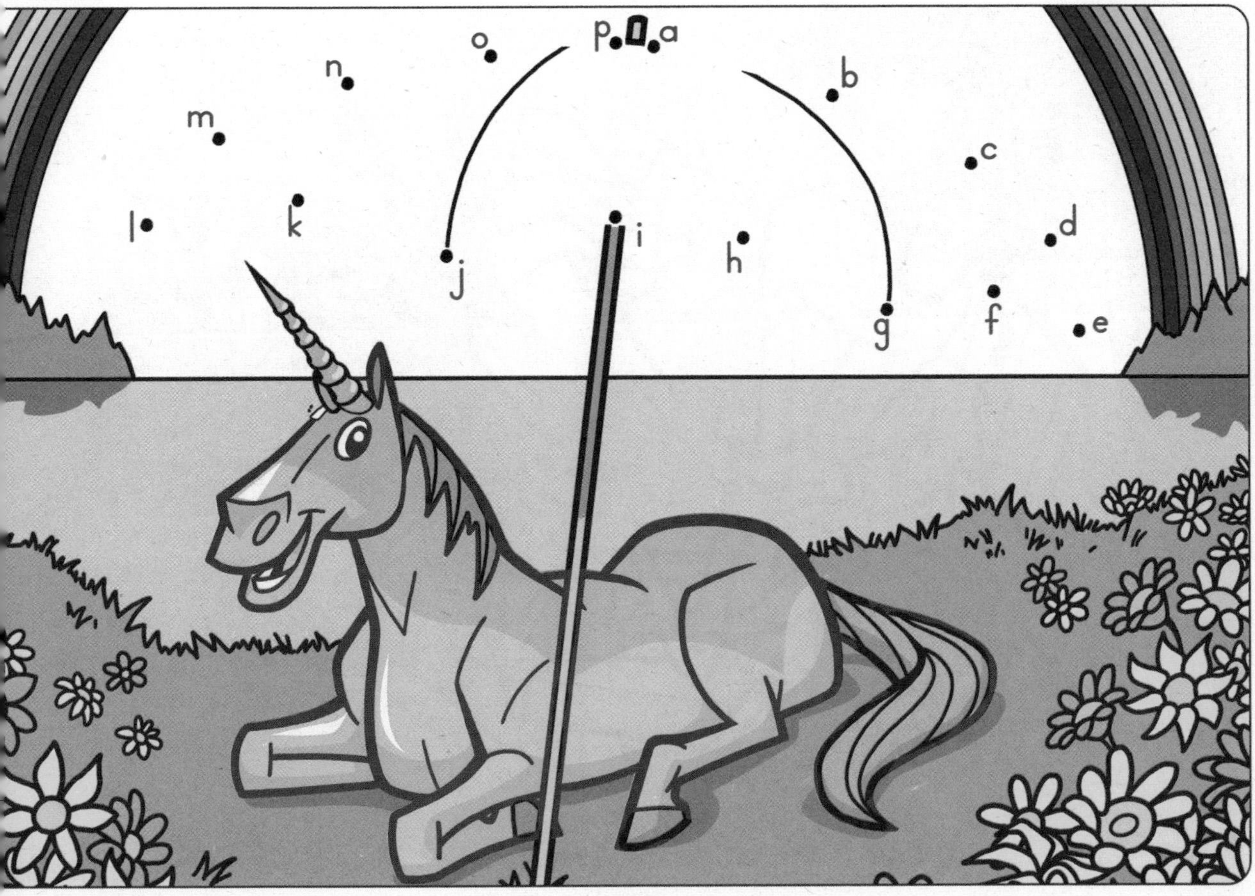
a
b
c
d
e
f
g
h
i
j
k
l
m
n
o
p

SEE, HEA
READ

V v

vegetables

Trace and print **V** and **v**.

A very relaxed vulture is on vacation.
Color the chair violet.

Ww

watermelon

ace and print **W** and **w**.

W W

W W

A warm whale swims in winter waters.
Draw a waterspout for the whale.

wax bean

Trace and print **X** and **x**.

Ray the x-ray fish meets Dexter.
Draw another x-ray fish.

yam

ace and print **Y** and **y**.

Y Y

y y

Yes, there's a yak in our yard.
Color the yak yellow.

Z z

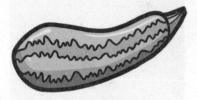

zucchini

Trace and print **Z** and **z**.

Z Z

Z Z

A zany zebra is at the zoo.
Draw **black** stripes on the zebra.

Draw lines to match the letter pairs.

Q R S T U

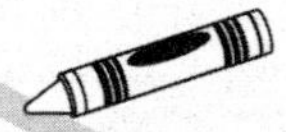

t u s q r

V W X Y Z

x v z w y

Learn the Alphabet!

Say the Alphabet.
Print the missing uppercase letters.

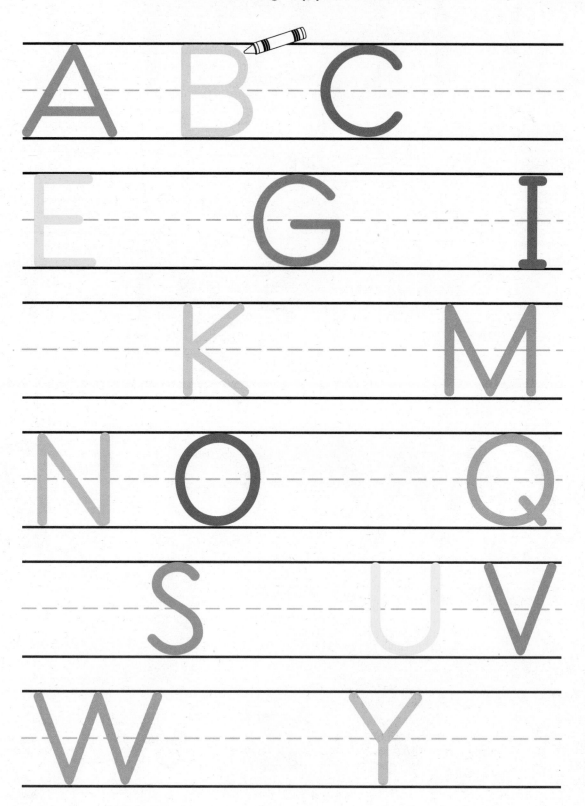

Say the Alphabet.
Print the missing lowercase letters.

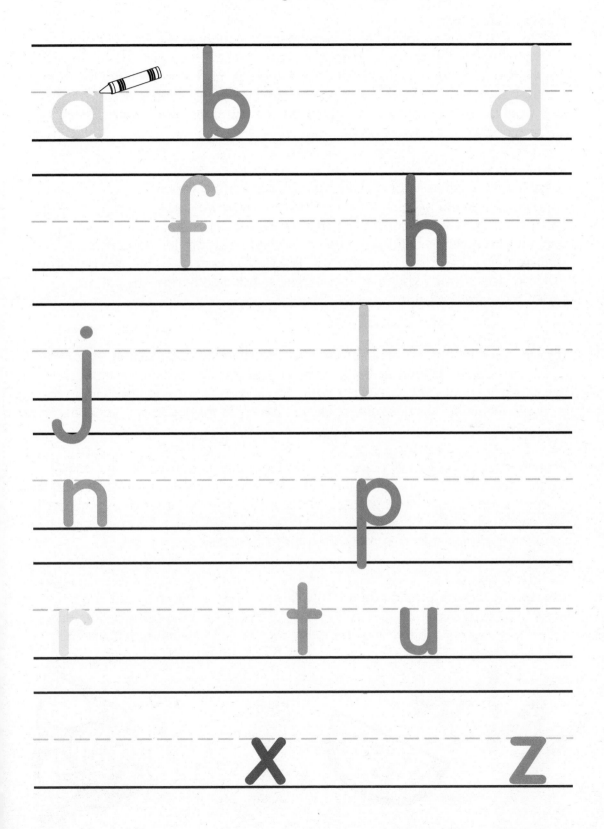

Fun Family Activities

The following activities will provide additional review of the concepts explored on the workbook pages.

1. **Puzzle Cards**
   Use 26 3″ x 5″ index cards. Write an uppercase alphabet letter on the left side of each card. Write the corresponding lowercase letter on the right side of the card. Cut the two letters apart using a different design for each card. Mix up the puzzle pieces. Help the child match the uppercase and lowercase letter pieces. The child may want to use the puzzle cuts as a guide until the upper and lowercase letters are memorized.

2. **Memory Game**
   Select five to seven pairs of alphabet puzzle cards. Turn the cards upside down on the table. Ask the child to turn over two cards. If they are a matching letter set, the child keeps the cards and draws again until a match is not made. The unmatched cards are turned back over. The turn then proceeds to the player to the left. Play continues until all pairs are matched. The player with the most cards wins. Additional letter sets can be added for more challenge.

3. **Visit the Library**
   Take the child to visit the local library. Find the alphabet book section. Help the child select different alphabet books to read. Ask your librarian if a young child can check out books with his or her own library card. If so, sign the child up for a card and let him or her select the books to take home for additional alphabet review.

4. **Alphabet Guessing Game**
   Write a letter on a piece of paper and fold the paper in half so that the letter is hidden. Tell the child you are thinking of a letter that is between two letters. Let the child try to guess your letter. If the child's guess is incorrect, offer clues such as "It is a vowel" or "It makes the first sound in the word ____." When the child correctly guesses your letter, take a turn guessing his or her letter.

5. **Reward Stickers**
   Use reward stickers to celebrate a job well done. You or the child can choose when to place a sticker on a specific page. Use a sticker as a reward when the child completes a page that requires extra care or is a little more difficult. The child can choose to place stickers on pages he or she is proud of completing.

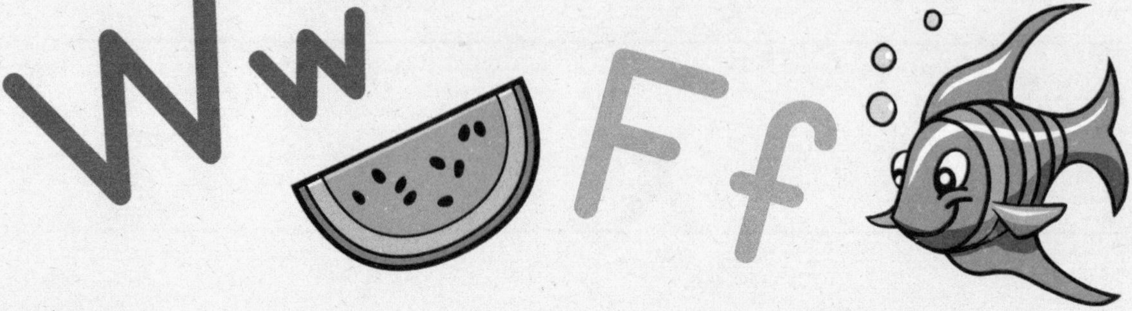
W w
F f

Illustrations by Greg Hardin